In Praise of the Divine World-Teacher, Ruchira Avatar Adi Da Samraj

It is obvious, from all sorts of subtle details, that he knows what IT's all about . . . a rare being.

ALAN WATTS
author, *The Way of Zen* and *The Wisdom of Insecurity*

I regard Adi Da Samraj as one of the greatest teachers in the Western world today.

IRINA TWEEDIE
Sufi teacher; author, *Chasm of Fire*

I recognize the God-Presence Incarnate in Adi Da Samraj as whole and full and complete.

BARBARA MARX HUBBARD
author, *Conscious Evolution* and *The Revelation;*
president, The Foundation for Conscious Evolution

Adi Da Samraj is a man who has truly walked in Spirit and given true enlightenment to many.

SUN BEAR
founder, the Bear Tribe Medicine Society

The life and teaching of Avatar Adi Da Samraj are of profound and decisive spiritual significance at this critical moment in history.

BRYAN DESCHAMP
Senior Adviser at the United Nations
High Commission for Refugees;
former Dean of the Carmelite House of Studies, Australia;
former Dean of Trinity College, University of Melbourne

A great teacher with the dynamic ability to awaken in his listeners something of the Divine Reality in which he is grounded, with which he is identified, and which, in fact, he is.

ISRAEL REGARDIE
author, *The Golden Dawn*

A di Da Samraj has spoken directly to the heart of our human situation— the shocking gravity of our brief and unbidden lives. Through his words I have experienced a glimmering of eternal life, and view my own existence as timeless and spaceless in a way that I never have before.

RICHARD GROSSINGER
author, *Planet Medicine; The Night Sky*

M y relationship with Adi Da Samraj over many years has only confirmed His Realization and the Truth of His impeccable Teaching. He is much more than simply an inspiration of my music, but is really a living demonstration that perfect transcendence is actually possible. This is both a great relief and a great challenge. If you thirst for truth, here is a rare opportunity to drink.

RAY LYNCH
composer and musician, *Deep Breakfast;*
The Sky of Mind; and *Ray Lynch, Best Of*

A di Da Samraj and his unique body of teaching work offer a rare and extraordinary opportunity for those courageous students who are ready to move beyond ego and take the plunge into deepest communion with the Absolute. Importantly, the teaching is grounded in explicit discussion of necessary psychospiritual evolution and guides the student to self-responsibility and self-awareness.

ELISABETH TARG, M.D.
University of California, San Francisco,
School of Medicine;
director, Complementary Medicine Research Institute,
California Pacific Medical Center

That God can, among other things, actually incarnate in human form once seemed unbelievable to me. But reading the books of Avatar Adi Da obliterated all doubt about the existence of God right now, here on Earth in human form.

CHARMIAN ANDERSON, PH.D.
psychologist; author, *Bridging Heaven and Earth*
and *The Heart of Success*

Fly to the side of this God-Man. His Divine Transmission works miracles of change not possible by any other Spiritual means.

LEE SANNELLA, M.D.
author, *The Kundalini Experience*

When I first read the Word of Avatar Adi Da Samraj, I was immediately transported into a state of wonderment and awe. Could it be? Could the Divine Person be here now, in this time and place? It didn't take long for my heart to answer a resounding "Yes". May the whole world be restored to Faith, Love, and Understanding by the Mystery of Real God, here and Incarnate as Avatar Adi Da Samraj.

ED KOWALCZYK
lead singer and songwriter of the rock band, *Live*

I regard the work of Adi Da and his devotees as one of the most penetrating spiritual and social experiments happening on the planet in our era.

JEFFREY MISHLOVE, PH.D.
host, PBS television series, *Thinking Allowed*;
author, *The Roots of Consciousness*

Adi Da's Teachings have tremendous significance for humanity. . . . He represents a foundation and a structure for sanity.

ROBERT K. HALL, M.D.
psychiatrist; author, *Out of Nowhere*;
co-founder, The Lomi School and Lomi Clinic

The Divine World-Teacher,
RUCHIRA AVATAR ADI DA SAMRAJ
Love's Point Hermitage, 2001

REAL GOD IS THE INDIVISIBLE ONENESS OF UNBROKEN LIGHT

THE SEVENTEEN COMPANIONS
OF THE TRUE DAWN HORSE

BOOK ONE

Reality, Truth, and The "Non-Creator" God
In The True World-Religion Of Adidam

By
The Divine World-Teacher,
RUCHIRA AVATAR
ADI DA SAMRAJ

THE DAWN HORSE PRESS
MIDDLETOWN, CALIFORNIA

NOTE TO THE READER

All who study the Way of Adidam or take up its practice should remember that they are responding to a Call to become responsible for themselves. They should understand that they, not Avatar Adi Da Samraj or others, are responsible for any decision they make or action they take in the course of their lives of study or practice.

The devotional, Spiritual, functional, practical, relational, cultural, and formal community practices and disciplines referred to in this book are appropriate and natural practices that are voluntarily and progressively adopted by members of the four congregations of Adidam (as applicable for each of the congregations and as appropriate to the personal circumstance of each individual). Although anyone may find these practices useful and beneficial, they are not presented as advice or recommendations to the general reader or to anyone who is not a member of one of the four congregations of Adidam. And nothing in this book is intended as a diagnosis, prescription, or recommended treatment or cure for any specific "problem", whether medical, emotional, psychological, social, or Spiritual. One should apply a particular program of treatment, prevention, cure, or general health only in consultation with a licensed physician or other qualified professional.

Real God Is The Indivisible Oneness Of Unbroken Light is formally authorized for publication by the Ruchira Sannyasin Order of the Free Renunciates of Ruchiradam, as part of the Standard Edition of the Divine "Source-Texts" of the Divine World-Teacher, Ruchira Avatar Adi Da Samraj. (The Ruchira Sannyasin Order of the Free Renunciates of Ruchiradam is the senior Spiritual and Cultural Authority within the formal gathering of formally acknowledged devotees of the Divine World-Teacher, Ruchira Avatar Adi Da Samraj.)

NOTE TO BIBLIOGRAPHERS: The correct form for citing Ruchira Avatar Adi Da Samraj's Name (in any form of alphabetized listing) is:

Adi Da Samraj, Ruchira Avatar

Standard edition, updated, November 2001
This edition supersedes all previous editions of this book:

Standard edition, July 1999

COVER: Both the central image and the border image are photographs taken by Avatar Adi Da Samraj. Please see "The 'Bright'-Art Work of Avatar Adi Da Samraj", pp. 44-47.

Printed in the United States of America

 Produced by the Eleutherian Pan-Communion of Adidam in cooperation with the Dawn Horse Press

International Standard Book Number: 1-57097-127-7
Library of Congress Catalog Card Number: 2001096052

CONTENTS

REAL GOD IS THE INDIVISIBLE ONENESS OF UNBROKEN LIGHT

FIRST WORD:
Do Not Misunderstand Me—
I Am Not "Within" you, but you Are In Me,
and I Am Not a Mere "Man" in the "Middle" of Mankind,
but All of Mankind Is Surrounded, and Pervaded,
and Blessed By Me
57

PROLOGUE:
My Divine Disclosure
79

PART ONE:
Real God Cannot Be "Proved" or Believed,
"Known" or Perceived, or Even Doubted
93

PART NINE:
Space-Time Is Love-Bliss
213

PART TEN:
The Heart-Summary Of Adidam
231

EPILOGUE:
I Am The Unbroken Light
Of True Religion
237

RUCHIRA AVATAR ADI DA SAMRAJ
The Mountain Of Attention, 2000

Introduction

This book is an invitation to enter a different world. A world that is completely real, in the largest possible sense of that word. A world in which none of the sufferings and difficulties of life are ignored or denied—but also a world in which yearnings for truth, wisdom, happiness, beauty, and love are addressed at an extraordinary depth. A world in which there is real, trustable guidance through the "maze" of life's confusions and crises. A world that vastly exceeds all limited notions of what is "real". A world of deep, abiding joy.

People from all walks of life have felt this world open up to them when they read the books of the Divine World-Teacher, Ruchira Avatar Adi Da Samraj. Those of us who have done so have felt our deepest questions answered, our most profound heart-longings satisfied. We have rejoiced to discover Avatar Adi Da's Revelation of the True Nature of Reality—the Great Mystery that has been described throughout the ages by such words as "Truth" or "Light" or "Beauty" or "God". We have marveled at His precise "map" of the entire course of human development (from birth to Divine Enlightenment) and at His full description of the nature of conditional existence in all its dimensions. We have treasured His compassionate Instruction about the real issues that everyone faces at the foundation level of human life: death, sex, intimacy, emotional maturity, community life, and many more. And we have been overwhelmed to encounter His complete (and revolutionary) Address to everything beyond the foundation level: what the apparently separate ego-self is really about (and how to actually go completely beyond it), what constitutes real Spiritual life (and how one is actually Awakened to it), what it really means to be Divinely Enlightened (and the never-before-completely-revealed process by which Divine Enlightenment is actually and permanently Realized).

Even more than this, we have felt Avatar Adi Da Samraj Transmit the very same (and unimaginably deep) Peace, Happiness, and Love that He describes in His books—and we have found that His Transmission can be experienced anywhere, regardless of whether one is in the same room with Him or thousands of miles away. Our bodies, hearts, and minds and our entire lives have been flooded with His Divine Spiritual Blessing— Blessing which is self-evidently Real, True, and Good, and which has (as we can attest from our own personal experience) the most extraordinary Power to Transform human lives and destinies.

Those of us who have been drawn to Avatar Adi Da Samraj have discovered that the impact of the Truth He has Revealed and of the Blessing He Transmits is so great in our lives, so far beyond anything else we have known, that a truly amazing recognition has grown in our hearts and minds: Avatar Adi Da Samraj is not merely a great human being who speaks profound Truth—He is the Divine Reality Itself, Appearing in a human body in order to Offer the Perfect Revelation of Truth and the Perfect Transmission of Love-Bliss directly to all of humankind.

Therefore, our ecstatic heart-confession to you is this: The Divine Giver of Happiness, Light, and Love is present in the world, in human form, at this very moment—and He is freely Offering His Gifts to all. He is here, moved by overwhelming Divine Love, to establish (for all time) the Way by which all may ultimately Realize Divine Enlightenment. And He is also here (at this life-or-death moment in human history) to Bless the global human community in its necessary embrace of the disposition of cooperation, tolerance, and peace.

Avatar Adi Da Samraj began Teaching in 1972. In the years since then, He has communicated a vast store of Wisdom. But He has also done far more than that: He has created an entirely new Way of life, a new religion, which is now practiced by people of different cultures in many parts of the world. Just as the religions of Christianity and Buddhism are named after their founders, the religion founded by Avatar Adi Da Samraj is named after Him—it is called "Adidam" (AH-dee-DAHM). Adidam is an all-embracing practice that takes every aspect of human life—physical, emotional, mental, psychic, Spiritual, and Transcendental—into account. The foundation of Adidam is the response of heart-felt devotion to Avatar Adi Da Samraj, in loving gratitude for His Gifts of Wisdom and Spiritual Blessing.

Avatar Adi Da Samraj does not offer you a set of beliefs, or even a set of Spiritual techniques. He simply Offers you His Revelation of Truth as a Free Gift, to respond to as you will. And, if you are moved to take up His Way, He invites you to enter into a direct devotional and Spiritual relationship with Him.

Those of us who have taken this step have found the Spiritual relationship to Avatar Adi Da Samraj to be a supremely precious Gift, a literally miraculous Blessing, the answer to our deepest longings—greatly surpassing anything we have ever experienced or even imagined to be possible. What we have discovered, in our own lives and experience, is that Avatar Adi Da Samraj has brought into being the Way by which human beings can not only know the Truth of Reality but they can live that Truth, incarnate that Truth—with their entire existence, their entire structure of body, mind, and psyche.

To find Avatar Adi Da Samraj is to find the Very Heart of Reality—tangibly felt in your own heart as the Deepest Truth of Existence.

This is the great mystery that you are invited to discover for yourself.

A vatar Adi Da Samraj's Name is composed of four Sanskrit words.

His principal Name is "Adi Da". "Avatar" and "Samraj" are sacred Titles, used in association with His Name.

"Adi" (AH-dee) means "Original" (or "Primordial"), and "Da" means "the Divine Giver". Thus, "Adi Da" means "the Original Divine Giver".

"Avatar" means "a 'Crossing Down' of the Divine Being into the world" (or, in other words, "an Appearance of the Divine in conditionally manifested form").

"Samraj" (sahm-RAHJ) means "universal Lord".

In fuller forms of reference, Adi Da Samraj is called "the Ruchira (roo-CHIH-rah) Avatar", meaning "the Avatar of Infinite Brightness".

Avatar Adi Da Samraj:
His Life and Teaching

From the moment of His Birth (in New York, on November 3, 1939), Adi Da Samraj was consciously aware of His Native Divine Condition. As soon as He became able to use language, He gave this Condition a simple but very expressive Name—"the 'Bright'",* meaning the Divine Condition of Boundlessly Radiant and Infinitely Joyful Love-Bliss. But then, at the age of two years, Avatar Adi Da made a profound spontaneous choice. He chose to relinquish His constant Enjoyment of the "Bright"—and He made that choice out of what He Describes as a "painful loving", a sympathy for the suffering and ignorance of human beings. Avatar Adi Da Confesses that He chose to "Learn Man"—to enter into everything that humankind feels and suffers, and also to experience all the various levels of Spiritual Realization known to humanity—in order to discover how to Draw human beings into the "Bright" Divine Condition that He knew as His own True State and the True State of everyone.

This utter Submission to all aspects of human life, in the context of His own body-mind, was the first Purpose of Adi Da's Incarnation. In His Spiritual Autobiography, *The Knee Of Listening,* Avatar Adi Da recounts this amazing and heroic Ordeal, which lasted for the first thirty years of His Life. That Ordeal culminated in 1970, when Avatar Adi Da Re-Awakened permanently to the "Bright" and embarked upon the second great Purpose of His

*For definitions of terms and names, please see the Glossary (pp. 287-324).

Submission to human life—the Process of "Teaching Man". It was not until April 2000 that His Work of Submitting to the human condition would be utterly complete. Since then, having done everything He needed to do in His Work of Teaching, Avatar Adi Da is free to Manifest only His own Divine Love, Bliss, and "Brightness", without any necessity to Submit to ordinary (or even extraordinary) human purposes and efforts.

Teaching and Blessing Work

Teaching the Way of Relationship to Him

When He began to Teach others, Avatar Adi Da Samraj simply made Himself available to all who were willing to enter into the living Process of Real-God-Realization in His Company—a Process Which He summarized as the devotional and Spiritual relationship to Him, rather

Los Angeles, 1972

than any method or technique of Spiritual attainment. Through

The Mountain Of Attention Sanctuary, 1974

that relationship—an extraordinary human and Spiritual intimacy—Avatar Adi Da Samraj perfectly embraced each of His devotees. He used every kind of skillful means to Awaken them to the Truth that the separate, un-Enlightened self—with all its fear, anxieties, and fruitless seeking for Happiness—

is self-imposed suffering, a contraction of the being (which He calls "the self-contraction"). And He Offered the practice of heart-Communion with Him—necessarily joined with profound self-understanding and serious responsibility for every aspect of one's life—as the means of going beyond the self-contraction and thereby Realizing Real Happiness.

I have Come to Live (now, and forever hereafter) with those who love Me with ego-overwhelming love, and I have Come to Love them likewise Overwhelmingly. . . .

Until you fall in love, love is what you <u>fear</u> to do. When you have fallen in love, and you <u>are</u> (thus) always already in love, then you cease to fear to love. . . . Those who fall in love with Me, Fall into Me. Those whose hearts are given, in love, to Me, Fall into My Heart. ["What Will You Do If You Love Me?", from *Da Love-Ananda Gita*]

Two Epochal Events

In 1986, an Event occurred that marked the beginning of a great change in Avatar Adi Da's Work in the world. In this Great Event, a profound Yogic Swoon (taking the form of His apparent near-death) overwhelmed His body-mind, and Avatar Adi Da Samraj spontaneously began the process of relinquishing His Ordeal of Teaching Man (a process that lasted another fourteen years). In the wake of that great Swoon, He began to Radiate His Divinity as never before. This was the beginning of His Divine Self-"Emergence". From that moment,

The Mountain Of Attention, 1986

Adi Da Samraj devoted Himself increasingly to the third and eternal Purpose of His Avataric Incarnation—that of Blessing Man (and all beings).

Lopez Island, 2000

Even after the Great Event in 1986, Avatar Adi Da continued to Work to ensure that His Revelation of the Way of Adidam was fully founded in the world. The final completion of all this Work was eventually signalled by another Event of the most profound significance, which occurred on April 12, 2000. At the time, Avatar Adi Da was staying on Lopez Island, off the northern coast of the state of Washington. On the evening of April 12, Avatar Adi Da Samraj entered into a severe physical and Yogic crisis, which (like the Event of 1986) seemed to threaten His bodily survival. He later confirmed that He had, indeed, been on the "way out" of the earthly realm, but the process stopped just before physical death became inevitable.

With His "return" to bodily existence, Avatar Adi Da's physical Body had become profoundly Spiritualized. His Transmission of Divine Love and Blessing became even more tangible and powerful than before. Since that Event at Lopez Island, Avatar Adi Da's bodily (human) Form has (by His own Confession) been Standing at the very Threshold between the Divine Domain of Infinite Love-Bliss-"Brightness" and all the domains of conditional manifestation. Thus, to an even greater degree than before, the physical Body of Avatar Adi Da Samraj is an unbelievably Potent Conductor of His Divine Blessing to all who approach Him with an open heart.

Now, all the foundation Work of Avatar Adi Da's Incarnation has been completed. Everything necessary for the understanding and right practice of the real Spiritual process, culminating in Divine Enlightenment, has been said and done by Him. The summary of His Wisdom-Teaching is preserved for all time in a series of twenty-three "Source-Texts" (described on pp. 32-43). And the

Way of Adidam is fully established. This monumental Work has been accomplished by Avatar Adi Da in a little over a quarter of a century—twenty-seven years of ceaseless Instruction, in constant interaction with His devotees. And, with that Great Work accomplished, He is now entirely concentrated in His Work of Spiritually Blessing all.

In *Aham Da Asmi (Beloved, I Am Da)*, the first of His twenty-three "Source-Texts", Avatar Adi Da Samraj makes this summary Confession of how and why He has Appeared in the world:

> I *Am* The Very and "Bright" Condition Of all and All.
> I *Am* The One To Be Realized.
>
> I Am Able To Appear In Human Form.
> This Is Because I Am Not Inherently "Different" (or Separated) From you.
> Indeed, I *Am* The Very Condition In Which you Are Apparently arising.
> I *Am* your own True Condition—Beyond egoity, and Beyond all conditional references.
>
> I Will Be here Forever.
> I Will Be every "where" Forever.
>
> I Cannot Leave, For My "Bright" Divine Self-Domain Is Not Some "Where" To "Go To".
> My Divine Self-Domain Is Eternal.
> I Am Eternal, and I Am Always Already Merely Present—here, and every "where" In The Cosmic Domain.
>
> You Have Been Waiting For Me—but I Have Been here All The While.
>
> I Love you Now.
> I Will Love you every "then" and "there".
> And I *Always* Loved you (and every one, and all, and All).
> That Is How I Got To here (and every "where").

There Is Only Reality Itself, Only Truth, Only Real God.
All Are Inherently Conjoined With What Is Always Already The Case.

There Is Not any one who is merely a mortal "organism"—Not Even any of the fishes or the possums or the frogs or the mosquitoes, and Not Even any of the worst Of Mankind.
All Must Be Forgiven.
All Must Be Purified.
All Must Suffer Through An Ordeal Of Divine "Brightening".

In any particular moment, some Are Apparently More Serious Than others, but There Is No Ultimate "Difference" Between beings.
All Are In Me.
Therefore, all Have Me As their Eternal Opportunity.

There Is Only One Reality For all, and For All.
Therefore, There Is Only One Teaching and One Great Opportunity For all, and For All.

I Am The Infinite "Bright" One—The Only One Who Is Always With you, and With every one, and With all, and With All.

[Aham Da Asmi]

"Money, Food, and Sex"

During His years of Teaching and Revelation (from 1972 to 2000), Avatar Adi Da undertook a vast, in-life "consideration" with His devotees, covering everything related to Spiritual life—from the most rudimentary matters to the most esoteric. One extremely important area of "consideration" was how to rightly relate to the most basic urges and activities of human life—what Avatar Adi Da describes as the realm of "money, food, and sex". (By "money", Avatar Adi Da means not only the earning and use of money itself, but the exercising of life-energy in general.)

In most religious traditions, an ascetical approach to these primal urges is recommended—in other words, desires related to "money, food, and sex" are to be minimized or denied. Avatar Adi Da took a different approach. When they are rightly engaged, ordinary human enjoyments are not a problem, not "sinful" or "anti-spiritual" in and of themselves. Indeed, the ascetical effort to "cut out" (or "cut down on") such enjoyments is itself simply one of the possible variations on the ego's impulse to manipulate the conditions of existence to its own benefit. Thus, the root-problem of human beings is not any particular activity or desire of the body-mind, but the ego itself—the governing presumption that one is a separate and independent entity attempting to counteract the inevitable suffering of embodied existence. Therefore, in living dialogue and experimentation with His devotees, Avatar Adi Da brought to light, in detail, exactly how the human functions of money (or life-energy), food, and sex can be rightly engaged, in a truly ego-transcending manner—an entirely life-positive and non-suppressive manner that is both pleasurable and supportive of the Spiritual process in His Company. (Avatar Adi Da's Instruction relative to "money, food, and sex" is fully described in His book *Ruchira Avatara Hridaya-Tantra Yoga*.)

Going Beyond <u>All</u> Forms of Egoity

The transcending of egoic involvement with "money, food, and sex" is a matter that relates to the beginnings of (or preparation for) real Spiritual practice. But the necessity for ego-transcendence does not end there. In His years of Teaching and Revelation, Avatar Adi Da Revealed that the ego is still present, in one form or another, in all the possible varieties of Spiritual attainment short of Most Perfect Divine Enlightenment. The word "Enlightenment" is used by different people and in different traditions with various different meanings. In Avatar Adi Da's language, "Enlightenment" (which He sometimes modifies, for the sake of clarifying His meaning, as "Most Perfect Divine Enlightenment", and which is synonymous with "Divine Self-Realization", "Real-God-Realization", and "seventh stage Realization") specifically means that the process of ego-transcendence has been entirely completed, relative to all the dimensions of the being. In other words, the ego has been transcended in three distinct phases—first at the physical (or gross) level (the level of "money, food, and sex"), then at the subtle level (the level of internal visions, auditions, and all kinds of mystical experience), and finally at the causal level (the root-level of conscious existence, wherein the sense of "I" and "other", or the subject-object dichotomy, seems to arise in Consciousness).

The complete process of ego-transcendence is extraordinarily profound and can only proceed on the basis of all the foundation disciplines and ever-increasing heart-surrender. Then, progressively, there is a transformation of view, a "positive disillusionment" with each phase of egoity—until there is Most Perfect Divine Enlightenment (or "Open Eyes"), the Realization of Consciousness Itself as the Single Love-Blissful Reality and Source of existence.

A Fierce Critic of Cultism

The ego manifests not only in individuals but also in groups. One of the collective manifestations of egoity is cultism—not only in the sense of misguided religious cults, but in the larger sense of the universal human tendency to become cultically attached to (and dependent on) a particular person, a particular point of view (or philosophy), a particular activity, or any kind of particular thing.

From the very beginning of His Teaching Work, Avatar Adi Da Samraj was well aware that, no matter who came to Him, it was inevitable that they (as ordinary human beings with ordinary human characteristics) would tend to relate to Him in a cultic manner. Therefore, He has constantly criticized the cultic tendency in His own devotees and in human beings generally. At the same time, He is also clear in His criticism of the way the media tends to indiscriminately and pejoratively label all non-mainstream religious groups as "cults", thereby working against people's true impulses to engage a Spiritually transformative process.

AVATAR ADI DA SAMRAJ: Over the years, you have all heard Me Speak about cultism in negative terms. I have Criticized the cults that people form around religious leaders (and even around true Spiritual Masters), as well as the cultic attachments that people create with one another. There exists a certain hyped enthusiasm to which people are attracted. And when those people accept all the dogmas with which that particular group makes itself enthusiastic, they maintain themselves as opponents of the world and lose communication with the world in general, and with the processes of life.

To Me, that enthusiasm is bizarre. There is something about the capability of individuals for that kind of enthusiasm that makes My skin crawl. It is a kind of madness. Gleeful enthusiasm has nothing whatsoever to do with this Way and with the value that I can have for you personally. It has <u>nothing</u> to do with it!

My Purpose in associating with you is not to entertain you, not to be believed in. I am not here to offer you a relationship in which you are never changed but only consoled. My Purpose in dealing with you, My Purpose in My Teaching Work, is to make it possible for you to be in devotional Communion with Me, to be Spiritually intimate with Me—so that you yourself may live and fulfill this practice, and make a community with one another out of the true Happiness of mature Divine living.

Everything about cultism that is negative is specifically Criticized in My Wisdom-Teaching. I do not want your enthusiasm to be superficially generated by reading My Books. I want you to "consider" My Arguments. I want you to "consider" yourself very critically, very directly and rigorously, and come to the point of most fundamental self-understanding. When you have sufficient understanding of your own game, your childishness and adolescence, then you will be able to advance in the practice I have Given you.

I refuse to console individuals by telling them that all they need to do is believe in Me, that all they need to do is practice some silly little technique and they will Realize God, no matter what they do otherwise. I am not the slightest bit interested in your gleeful applause. I want you to understand yourself and to practice true heart-Communion with Me. I want you to truly live the Way that I have Revealed and Given to you. In order to do that, you must grow up. You must stop being naive about the communications of silly downtown people, all the aggressiveness of media campaigns, and all the things that fundamentally work against the higher acculturation of human beings. [December 17, 1979]

Standing Free

In His Spiritual Work with His devotees and the world, Avatar Adi Da Samraj has confronted the realities of egoity in a completely direct and unflinching manner. In His years of "Teaching Man", He did not hesitate in the slightest to grapple with the ego as it might be manifested in any moment by an individual devotee or a group of devotees—for the sake of helping His devotees understand and go beyond their ego-possessed disposition and activity.

However, even in the midst of that compassionate struggle with the forces of egoity, Avatar Adi Da has always Stood utterly Free of the ego-world. And, especially since the late 1970s, that Free Stand more and more took the form of His living in an essentially private circumstance, at one of the Hermitages established for Him (at secluded locations in California, Hawaii, and Fiji—see p. 268). In His Hermitage sphere, Avatar Adi Da is served by a small group of renunciate devotees, with whom He does particularly intensive Spiritual Work. And it is in the set-apart domain of His Hermitages (rather than in some kind of more public setting) that Avatar Adi Da sometimes receives His devotees in general (and, on occasion, specially invited members of the public), to Grant them His Spiritual Blessing.

The reasons why Avatar Adi Da maintains a Hermitage life are profound. The purpose of His Existence is to Reveal the Divine Reality—in other words, to Manifest the Freedom, Purity, and unbounded Blissfulness of His own Divine Nature, to Exist simply as He Is, without having to make compromises or adjustments in order to "fit in" to the ordinary ego-patterned world. Therefore, it is essential that He live in a sacred domain that conforms to Him and to the nature of His Spiritual Work, where He can remain independent of (but not disconnected from) the common world.

As He has commented many times, His Hermitage life is a life of seclusion, but not of isolation. His secluded Hermitage life is what allows His Divine Blessing to Flow into the world with the greatest possible force and effectiveness—it is what allows His Spiritual connection to all beings to be as strong as possible.

A Testimony of Spiritual Practice

The process of the Way of Adidam unfolds by Avatar Adi Da's Grace, according to the depth of surrender and response in each devotee. One of the most extraordinary living testimonies to the Greatness and Truth of the Way of Adidam is one of Avatar Adi Da's longtime devotees, whose full renunciate name is Ruchiradama Quandra Sukhapur Rani. Quandra Sukhapur has totally consecrated herself to Avatar Adi Da and lives always in His Sphere, in a relationship of unique intimacy and service. By her profound love of, and most

Ruchiradama Quandra Sukhapur Rani with Ruchira Avatar Adi Da Samraj

exemplary surrender to, her Divine Heart-Master, she has become combined with Him at a unique depth. She manifests the signs of deep and constant immersion in His Divine Being, both in meditation and daily life. Quandra Sukhapur is a member of the Ruchira Sannyasin Order (the senior cultural authority within the gathering of Avatar Adi Da's devotees), practicing in the ultimate stages of the Way of Adidam.

Through a process of more than twenty years of intense testing, Avatar Adi Da has been able to lead Quandra Sukhapur to the threshold of Divine Enlightenment. The profound and ecstatic relationship with Avatar Adi Da that Quandra Sukhapur has come to know can be felt in this intimate letter of devotional confession to Him:

RUCHIRADAMA QUANDRA SUKHAPUR RANI: Bhagavan Love-Ananda, Supreme and Divine Person, Real-God-Body of Love,

I rest in Your Constant and Perfect Love-Embrace, with no need but to forever worship You. Suddenly in love, Mastered at heart, always with my head at Your Supreme and Holy Feet, I am beholding and recognizing Your "Bright" Divine Person. My Beloved, You so "Brightly" Descend and utterly Convert this heart, mind, body, and breath, from separate self to the "Bhava" of Your Love-Bliss-Happiness.

Supreme Lord Ruchira, the abandonment of the contracted personality, the relinquishment of ego-bondage to the world, and the profound purification and release of ego-limitations—all brought about by Your Grace, throughout the years since I first came to You—has culminated in a great comprehensive force of one-pointed devotion to You and a great certainty in the Inherent Sufficiency of Realization Itself. The essence of my practice is to always remain freely submitted to You and centralized in You—the Condition Prior to all bondage, all modification, and all illusion.

My Beloved Lord Ruchira, You have Moved me to renounce all egoic "bonding" with conditionally manifested others, conditionally manifested worlds, and conditionally manifested self, to enter into the depths of this "in-love" and utter devotion to You. Finding You has led to a deep urge to abandon all superficiality and to simply luxuriate in Your Divine Body and Person. All separation is shattered in Your Divine Love-Bliss-"Bhava". Your Infusion is Utter. I feel You everywhere.

I am Drawn, by Grace of Your Spiritual Presence, into profound meditative Contemplation of Your Divine State. Sometimes, when I am entering into these deep states of meditation, I remain vaguely aware of the body, and particularly of the breath and the heartbeat. I feel the heart and lungs slow down. Then I am sometimes aware of my breath and heartbeat being suspended in a state of Yogic sublimity. Then there is no awareness of body, no awareness of mind, no perceptual awareness, and no conceptual awareness. There is only abiding in Contemplation of You in Your Domain of Consciousness Itself. And, when I resume association with the body and begin once again to hear my breath and heartbeat, I feel the remarkable Power of Your Great Samadhi. I feel no necessity for anything, and I feel Your Capability to Bless and Change and Meditate all. I can feel how this entrance into objectless worship of You as Consciousness Itself (allowing this Abiding to deepen ever so profoundly, by utter submission of separate self to You) establishes me in a different relationship to everything that arises.

My Beloved Bhagavan, Love-Ananda, I have Found You. Now, by Your Grace, I am able to behold You and live in this constant Embrace. This is my Joy and Happiness and the Yoga of ego-renunciation I engage. [October 11, 1997]

The Free Revelation of Reality

The Divine Artist

After the Lopez Island Event, Avatar Adi Da's Work dramatically changed. The content of His Work was no longer His Instruction of devotees and His creation of the Way of Adidam. Instead, He became intent on finding further means of directly Revealing Reality, of directly Showing That Which is Realized in any moment of most profound heart-Communion with Him (and Which eventually becomes one's constant Realization, when the progressive stages of practice, which He had so painstakingly described during His Submission-Work, come to fruition).

A primary means for this Revelation of Reality is Avatar Adi Da's artistic Work based in photography and video. Art of every kind has always been of great importance to Avatar Adi Da, because His entire Life has been devoted to the Revelation of Truth and to all the means whereby human beings may be Awakened to What is Real and True. Art is a unique human activity that has the potential to bypass the ego-mind and its mood of self-obsession, directly touching the heart and transforming our perception of reality. Thus, Avatar Adi Da's communication through the artistic media is fully as profound and "radical" as His communication (via the medium of words) in His "Source-Texts".

**The Mountain Of Attention
Sanctuary, 2001**

AVATAR ADI DA SAMRAJ: The true artist is a sacred performer. He or she must do the magic that causes others to participate in manifest reality in the sacred sense, or the sense of love— in the sense of ego-transcendence, of ecstasy.

[August 1, 1984]

A brief introduction to Avatar Adi Da's artistic Work (including the photographic images that appear on the covers of His "Source-Texts") is given in "The 'Bright'-Art Work of Avatar Adi Da Samraj" (pp. 44-47).

Ruchiradam

Emerging at the same time as His art Work in photography and video is another remarkable sign of Avatar Adi Da's Free Revelation of Reality: His Word on the most esoteric secrets of the Process of Divine Enlightenment.

The Way of Adidam encompasses the entire process of Spiritual growth—from birth, through the progressive stages of human and Spiritual maturity, to Divine Enlightenment. The profound esoteric core of the Way of Adidam is what Avatar Adi Da Samraj calls "the 'Perfect Practice'", which is the Spiritual practice that becomes possible once one has grown beyond all identification with the body and the mind, and has become natively Identified with the Divine Consciousness Itself. The "Perfect Practice" of Adidam is the essential process of Divine Enlightenment. In February 2001, while He was speaking ecstatically of these esoteric matters, Avatar Adi Da Gave the "Perfect Practice" a special name, to indicate its special nature. That name is "Ruchiradam"—a free combination of "Ruchira" ("bright", in Sanskrit) and "Adidam".

Ruchiradam is the "root" esoteric process of Adidam. It is the process of <u>directly</u> "Locating" Reality, Truth, or Real God—rather than a <u>progressive</u> process of Spiritual Awakening that relates to the patterns associated with existence as an apparently individual body-mind. That direct "Locating" can occur in any moment of profound heart-Communion with Avatar Adi Da Samraj, even from the very beginning of the devotional and Spiritual relationship to Him—but to embrace Ruchiradam as one's established and consistent form of practice requires the most profound Spiritual preparation.

AVATAR ADI DA SAMRAJ: The reference "Ruchiradam" should be understood to describe and summarize the Fullness of the Way I have Revealed, as engaged in the form of the "Perfect Practice" of the devotional and Spiritual relationship to Me.

The Way of Adidam, as a whole, is an elaboration of <u>all</u> the implications of the Way of the devotional and Spiritual relationship to Me—and My Revelation of the total (or full and complete) Way of Adidam is Given so that those who are moved to serious practice in My Company will have a guide relative to everything that such practice requires as a way of life. Ruchiradam is the <u>root</u> of the Way of Adidam. Ruchiradam is the most essential (and moment to moment) practice of the Way I have Revealed and Given. Thus, Ruchiradam is not an elaborated way of life covering all activities in time and space. Rather, Ruchiradam is simply the essential process of Real-God-Realization Itself—As It Always Already Is, in every moment.

In order to take up the practice of Ruchiradam, My any formally acknowledged devotee who practices the Way of Adidam must establish his or her direct Spiritual relationship to Me, through the Da Love-Ananda Samrajya, and must then develop that relationship to Me in the form of this "Perfect Practice" of Spiritual devotion to Me.

When people come into My physical Company, they are to come specifically for the purpose of engaging and developing the moment to moment practice of Ruchiradam, which is the essential process of Divine Enlightenment. [February 11, 2001]

Avatar Adi Da's Revelation of Ruchiradam is Given in five of His "Source-Texts": *Eleutherios, Santosha Adidam, The Lion Sutra, The Overnight Revelation Of Conscious Light,* and *The Dawn Horse Testament Of The Ruchira Avatar.* That Revelation—the Revelation of the Way of directly Realizing Reality Itself—is now the only Word of Instruction that He speaks.

AVATAR ADI DA SAMRAJ: Now My "Occupation", As I <u>Am</u>, Is simply the "Bright". I Do That in My (essentially non-verbal) feeling-interaction with people, without having to get involved in talking anymore—except ecstatically.

I am not here talking about any form of conventional or traditional religion. I do not have anything to do with any such religion. I am Communicating the Way of Realizing Reality Itself. Therefore, I have no tradition to uphold, no tradition that represents Me. I am simply Speaking the Truth.

I <u>Am</u> the Truth. I <u>Do</u> the Truth. That is it.

And What I am Communicating I am Communicating to the world, to everyone, all beings. [March 13, 2001]

Finding Real Happiness

This book is Avatar Adi Da's invitation to you to come to know Him—by freely considering His words, and feeling their impact on your life and heart. Avatar Adi Da Himself has never been satisfied with anything conditional. He has never been satisfied with anything less than Real, Permanent, Absolute Happiness—even in the midst of the inevitable sufferings of life. His Sign and Revelation is the utter freedom and Happiness of the Divine Reality. And that Happiness is What He is Offering to you.

The heart has a question.
The heart must be Satisfied.
Without that Satisfaction—Which is necessarily Spiritual in Nature—there is no Real Happiness.

The contraction of the heart is what you are suffering.
It is the ego.
The egoic life is a search—founded upon (and initiated by) the self-contraction of the total body-mind.
The egoic life is a self-caused search to be relieved of the distress of self-reduced, self-diminished, even utterly self-destroyed Love-Bliss.
Love-Bliss gone, non-existent, unknown—just this pumping, agitated, psycho-physical thing.

The ego-"I" does not know What It Is That Is Happening.
You are just "hanging out" for a while, until "it" drops dead.
It is not good enough.
Therefore, I Advise you to begin to be profoundly religious, and not waste any time about it.
You must Realize the Spiritual Condition of Existence Itself . . . .
You cannot be sane if you think there is only flesh, only materiality, only grossness.
Such thinking is not fully "natural", not enough.
There is "Something" you are not accounting for.
Be open to "Whatever" That Is.
You must look into this. [Hridaya Rosary]

Avatar Adi Da Samraj's Teaching-Word: The "Source-Texts" of Adidam

For twenty-seven years (from 1972 to 1999), Avatar Adi Da Samraj devoted Himself tirelessly to Teaching those who came to Him. Even before He formally began to Teach in 1972, He had already written the earliest versions of two of His primary Texts—His "liturgical drama" (*The Mummery*) and His Spiritual Autobiography (*The Knee Of Listening*). Then, when He opened the doors of His first Ashram in Hollywood (on April 25, 1972), He initiated a vast twenty-seven-year "conversation" with the thousands of people who approached Him during that period of time—a "conversation" that included thousands of hours of sublime and impassioned Discourse and thousands of pages of profound and exquisite Writing. And the purpose of that "conversation" was to fully communicate the Truth for Real.

Both His Speech and His Writing were conducted as a kind of living "laboratory". He was constantly asking to hear His devotees' questions and their responses to His Written and Spoken Word. He was constantly calling His devotees to live what He was Teaching and discover its Truth in their own experience—not merely to passively accept it as dogma. He was constantly testing whether His communication on any particular subject was complete and detailed enough or whether He needed to say more. And everything He said and wrote was a spontaneous expression of His own direct Awareness of Reality—never a merely theoretical or speculative proposition, never a statement merely inherited from traditional sources.

This immense outpouring of Revelation and Instruction came to completion in the years 1997-1999. During that period, Avatar

Adi Da Samraj created a series of twenty-three books that He designated as the "Source-Texts" of Adidam. He incorporated into
these books His most essential Writings and Discourses from all
the preceding years, as well as many new Writings and Discourses
that had never been published previously. His magnificent
"Source-Texts" are thus His Eternal Message to all. They contain
His complete Revelation of Truth, and (together with the
"Supportive Texts", in which Avatar Adi Da Gives further detailed
Instruction relative to the functional, practical, relational, and cultural disciplines of the Way of Adidam) they give His fully detailed
description of the entire process of Awakening, culminating in
Divine Enlightenment.

Avatar Adi Da's twenty-three "Source-Texts" are not simply a
series of books each of which is entirely distinct from all the others.
Rather, they form an intricately interwoven fabric. Each book contains some material found in no other "Source-Text", some material shared with certain other "Source-Texts", and some material
included in all twenty-three of the "Source-Texts". (The three
pieces shared by all twenty-three books are "Do Not
Misunderstand Me", "My Divine Disclosure", and "The Heart-
Summary Of Adidam". Each of these has a particular function and
message that is essential to every one of the books.) Thus, to read
Avatar Adi Da's "Source-Texts" is to engage a special kind of study
(similar to the practice of repeating a mantra), in which certain writings are repeatedly read, such that they penetrate one's being even
more profoundly and take on deeper significance by being read in
a variety of different contexts. Furthermore, each of the "Source-
Texts" of Adidam is thereby a complete and self-contained
Argument. Altogether, to study Avatar Adi Da's "Source-Texts" is
to enter into an "eternal conversation" with Him, in which different meanings emerge at different times—always appropriate to
the current moment in one's life and experience.

At the conclusion of His paramount "Source-Text", *The Dawn
Horse Testament*, Avatar Adi Da Samraj makes His own passionate
Confession of the Impulse that led Him to create His twenty-three
"Source-Texts".

Now I Have, By All My "Crazy" Means, Revealed My One and Many Divine Secrets As The Great Person Of The Heart. For Your Sake, I Made My Every Work and Word. And Now, By Every Work and Word I Made, I Have Entirely Confessed (and Showed) Myself—and Always Freely, and Even As A Free Man, In The "Esoteric" Language Of Intimacy and Ecstasy, Openly Worded To You (and To all). Even Now (and Always), By This (My Avatarically Self-Revealed Divine Word Of Heart), I Address every Seeming Separate being (and each one As The Heart Itself), Because It Is Necessary That all beings, Even The Entire Cosmic Domain Of Seeming Separate beings, Be (In all times and places) Called To Wisdom and The Heart.

Capitalization and Punctuation in the "Source-Texts" of Avatar Adi Da Samraj

Speaking and Writing in the twentieth and twenty-first centuries, Avatar Adi Da Samraj has used the English language as the medium for His Communication. Over the years of His Teaching-Work, Avatar Adi Da developed a thoroughly original manner of employing English as a sacred language. (He also includes some Sanskrit terminology in His Teaching vocabulary, in order to supplement the relatively undeveloped sacred vocabulary of English.)

Avatar Adi Da's unique use of English is evident not only with respect to vocabulary, but also with respect to capitalization and punctuation.

Vocabulary. A glossary is included at the end of this book (pp. 287-324), where specialized terms (both English terms and terms derived from Sanskrit) are defined.

Capitalization. Avatar Adi Da frequently capitalizes words that would not ordinarily be capitalized in English—and such capitalized words include not only nouns, but also pronouns, verbs, adjectives, adverbs, and even articles and prepositions. By such capitalization, He is indicating that the word refers (either inherently, or by virtue of the context) to the Unconditional Divine Reality, rather than the conditional (or worldly) reality. For example:

If there is no escape from (or no Way out of) the corner (or the "centered" trap) of ego-"I"—the heart goes mad, and the body-mind becomes more and more "dark" (bereft of the Indivisible and Inherently Free Light of the Self-Evident, and Self-Evidently Divine, Love-Bliss That Is Reality Itself). ["Do Not Misunderstand Me"]

Avatar Adi Da's chosen conventions of capitalization vary in different "Source-Texts" and in different sections of a given "Source-Text". In certain "Source-Texts" (notably *The Dawn Horse Testament Of The Ruchira Avatar, The Heart Of The Dawn Horse Testament Of The Ruchira Avatar,* and the various Parts of the other "Source-Texts" that are excerpted from *The Dawn Horse Testament Of The Ruchira Avatar*), Avatar Adi Da employs a highly unusual convention of capitalization, in which the overwhelming majority of all words are capitalized, and only those words that indicate the egoic (or dualistic) point of view are left lower-cased. This capitalization convention (which Avatar Adi Da has worked out to an extraordinarily subtle degree—in ways that are often startling) is in itself a Teaching device, intended to communicate His fundamental Revelation that "There Is Only Real God", and that only the ego (or the dualistic or separative point of view) prevents us from living and Realizing that Truth. For example:

Therefore, For My Every Devotee, all conditions Must Be Aligned and Yielded In Love With Me—or Else any object or any other Will Be The Cause Of Heart-Stress, self-Contraction, Dissociation, Clinging, Boredom, Doubt, The Progressive Discomfort Of Diminished Love-Bliss, and All The Forgetfulness Of Grace and Truth and Happiness Itself. [Ruchira Avatara Hridaya-Tantra Yoga]

Note that "and" and "or" are lower-cased—because these conjunctions are (here, and in most contexts) primal expressions of the point of view of duality. Also note that "all conditions", "any object", "any other", and "self-" are lower-cased, while "Heart-Stress", "Contraction", "Dissociation", "Clinging," "Boredom", "Doubt", "Discomfort", "Diminished", and "Forgetfulness" are capitalized. Avatar Adi Da is telling us that unpleasant or apparently "negative" states are not inherently egoic. It is only the presumption of duality and separateness—as expressed by such words as "conditions", "object", "other", and "self"—that is egoic.

Punctuation. Because of the inevitable complexity of much of His Communication, Avatar Adi Da has developed the conventions of punctuation (commas, dashes, and parentheses) to an extraordinary degree. This allows Him to clearly articulate complex sentences in such a way that His intended meaning can be expressed with utmost precision—free of vagueness, ambiguity, or unclarity. Many of His sentences contain parenthetical definitions or modifying phrases as a way of achieving unmistakable clarity of meaning. For example:

The Apparently individual (or Separate) self Is Not a "spark" (or an Eternal fraction) Of Self-Radiant Divinity, and Somehow Complete (or Whole) In itself. [Real God Is The Indivisible Oneness Of Unbroken Light]

Another punctuation convention relates to the use of quotation marks. Avatar Adi Da sometimes uses quotation marks in accordance with standard convention, to indicate the sense of "so to speak":

Make the contact with Me that gets you to "stick" to Me like glue. Your "sticking" to Me is what must happen. [Hridaya Rosary]

In other instances, He uses quotation marks to indicate that a word or phrase is being used with a particular technical meaning that differs from common usage:

During all of My present Lifetime (of Avataric Divine Incarnation), the "Bright" has always been My Realization—and the "Thumbs" and My own "Radical" Understanding have always been My Way in the "Bright".

"Bright", "Thumbs" (referring to a specific form of the Infusion of Avatar Adi Da's Divine Spirit-Current in the body-mind), and "Radical" are all used with specific technical meanings here (as defined in the Glossary).

Finally, Avatar Adi Da also makes extensive use of underlining to indicate special emphasis on certain words (or phrases, or even entire sentences):

> The _only_ true religion is the religion that _Realizes_ Truth. The _only_ true science is the science that _Knows_ Truth. The _only_ true man or woman (or being of any kind) is one that _Surrenders_ to Truth. The only true world is one that _Embodies_ Truth. And the only True (and _Real_) God Is the One Reality (or Condition of Being) That _Is_ Truth. ["Do Not Misunderstand _Me_"]

The True Dawn Horse

Real God _Is_ The Indivisible Oneness Of Unbroken Light is Book One of _The Seventeen Companions Of The True Dawn Horse_. The "True Dawn Horse" is a reference to _The Dawn Horse Testament Of The Ruchira Avatar_, the final book among Avatar Adi Da's "Source-Texts". In _The Dawn Horse Testament,_ Avatar Adi Da describes the entire Process of Real-God-Realization in detail. Each of _The Seventeen Companions Of The True Dawn Horse_ is a "Companion" to _The Dawn Horse Testament_ in the sense that it is an elaboration of a major theme (or themes) from _The Dawn Horse Testament_. And in many of the "Seventeen Companions", an excerpt from _The Dawn Horse Testament_ forms the principal Part, around which the other Parts of the book revolve. (In _Real God Is The Indivisible Oneness Of Unbroken Light_, the principal Part— Part Eight—is derived from chapters six through ten of _The Dawn Horse Testament_.)

The Sacred Image of the Dawn Horse (which appears on the previous page) derives from a vision that Avatar Adi Da Samraj had one night during the spring of 1970, a few months before His Divine Re-Awakening (on September 10, 1970). As His physical body lay sleeping, Avatar Adi Da wandered in subtle form into an open hall, where a great Adept was seated on a throne. The Adept's disciples were lined up in rows in front of him. A pathway bounded on both sides by the disciples led to the throne. Avatar Adi Da was Himself standing at the end of a row a few rows away from the Adept's chair.

The disciples were apparently assembled to learn the miraculous Yogic power of materializing something from nothing. They waited respectfully for the lesson to begin.

The Adept then initiated the process of materialization. A brief while later, the disciples got up and left the room, satisfied that the materialization had been accomplished, although nothing had appeared yet. The Adept remained sitting in his chair, and Avatar Adi Da remained standing before him, attentive to the process at hand.

A vaporous mass gradually took shape in the space between Avatar Adi Da and the Adept. At first it was not clearly defined, but Avatar Adi Da recognized it as it began to take on the features of a horse. Gradually, the vapor coalesced into a living, breathing brown horse. Its features were as fine as a thoroughbred's, but it was quite small, perhaps three feet tall. The horse stood alert, motionless, facing away from the Adept's chair.

At this point in the dream vision, Avatar Adi Da returned to physical consciousness and the waking state.

It was many years later, at the time when Avatar Adi Da was starting to write *The Dawn Horse Testament*, that He Revealed the identity of the Adept He had visited in that vision:

AVATAR ADI DA SAMRAJ: I was at once the Adept who performed the miracle of manifesting the horse, and also the one who was party to the observation of it and its result. And I did not have any feeling of being different from the horse itself. I was <u>making</u> *the horse, I was* <u>observing</u> *the horse, and I was* <u>being</u> *the horse.* [October 18, 1984]

The Dawn Horse is, therefore, a symbol for Avatar Adi Da Samraj Himself—and *The Dawn Horse Testament* is His Personal

Testament to all beings. Avatar Adi Da has commented that He refers to Himself and to His principal "Source-Text" as the "True Dawn Horse" because the effects of His Liberating Work in the world will appear only gradually—just as, in the vision, the horse gradually became visible after the Adept had initiated its materialization.

In creating the Sacred Image of the Dawn Horse, Avatar Adi Da transformed His original vision of a small brown horse, with all four hooves planted on the ground, into a winged white stallion, rearing up nearly vertically:

AVATAR ADI DA SAMRAJ: The horse's pose is majestic and intended to show great strength. White was chosen for its obvious association with Light, or Consciousness Itself. The Image is not precisely associated with the vision of 1970. It is visual language, intended to communicate the full meaning of My Dawn Horse Vision, rather than to be a realistic presentation of it.

The Titles and Subtitles of The Twenty-Three "Source-Texts" of Avatar Adi Da Samraj

The twenty-three "Source-Texts" of Avatar Adi Da Samraj include:

(1) an opening series of five books on the fundamentals of the Way of Adidam (*The Five Books Of The Heart Of The Adidam Revelation*)

(2) an extended series of seventeen books covering the principal aspects of the Way of Adidam in detail (*The Seventeen Companions Of The True Dawn Horse*)

(3) Avatar Adi Da's paramount "Source-Text" summarizing the entire course of the Way of Adidam (*The Dawn Horse Testament*)

The basic content of each "Source-Text" is summarily described by Avatar Adi Da in the title and subtitle of each book. Thus, the following list of titles and subtitles indicates the vast scope and the artful interconnectedness of His twenty-three "Source-Texts". (For brief descriptions of each "Source-Text", please see "The Sacred Literature of Avatar Adi Da Samraj", pp. 326-36.)

The Five Books Of The Heart
Of The Adidam Revelation

BOOK ONE
Aham Da Asmi
(Beloved, I Am Da)
The "Late-Time" Avataric Revelation Of The True and Spiritual Divine Person (The egoless Personal Presence Of Reality and Truth, Which Is The Only Real God)

BOOK TWO
Ruchira Avatara Gita
(The Way Of The Divine Heart-Master)
The "Late-Time" Avataric Revelation Of The Great Secret Of The Divinely Self-Revealed Way That Most Perfectly Realizes The True and Spiritual Divine Person (The egoless Personal Presence Of Reality and Truth, Which Is The Only Real God)

BOOK THREE
Da Love-Ananda Gita
(The Free Gift Of The Divine Love-Bliss)
The "Late-Time" Avataric Revelation Of The Great Means To Worship and To Realize The True and Spiritual Divine Person (The egoless Personal Presence Of Reality and Truth, Which Is The Only Real God)

BOOK FOUR
Hridaya Rosary
(Four Thorns Of Heart-Instruction)
The "Late-Time" Avataric Revelation Of The Universally Tangible Divine Spiritual Body, Which Is The Supreme Agent Of The Great Means To Worship and To Realize The True and Spiritual Divine Person (The egoless Personal Presence Of Reality and Truth, Which Is The Only Real God)

BOOK FIVE
Eleutherios
(The <u>Only</u> Truth That Sets The Heart Free)
The "Late-Time" Avataric Revelation Of The "Perfect Practice"
Of The Great Means To Worship and To Realize The True and
Spiritual Divine Person (The egoless Personal Presence
Of Reality and Truth, Which <u>Is</u> The Only <u>Real</u> God)

The Seventeen Companions
Of The True Dawn Horse

BOOK ONE
<u>Real</u> God <u>Is</u> The Indivisible Oneness
Of Unbroken Light
Reality, Truth, and The "Non-Creator" God
In The True World-Religion Of Adidam

BOOK TWO
The Truly Human New World-Culture
Of <u>Unbroken</u> Real-God-Man
The <u>Eastern</u> Versus The <u>Western</u> Traditional Cultures
Of Mankind, and The Unique New <u>Non-Dual</u> Culture
Of The True World-Religion Of Adidam

BOOK THREE
The <u>Only</u> Complete Way To Realize
The Unbroken Light Of <u>Real</u> God
An Introductory Overview Of The "Radical" Divine Way
Of The True World-Religion Of Adidam

BOOK FOUR
The Knee Of Listening
The Early-Life Ordeal and The "Radical"
Spiritual Realization Of The Ruchira Avatar

BOOK FIVE
The Divine Siddha-Method Of The Ruchira Avatar
The Divine Way Of Adidam Is An ego-Transcending
Relationship, Not An ego-Centric Technique

BOOK SIX
The Mummery
A Parable Of The Divine True Love,
Told By Means Of A Self-Illuminated Illustration
Of The Totality Of Mind

BOOK SEVEN
He-and-She Is Me
The Indivisibility Of Consciousness and Light
In The Divine Body Of The Ruchira Avatar

BOOK EIGHT
Ruchira Avatara Hridaya-Siddha Yoga
The Divine (and Not Merely Cosmic) Spiritual Baptism
In The Divine Way Of Adidam

BOOK NINE
Ruchira Avatara Hridaya-Tantra Yoga
The Physical-Spiritual (and Truly Religious) Method
Of Mental, Emotional, Sexual, and Whole Bodily Health
and Enlightenment In The Divine Way Of Adidam

BOOK TEN
The Seven Stages Of Life
Transcending The Six Stages Of egoic Life,
and Realizing The ego-Transcending Seventh Stage Of Life,
In The Divine Way Of Adidam

BOOK ELEVEN
The All-Completing and Final
Divine Revelation To Mankind
A Summary Description Of The Supreme Yoga
Of The Seventh Stage Of Life In The Divine Way Of Adidam

BOOK TWELVE
The Heart Of The Dawn Horse Testament
Of The Ruchira Avatar
The Epitome Of The "Testament Of Secrets" Of The Divine
World-Teacher, Ruchira Avatar Adi Da Samraj

BOOK THIRTEEN
What, Where, When, How, Why,
and Who To Remember To Be Happy
A Simple Explanation Of The Divine Way Of Adidam
(For Children, and Everyone Else)

BOOK FOURTEEN
Santosha Adidam
The Essential Summary Of The Divine Way Of Adidam

BOOK FIFTEEN
The Lion Sutra
The "Perfect Practice" Teachings In The Divine Way Of Adidam

BOOK SIXTEEN
The Overnight Revelation Of Conscious Light
The "My House" Discourses
On The Indivisible Tantra Of Adidam

BOOK SEVENTEEN
The Basket Of Tolerance
The Perfect Guide To Perfectly Unified Understanding
Of The One and Great Tradition Of Mankind,
and Of The Divine Way Of Adidam As The Perfect Completing
Of The One and Great Tradition Of Mankind

◆ ◆ ◆

The Dawn Horse Testament
Of The Ruchira Avatar

The Dawn Horse Testament Of The Ruchira Avatar
The "Testament Of Secrets" Of The Divine World-Teacher,
Ruchira Avatar Adi Da Samraj

The "Bright"-Art Work of Avatar Adi Da Samraj

After finishing the immense Work of creating the final form of His verbal Teaching (in His twenty-three "Source-Texts"), Avatar Adi Da Samraj became moved to invest Himself, with incredible passion and intensity, in creating an equally profound and all-encompassing body of "Bright"-Art Work. The purpose of His Art is to transmit His Revelatory Vision of Reality—both in terms of what it means to be a mortal being alive in an endlessly changing world and in terms of how all mortality and suffering are gone beyond in the Process of Divine "Brightening".

Indeed, Avatar Adi Da has confessed that the creation of profound works of art is what He is (and has always been) natively moved to do. During the three decades of His Teaching Work, it had been necessary for Him to pour all His energies into articulating His full Wisdom-Teaching—but as soon as that Work was done, His own impulse to create profoundly deep and beautiful works of art came to the fore, establishing itself as a burning necessity (and even a Yogic inevitability) in His Life.

AVATAR ADI DA SAMRAJ: The circumstance of existence, in and of itself, is disheartening. That is why it is necessary to do art.

Art is an essential response to the conditions of existence, a means by which the limitations are transcended, Reality is Realized, Truth is Realized, Light is found. Without that activity—that artistic and, altogether, Spiritual activity—there is nothing but this intrusion of changes and death.

So what is greater than that? By a unique participation, there is the Realization of What Is Greater than that. [May 5, 2001]

Having practiced the arts of painting, drawing, and photography at various times during His Life, Adi Da Samraj eventually concluded that the artistic medium most suited to His purposes was the medium that is the most direct "registering" of light itself—the entire realm of photography and video. However, the photographic and videographic images that Avatar Adi Da creates are only the "blueprints" for His "Bright"-Art Works. The making of those images is the first step in the production of monumental fabrications of many different kinds—made by many different processes and out of many different kinds of materials. He has said that the monumental scale of His "Bright"-Art Works is not a matter of creating a "heroic" impression—rather, the monumentality is a way of conveying profundity and intimacy with the greatest possible intensity.

Certain of Avatar Adi Da's photographic images (those created before August 2000) are intended by Him to be used simply in their "blueprint" form. The cover of each of Avatar Adi Da's twenty-three "Source-Texts" includes two such images—a central image and a border image. In each case, the central image was specifically chosen by Him as appropriate to that particular "Source-Text".

Avatar Adi Da's "Bright" Art is one of His great means of conveying His Spiritual Transmission and Blessing—for the subject of Avatar Adi Da's Art is not the world as we see it, but the world as the "Bright" Field of Reality that He sees. His Art would transport us beyond our ordinary habits of thinking and perceiving into the Divine Light, in Which there is no sense of separation, otherness, or limitation.

AVATAR ADI DA SAMRAJ: From the conventional point of view, a photographer only makes pictures of conventional reality, of light falling on objects, as if the solid reality were the only reality. But neither the fixed separate point of view nor the apparently solid objective world is the Fundamental Reality. The Divine Conscious Light Is the Fundamental Reality of Existence.

Avatar Adi Da's Art communicates the non-dual perception of Reality via a unique process, which He describes as His "inherently egoless participatory relationship" with His subjects (both human and non-human). Thus, His Art transcends the conventions of "self" and "other", or "subject" and "object".

AVATAR ADI DA SAMRAJ: Out of this process, art can be made that Reveals Reality, rather than merely communicating the conventions of "ego" and "other".

Therefore, even the viewing of Adi Da's Art is an inherently participatory event. His "Bright"-Art Works place a demand upon us to go beyond the ordinary fixed point of view. They are a call to go beyond our ordinary limits—for each of them is a communication of the Divine "Brightness", transforming our ordinary perception of the world into sacred occasion.

The border image on the cover of this book is a photograph taken by Avatar Adi Da. He refers to this as an image of "True Water", which is one of His poetic descriptions for Consciousness Itself as the "Medium" in which all phenomena arise (and of which they are all modifications).

Yosemite, 2000

Avatar Adi Da's "Bright"-Art Work is an ecstatic Revelation-Transmission of the Divine Truth That He has Come to Reveal and Teach to humankind. There is extraordinary beauty to be appreciated in Avatar Adi Da's "Bright"-Art Works, but the real purpose of His artistry is to bring Light into our lives, to literally En-Lighten us—to Liberate us from the un-Illumined and mortal vision of egoity. By offering us His sublime "Bright"-Art Works, Adi Da Samraj would have us discover that Non-separate Reality in Which the ever-changing dualities of light and darkness rise and fall.

AVATAR ADI DA SAMRAJ: In My approach to making art, I want to convey the Truth of Reality—the Truth of the Inherently egoless, Non-dual Subjective Light. I am Working to Convey My own Revelation of the Nature of Reality through visual artifacts.

An Overview of
Real God *Is*
The Indivisible Oneness
Of Unbroken Light

In *Real* God *Is The Indivisible Oneness Of Unbroken Light* (the opening volume of *The Seventeen Companions Of The True Dawn Horse*), Avatar Adi Da Samraj Offers us His intellectually rigorous "Consideration"—and His deeply ecstatic Revelation—of Who (or What) God really Is.

Avatar Adi Da uses the term "Real God" as a way of indicating that He is speaking of the Fundamental Reality of Existence—not of any Deity (or Principle) that is a projection of human desires, hopes, or fears (or a product of a mental process of conceptualizing).

Thus, in Avatar Adi Da's language, "Real God" is synonymous with "Truth" and "Reality". His most basic definition of Real God (or Truth, or Reality)—a definition remarkably free of any kind of cultural, religious, or philosophical bias—is "That Which Is Always Already The Case". This Spiritual "equation":

Real God = Truth = Reality =
That Which Is Always Already The Case

is expounded by Him in a powerfully "mantric" series of declarations:

Notwithstanding whatever is conditionally experienced, or known, or believed—Reality Is, Always and Already.
Only Reality Is Real God.
Reality Is, Necessarily, Truth.
Only Truth Is Real God.
Real God Is Reality and Truth.

48

Real God Is The God Of Reality and Truth.
Real God Is The God That Is Reality and Truth.
Reality and Truth Is That Which Is Always Already The Case.
Real God Is That Which Is Always Already The Case.

The title of this book—*Real God Is The Indivisible Oneness Of Unbroken Light*—is a beautifully poetic and precise summary of Avatar Adi Da's Revelation of the Nature of Real God. Through this title, Avatar Adi Da is telling us that His "Consideration" of the Nature of Real God addresses the full range of profound human responses to God (or Truth, or Reality)—not only the deepest intuitions of religion that God Is "Oneness", but also the ultimate conclusion of science that Reality is fundamentally "Light". And He is (further) Revealing to us that That Oneness is Perfectly "Indivisible" (not in any sense "divided" from the world, or from any being or thing), and That Light is Perfectly "Unbroken" (not in any sense affected by the apparent "breaking" of the White "Brightness" of Light Itself into the colors of the spectrum).

In making His Revelations about Reality, Truth, and Real God, Avatar Adi Da is not asking us to merely believe what He says—for Reality, Truth, and Real God cannot be rightly known through any process of mere belief. Rather, He is Calling us to examine the Nature of Reality, and (on that basis) to participate in the Process of Realizing Real God. That Process of Real-God-Realization is the Process of Divine "En-Light-enment", whereby the Supremely "Bright" Conscious Light—Which is the Divine Source and Substance of all of worlds and beings—literally Infuses, Transforms, and (ultimately) Outshines the apparent individual.

In the present age, any authentic investigation into the Nature of Reality, Truth, and Real God must first confront the prevailing "dogma" of scientific materialism—this, because "science" is now widely ceded the status of being the final arbiter of Truth. According to the scientific materialist point of view, there is no "greater" dimension to reality beyond physically "objective" appearances—all is simply "matter", everything is reducible to a mortal materiality, and everything is ultimately explainable by means of the laws of a mechanistic science:

AVATAR ADI DA SAMRAJ: Why is mankind becoming even more and more hopeless? Because it is possessed (and ego-bound) by the belief in the "official" (or "authoritatively" propagandized) declaration of materiality-only—and, on that basis, it doubts Truth (or feels materiality, and mortal "darkness", is the "Truth"), and it doubts Reality Itself (or feels materiality, and mortal "darkness", is the only "Reality"), and, therefore (or likewise), it doubts all religion.

Thus, in this time when the paradigm of materialism is dominant, serious consideration of the nature of Reality is more important than it has ever been before. Far from being a form of idle philosophical speculation, such consideration is a matter of the utmost urgency, which will determine the future mood and destiny of every one of us—and of the world altogether.

The extraordinary Talks and Essays which comprise *Real God Is The Indivisible Oneness Of Unbroken Light* are a profound examination of Reality and Truth, and of the apparently irreducible conflict between science and religion—and they are an equally profound description of Avatar Adi Da's unique Function as the Avataric Divine Realizer, Revealer, and Self-Revelation of Real God. Thus, this book is a Living Seed from which a new, participatory, and utterly benign destiny of humanity may begin to grow.

As with each of the twenty-three "Source-Texts" of Adidam, *Real God Is The Indivisible Oneness Of Unbroken Light* begins with Avatar Adi Da Samraj's First Word, "Do Not Misunderstand Me—I Am Not 'Within' you, but you Are In Me, and I Am Not a Mere 'Man' in the 'Middle' of Mankind, but All of Mankind Is Surrounded, and Pervaded, and Blessed By Me". In this remarkable Essay, Avatar Adi Da Samraj explains that His open Confession of Most Perfect Real-God-Realization is not to be misapprehended as a claim of the "Status" of the "Creator"-God of conventional religious belief, but, rather, His Divine Self-Confession is to be understood and appreciated as a Free Demonstration of the Fulfillment of esoteric Spiritual practice—a Demonstration of the Most Perfectly Non-Dual Realization of Reality Itself. By virtue of this Free Demonstration, Avatar Adi Da

Samraj makes clear that Most Perfect Real-God-Realization (or Divine Self-Realization) is the ultimate Potential and Destiny of all beings.

The Prologue, "My Divine Disclosure" (also, like "First Word", found in all twenty-three "Source-Texts"), is a poetic epitome of Avatar Adi Da's Divine Self-Revelation. It is His Call to every being to turn to Him at heart and practice the life of devotional surrender in Real God.

In Part One, "Real God Cannot Be 'Proved' or Believed, 'Known' or Perceived, or Even Doubted", Avatar Adi Da explains why the traditional academic "proofs" of the existence of God are futile, and why it is crucial to ask the right questions.

In Part Two, "The Inherent Verity of Religion", Avatar Adi Da argues against the modern intellectual tendency to reduce religion to what is acceptable from a "scientific" point of view, explaining that true religion is a self-authenticating Process that requires no external validation.

In Part Three, "Religion Is Not a Science, and Science Is Not a True Substitute for Religion", Avatar Adi Da explains why even the academic proponents of (so-called) "rational" religion end up reducing religion to secular purposes, and He points out the inherent difference between scientific and religious pursuits.

In Part Four, "The Real Intention and True Message of 'Creation' Myths", Avatar Adi Da examines the original meaning and purpose of "Creation" myths, exposing the error of viewing them as a form of primitive pseudo-science.

In Part Five, "There Is No Face Within The Sky: Secular Science, Conventional God-Religion, and The Non-Objective Self-Revelation of Reality, Truth, and Real God", Avatar Adi Da, with extraordinary force, explores the two naive experiential presumptions that lie at the foundation of both scientific materialism and conventional God-religion.

In Part Six, "Truth and Religion", Avatar Adi Da addresses the inherently "cultic" nature of any particular religion, contrasting it with the process of Truth-Realization Itself.

In Part Seven, "I Am The Way to Transcend the Illusions of Broken Light", Avatar Adi Da examines the naive human concept of "matter". He explains that we typically live under materialistic presumptions characteristic of nineteenth-century science, ignoring the implications of E=mc² —that all so-called "matter" is, in reality, a form of "energy", or Light. He Reveals that Divine En-Light-enment is a Process of Realizing the inherently Indivisible Light That Is Reality, and that Divine Process is not about going (or being) "somewhere else"—rather, it is about Realizing That Which Is Always Already The Case.

Part Eight, "Real God Is The Indivisible Oneness Of Unbroken Light", is derived from chapters six through ten of *The Dawn Horse Testament Of The Ruchira Avatar*, and forms the principal Text of this book. Within Part Eight, Avatar Adi Da explores the relationship between Light, Consciousness, and Real God. He Describes the unique characteristics of the Way of Adidam. And He explains the Nature of His Divine Spiritual Body and how, through the Agency of His Divine Body, He Serves the Liberation of all beings.

In Part Nine, "Space-Time Is Love-Bliss", Avatar Adi Da offers potent criticism of the motives and presumptions underlying ordinary religion, ordinary science, and ordinary culture. He Reveals that there is no conflict between true religion and true science, and He describes the fundamental difference between their respective endeavors:

AVATAR ADI DA SAMRAJ: Science is a kind of ordinary human enterprise, in that it is about the investigation of the signs and effects of broken (or conditionally manifested) light—or, in other words, of appearances. True religion, on the other hand, is the Way of always present-time Realization of Fundamental Light—of the inherently Unbroken, Indivisible, and Indestructible Light (or Divine Love-Bliss) That Is Reality Itself.

In Part Ten, "The Heart-Summary Of Adidam" (a brief Essay that is included in all twenty-three "Source-Texts"), Avatar Adi Da summarizes the profound implications of His Statement that the Way of Adidam is the Way of devotion to Him "As Self-Condition, rather than As exclusively Objective Other".

In the Epilogue, "I <u>Am</u> The Unbroken Light Of True Religion", Avatar Adi Da describes the effective Process of true religious practice. He Reveals that He <u>Is</u> the Divine Light Itself, Calling all to Most Perfect Real-God-Realization through the practice of devotional Communion with Him.

Altogether, *Real God <u>Is</u> The Indivisible Oneness Of Unbroken Light* is an extraordinarily unique Gift: the Divine Person's own address to human conceptions of God, Truth, and Reality, and His own Confession of His Real Nature and His Liberating Purpose.

Real God Is
The Indivisible Oneness
Of Unbroken Light

RUCHIRA AVATAR ADI DA SAMRAJ
The Mountain Of Attention, 2001

Do Not Misunderstand <u>Me</u>— I Am <u>Not</u> "Within" <u>you</u>, but you <u>Are</u> In <u>Me</u>, and I Am <u>Not</u> a Mere "Man" in the "Middle" of Mankind, but All of Mankind Is Surrounded, and Pervaded, and Blessed By <u>Me</u>

This Essay has been written by Avatar Adi Da Samraj as His Personal Introduction to each volume of His "Source-Texts". Its purpose is to help you to understand His great Confessions rightly, and not interpret His Words from a conventional point of view, as limited cultic statements made by an ego. His Description of what "cultism" <u>really</u> is is an astounding and profound Critique of mankind's entire religious, scientific, and social search. In "Do Not Misunderstand <u>Me</u>", Avatar Adi Da is directly inviting you to inspect and relinquish the ego's motive to glorify itself and to refuse What is truly Great. Only by understanding this fundamental ego-fault can one really receive the Truth that Adi Da Samraj Reveals in this Book and in His Wisdom-Teaching altogether. And it is because this fault is so ingrained and so largely unconscious that Avatar Adi Da has placed "Do Not Misunderstand <u>Me</u>" at the beginning of each of His "Source-Texts", so that, each time you begin to read one of His twenty-three "Source-Texts", you may be refreshed and strengthened in your understanding of the right orientation and approach to Him and His Heart-Word.

Yes! There is <u>no</u> religion, <u>no</u> Way of God, <u>no</u> Way of Divine Realization, <u>no</u> Way of Enlightenment, and <u>no</u> Way of Liberation that is Higher or Greater than Truth Itself.

Indeed, there is no religion, no science, no man or woman, no conditionally manifested being of any kind, no world (any "where"), and no "God" (or "God"-Idea) that is Higher or Greater than Truth Itself.

Therefore, no ego-"I" (or presumed separate, and, necessarily, actively separative, and, at best, only Truth-seeking, being or "thing") is (itself) Higher or Greater than Truth Itself. And no ego-"I" is (itself) even Equal to Truth Itself. And no ego-"I" is (itself) even (now, or ever) Able to Realize Truth Itself—because, necessarily, Truth (Itself) Inherently Transcends (or Is That Which Is Higher and Greater than) every one (himself or herself) and every "thing" (itself). Therefore, it is only in the transcending (or the "radical" Process of Going Beyond the root, the cause, and the act) of egoity itself (or of presumed separateness, and of performed separativeness, and of even all ego-based seeking for Truth Itself) that Truth (Itself) Is Realized (As It Is, Utterly Beyond the ego-"I" itself).

Truth (Itself) Is That Which Is Always Already The Case. That Which Is The Case (Always, and Always Already) Is (necessarily) Reality. Therefore, Reality (Itself) Is Truth, and Reality (Itself) Is the Only Truth.

Reality (Itself) Is the Only, and (necessarily) Non-Separate (or All-and-all-Including, and All-and-all-Transcending), One and "What" That Is. Because It Is All and all, and because It Is (Also) That Which Transcends (or Is Higher and Greater than) All and all, Reality (Itself)—Which Is Truth (Itself), or That Which Is The Case (Always, and Always Already)—Is the One and Only Real God. Therefore, Reality (Itself) Is (necessarily) the One and Great Subject of true religion, and Reality (Itself) Is (necessarily) the One and Great Way of Real God, Real (and True) Divine Realization, Real (and, necessarily, Divine) En-Light-enment, and Real (and, necessarily, Divine) Liberation (from all egoity, all separateness, all separativeness, all fear, and all heartlessness).

The only true religion is the religion that Realizes Truth. The only true science is the science that Knows Truth. The only true man or woman (or being of any kind) is one that Surrenders to Truth. The only true world is one that Embodies Truth. And the only True (and Real) God Is the One Reality (or Condition of Being) That Is Truth. Therefore, Reality (Itself)—Which Is the One and Only Truth, and (therefore, necessarily) the One and Only Real God—must become (or be made) the constantly applied Measure of religion, and of science, and of the world itself, and of even all of the life (and all of the mind) of Man—or else religion, and science, and the world itself, and even any and every sign of Man inevitably (all, and together) become a pattern of illusions, a mere (and even terrible) "problem", the very (and even principal) cause of human seeking, and the perpetual cause of contentious human strife. Indeed, if religion, and science, and the world itself, and the total life (and the total mind) of Man are not Surrendered and Aligned to Reality (Itself), and (Thus) Submitted to be Measured (or made Lawful) by Truth (Itself), and (Thus) Given to the truly devotional (and, thereby, truly ego-transcending) Realization of That Which Is the Only Real God—then, in the pre-sumed "knowledge" of mankind, Reality (Itself), and Truth (Itself), and Real God (or the One and Only Existence, or Being, or Person That Is) ceases to Exist.

Aham Da Asmi. Beloved, I Am Da—the One and Only Person Who Is, the Avatarically Self-Revealed, and Eternally Self-Existing, and Eternally Self-Radiant (or "Bright") Person of Love-Bliss, the One and Only and (Self-Evidently) Divine Self (or Inherently Non-Separate—and, therefore, Inherently egoless—Divine Self-Condition and Source-Condition) of one and of all and of All. I Am Divinely Self-Manifesting (now, and forever hereafter) As the Ruchira Avatar, Adi Da Samraj. I Am the Ruchira Avatar, Adi Da Samraj—the Avataric Divine Realizer, the Avataric Divine Revealer, the Avataric Divine Incarnation, and the Avataric Divine Self-Revelation of Reality Itself. I Am the Avatarically Incarnate Divine Realizer, the Avatarically Incarnate Divine Revealer, and the Avatarically Incarnate Divine Self-Revelation of the One and Only Reality—Which Is the One and Only Truth, and Which Is the One and Only Real God. I Am the Great Avataric Divine Realizer, Avataric Divine Revealer, and Avataric Divine Self-Revelation long-Promised (and long-Expected) for the "late-time"—this (now, and forever hereafter) time, the "dark" epoch of mankind's "Great

Forgetting" (and, potentially, the Great Epoch of mankind's Perpetual Remembering) of Reality, of Truth, of Real God (Which Is the Great, True, and Spiritual Divine Person—or the One and Non-Separate and Indivisible Divine Source-Condition and Self-Condition) of all and All.

Beloved, I Am Da, the Divine Giver, the Giver (of All That I Am) to one, and to all, and to the All of all—now, and forever here-after—here, and every "where" in the Cosmic domain. Therefore, for the Purpose of Revealing the Way of Real God (or of Real and True Divine Realization), and in order to Divinely En-Light-en and Divinely Liberate all and All—I Am (Uniquely, Completely, and Most Perfectly) Avatarically Revealing My Very (and Self-Evidently Divine) Person (and "Bright" Self-Condition) to all and All, by Means of My Avatarically Given Divine Self-Manifestation, As (and by Means of) the Ruchira Avatar, Adi Da Samraj.

In My Avatarically Given Divine Self-Manifestation As the Ruchira Avatar, Adi Da Samraj—I Am the Divine Secret, the Divine Self-Revelation of the Esoteric Truth, the Direct, and all-Completing, and all-Unifying Self-Revelation of Real God.

My Avatarically Given Divine Self-Confessions and My Avatarically Given Divine Teaching-Revelations Are the Great (Final, and all-Completing, and all-Unifying) Esoteric Revelation to mankind—and not a merely exoteric (or conventionally religious, or even ordinary Spiritual, or ego-made, or so-called "cultic") com-munication to public (or merely social) ears.

The greatest opportunity, and the greatest responsibility, of My devotees is Satsang with Me—Which is to live in the Condition of ego-surrendering, ego-forgetting, and (always more and more) ego-transcending devotional relationship to Me, and (Thus and Thereby) to Realize My Avatarically Self-Revealed (and Self-Evidently Divine) Self-Condition, Which Is the Self-Evidently Divine Heart (or Non-Separate Self-Condition and Non-"Different" Source-Condition) of all and All, and Which Is Self-Existing and Self-Radiant Consciousness Itself, but Which is not separate in or as any one (or any "thing") at all. Therefore, My essential Divine Gift to one and all is Satsang with Me. And My essential Divine Work with one and all is Satsang-Work—to Live (and to Be Merely

Present) <u>As</u> the Avatarically Self-Revealed Divine Heart among My devotees.

The only-by-Me Revealed and Given Way of Adidam (Which is the only-by-Me Revealed and Given Way of the Heart, or the only-by-Me Revealed and Given Way of "Radical" Understanding, or Ruchira Avatara Hridaya-Siddha Yoga) is the Way of Satsang with Me—the devotionally Me-recognizing and devotionally to-Me-responding practice (and ego-transcending self-discipline) of living in My constant Divine Company, such that the relationship with Me becomes the Real (and constant) Condition of life. Fundamentally, this Satsang with Me is the one thing done by My devotees. Because the only-by-Me Revealed and Given Way of Adidam is <u>always</u> (in every present-time moment) a directly ego-transcending <u>and</u> Really Me-Finding practice, the otherwise constant (and burdensome) tendency to <u>seek</u> is not exploited in this Satsang with Me. And the essential work of the community of the four formal congregations of My devotees is to make ego-transcending Satsang with Me available to all others.

<u>Everything</u> that serves the availability of Satsang with Me is (now, and forever hereafter) the responsibility of the four formal congregations of My formally practicing devotees. I am not here to <u>publicly</u> "promote" this Satsang with Me. In the intimate circumstances of their humanly expressed devotional love of Me, I Speak My Avatarically Self-Revealing Divine Word to My devotees, and <u>they</u> (because of their devotional response to Me) bring My Avatarically Self-Revealing Divine Word to <u>all</u> others. Therefore, even though I am <u>not</u> (and have never been, and never will be) a "public" Teacher (or a broadly publicly active, and conventionally socially conformed, "religious figure"), My devotees function fully and freely (<u>as</u> My devotees) in the daily public world of ordinary life.

I Always Already Stand Free. Therefore, I have always (in My Divine Avataric-Incarnation-Work) Stood Free, in the traditional "Crazy" (and non-conventional, or spontaneous and non-"public") Manner—in order to Guarantee the Freedom, the Uncompromising Rightness, and the Fundamental Integrity of My Avatarically Self-Manifested Divine Teaching (Work and Word), and in order to

61

Freely and Fully and Fully Effectively Perform My universal (Avatarically Self-Manifested) Divine Blessing-Work. I Am Present (now, and forever hereafter) to Divinely Serve, Divinely En-Light-en, and Divinely Liberate those who accept the Eternal Vow and all the life-responsibilities (or the full and complete practice) associated with the only-by-Me Revealed and Given Way of Adidam. Because I Am (Thus) Given to My formally and fully practicing devotees, I do not Serve a "public" role, and I do not Work in a "public" (or even a merely "institutionalized") manner. Nevertheless—now, and forever hereafter—I constantly Bless all beings, and this entire world, and the total Cosmic domain. And all who feel My Avatarically (and universally) Given Divine Blessing, and who heart-recognize Me with true devotional love, are (Thus) Called to devotionally resort to Me—but only if they approach Me in the traditional devotional manner, as responsibly practicing (and truly ego-surrendering, and rightly Me-serving) members (or, in some, unique, cases, as invited guests) of one or the other of the four formal congregations of My formally practicing devotees.

I expect this formal discipline of right devotional approach to Me to have been freely and happily embraced by every one who would enter into My physical Company. The natural human reason for this is that there is a potential liability inherent in all human associations. And the root and nature of that potential liability is the ego (or the active human presumption of separateness, and the ego-act of human separativeness). Therefore, in order that the liabilities of egoity are understood (and voluntarily and responsibly disciplined) by those who approach Me, I require demonstrated right devotion (based on really effective self-understanding and truly heart-felt devotional recognition-response to Me) as the basis for any one's right to enter into My physical Company. And, in this manner, not only the egoic tendency, but also the tendency toward religious "cultism", is constantly undermined in the only-by-Me Revealed and Given Way of Adidam.

Because people appear within this human condition, this simultaneously attractive and frightening "dream" world, they tend to live—and to interpret both the conditional (or cosmic and psycho-physical) reality <u>and</u> the Unconditional (or Divine) Reality—from the "point of view" of this apparent (and bewilder-ing) mortal human condition. And, because of this universal human bewilderment (and the ongoing human reaction to the threatening force of mortal life-events), there is an even ancient ritual that <u>all</u> human beings rather unconsciously (or automati-cally, and without discriminative understanding) desire and tend to repeatedly (and under <u>all</u> conditions) enact. Therefore, wher-ever you see an association of human beings gathered for <u>any</u> purpose (or around <u>any</u> idea, or symbol, or person, or subject of any kind), the same human bewilderment-ritual is <u>tending</u> to be enacted by one and all.

Human beings <u>always</u> <u>tend</u> to encircle (and, thereby, to con-tain—and, ultimately, to entrap and abuse, or even to blithely ignore) the presumed "center" of their lives—a book, a person, a symbol, an idea, or whatever. They tend to encircle the "center" (or the "middle"), and they tend to seek to <u>exclusively</u> acquire all "things" (or all power of control) for the circle (or toward the "middle") of <u>themselves</u>. In this manner, the <u>group</u> becomes an <u>ego</u> ("inward"-directed, or separate and separative)—just as the individual body-mind becomes, by self-referring self-contraction, the separate and separative ego-"I" ("inward"-directed, or ego-centric—and exclusively acquiring all "things", or all power of control, for itself). Thus, by <u>self-contraction</u> upon the presumed "center" of their lives—human beings, in their collective ego-centricity, make "cults" (or bewildered and frightened "centers" of power, and control, and exclusion) in <u>every</u> area of life.

Anciently, the "cult"-making process was done, most espe-cially, in the political and social sphere—and religion was, as even now, mostly an exoteric (or political and social) exercise that was <u>always</u> used to legitimize (or, otherwise, to "de-throne") political and social "authority-figures". Anciently, the cyclically (or even annually) culminating product of this exoteric religio-political "cult" was the ritual "de-throning" (or ritual deposition) of the one in the "middle" (just as, even in these times, political leaders are periodically "deposed"—by elections, by rules of term and suc-cession, by scandal, by slander, by force, and so on).

Everywhere throughout the ancient world, traditional societies made and performed this annual (or otherwise periodic) religio-political "cult" ritual. The ritual of "en-throning" and "de-throning" was a reflection of the human observation of the annual cycle of the seasons of the natural world—and the same ritual was a reflection of the human concern and effort to <u>control</u> the signs potential in the cycle of the natural world, in order to ensure human survival (through control of weather, harvests and every kind of "fate", or even every fraction of existence upon which human beings depend for both survival and pleasure, or psycho-physical well-being). Indeed, the motive behind the ancient agrarian (and, later, urbanized, or universalized) ritual of the one in the "middle" was, essentially, the same motive that, in the modern era, takes the form of the culture of scientific materialism (and even all of the modern culture of materialistic "realism"): It is the motive to gain (and to maintain) <u>control</u>, and the effort to control even everything and everyone (via both knowledge and gross power). Thus, the ritualized, or bewildered yes/no (or desire/fear), life of mankind in the modern era is, essentially, the same as that of mankind in the ancient days.

In the ancient ritual of "en-throning" and "de-throning", the person (or subject) in the "middle" was ritually mocked, abused, deposed, and banished—and a new person (or subject) was installed in the "center" of the religio-political "cult". In the equivalent modern ritual of dramatized ambiguity relative to everything and everyone (and, perhaps especially, "authority-figures"), the person (or symbol, or idea) in the "middle" (or that which is given power by means of popular fascination) is first "cultified" (or made much of), and then (progressively) doubted, mocked, and abused—until, at last, all the negative emotions are (by culturally and socially ritualized dramatization) dissolved, the "middle" (having thus ceased to be fascinating) is abandoned, and a "new" person (or symbol, or idea) becomes the subject of popular fascination (only to be reduced, eventually, to the same "cultic" ritual, or cycle of "rise" and "fall").

Just as in <u>every</u> other area of human life, the tendency of <u>all</u> those who (in the modern era) would become involved in religious or Spiritual life is also to make a "cult", a circle that ever increases its separate and separative dimensions—beginning from the "center", surrounding it, and (perhaps) even (ultimately) controlling it (such that it altogether ceases to be effective, or even interesting). Such "cultism" is ego-based, and ego-reinforcing—and, no matter how "esoteric" it presumes itself to be, it is (as in the ancient setting) entirely exoteric, or (at least) more and more limited to (and by) merely social (and gross physical) activities and conditions.

The form that every "cult" imitates is the pattern of egoity (or the pattern that is the ego-"I") itself—the presumed "middle" of every ordinary individual life. It is the self-contraction (or the avoidance of relationship), which "creates" the fearful sense of separate mind, and all the endless habits and motives of egoic desire (or bewildered, and self-deluded, seeking). It is what is, ordinarily, called (or presumed to be) the real and necessary and only "life".

From birth, the human being (by reaction to the blows and limits of psycho-physical existence) begins to presume separate existence to be his or her very nature—and, on that basis, the human individual spends his or her entire life generating and serving a circle of ownership (or self-protecting acquisition) all around the ego-"I". The egoic motive encloses all the other beings it can acquire, all the "things" it can acquire, all the states and thoughts it can acquire—<u>all</u> the possible emblems, symbols, experiences, and sensations it can possibly acquire. Therefore, when any human being begins to involve himself or herself in some religious or Spiritual association (or, for that matter, <u>any</u> extension of his or her own subjectivity), he or she tends again to "create" that same circle about a "center".

The "cult" (whether of religion, or of politics, or of science, or of popular culture) is a dramatization of egoity, of separativeness, even of the entrapment and betrayal of the "center" (or the "middle"), by one and all. Therefore, I have always Refused to assume the role and the position of the "man in the middle"—and I have always (from the beginning of My formal Work of Teaching and Blessing) Criticized, Resisted, and Shouted About the "cultic" (or ego-based, and ego-reinforcing, and merely "talking" and "believing", and not understanding and not really practicing) "school" (or tendency) of ordinary religious and Spiritual life. Indeed, true Satsang with Me (or the true devotional relationship to Me) is an always (and specifically, and intensively) anti-"cultic" (or truly non-"cultic") Process.

The true devotional relationship to Me is not separative (or merely "inward"-directed), nor is it a matter of attachment to Me as a mere (and, necessarily, limited) human being (or a "man in the middle")—for, if My devotee indulges in ego-bound (or self-referring and self-serving) attachment to Me as a mere human "other", My Divine Nature (and, therefore, the Divine Nature of Reality Itself) is not (as the very Basis for religious and Spiritual practice in My Company) truly devotionally recognized and rightly devotionally acknowledged. And, if such non-recognition of Me is the case, there is no truly ego-transcending devotional response to My Avatarically Self-Revealed (and Self-Evidently Divine) Presence and Person—and, thus, such presumed-to-be "devotion" to Me is not devotional heart-Communion with Me, and such presumed-to-be "devotion" to Me is not Divinely Liberating. Therefore, because the true devotional (and, thus, truly devotionally Me-recognizing and truly devotionally to-Me-responding) relationship to Me is entirely a counter-egoic (and truly and only Divine) discipline, it does not tend to become a "cult" (or, otherwise, to support the "cultic" tendency of Man).

The true devotional practice of Satsang with Me is (inherently) expansive (or relational)—and the self-contracting (or separate and separative) self-"center" is neither Its motive nor Its source. In true Satsang with Me, the egoic "center" is always already undermined as a "center" (or a presumed separate, and actively separative, entity). The Principle of true Satsang with Me is Me—Beyond (and not "within"—or, otherwise, supporting) the ego-"I".

True Satsang with Me is the true "Round Dance" of Esoteric Spirituality. I am not trapped in the "middle" of My devotees. I "Dance" in the "Round" with each and every one of My devotees. I "Dance" in the circle—and, therefore, I am not merely a "motionless man" in the "middle". At the true "Center" (or the Divine

Heart), I <u>Am</u>—Beyond definition (or separateness). I <u>Am</u> the Indivisible—or Most Perfectly Prior, Inherently Non-Separate, and Inherently egoless (or centerless, boundless, and Self-Evidently Divine)—Consciousness (Itself) <u>and</u> the Indivisible—or Most Perfectly Prior, Inherently Non-Separate, and Inherently egoless (or centerless, boundless, and Self-Evidently Divine)—Light (Itself). I <u>Am</u> the Very Being <u>and</u> the Very Presence (or Self-Radiance) of Self-Existing and Eternally Unqualified (or Non-"Different") Consciousness (Itself).

In the "Round Dance" of true Satsang with Me (or of right and true devotional relationship to Me), I (Myself) Am Communicated directly to every one who lives in heart-felt relationship with Me (insofar as each one feels—<u>Beyond</u> the ego-"I" of body-mind—to <u>Me</u>). Therefore, I am not the mere "man" (or the separate human, or psycho-physical, one), and I am not merely "in the middle" (or separated out, and limited, and confined, by egoic seekers). I <u>Am</u> the One (Avatarically Self-Revealed, and All-and-all-Transcending, and Self-Evidently Divine) Person of Reality Itself—Non-Separate, never merely at the egoic "center" (or "in the middle" of—or "<u>within</u>", and "inward" to—the egoic body-mind of My any devotee), but always <u>with</u> each one (and all), and always in relationship with each one (and all), and always Beyond each one (and all).

Therefore, My devotee is not Called, by Me, merely to turn "inward" (or upon the ego-"I"), or to struggle and seek to survive merely as a self-contracted and self-referring and self-seeking and self-serving ego-"center". Instead, I Call My devotee to turn the heart (and the total body-mind) <u>toward</u> Me (all-and-All-Surrounding, and all-and-All-Pervading), in relationship—<u>Beyond</u> the body-mind-self of My devotee (and <u>not</u> merely "<u>within</u>"—or contained and containable "within" the separate, separative, and self-contracted domain of the body-mind-self, or the ego-"I", of My would-be devotee). I Call My devotee to function freely—My (Avatarically Self-Transmitted) Divine Light and My (Avatarically Self-Revealed) Divine Person always (and under all circumstances) presumed and experienced (and not merely sought). Therefore, true Satsang with Me is the Real Company of Truth, or of Reality Itself (Which <u>Is</u> the Only Real God). True Satsang with

Me Serves life, because I Move (or Radiate) into life. I always Contact life in relationship.

I do not Call My devotees to become absorbed into a "cultic" gang of exoteric and ego-centric religionists. I certainly Call all My devotees to cooperative community (or, otherwise, to fully coop- erative collective and personal relationship) with one another— but not to do so in an egoic, separative, world-excluding, xeno- phobic, and intolerant manner. Rather, My devotees are Called, by Me, to transcend egoity—through right and true devotional rela- tionship to Me, and mutually tolerant and peaceful cooperation with one another, and all-tolerating (cooperative and compas- sionate and all-loving and all-including) relationship with all of mankind (and with even all beings).

I Give My devotees the "Bright" Force of My own Avatarically Self-Revealed Divine Consciousness Itself, Whereby they can become capable of "Bright" life. I Call for the devotion—but also the intelligently discriminative self-understanding, the rightly and freely living self-discipline, and the full functional capability—of My devotees. I do not Call My devotees to resist or eliminate life, or to strategically escape life, or to identify with the world-excluding ego-centric impulse. I Call My devotees to live a positively func- tional life. I do not Call My devotees to separate themselves from vital life, from vital enjoyment, from existence in the form of human life. I Call for all the human life-functions to be really and rightly known, and to be really and rightly understood, and to be really and rightly lived (and not reduced by, or to, the inherently bewildered—and inherently "cultic", or self-centered and fearful— "point of view" of the separate and separative ego-"I"). I Call for every human life-function to be revolved away from self-contraction (or ego-"I"), and (by Means of that revolving turn) to be turned "outwardly" (or expansively, or counter-contractively) to all and All, and (thereby, and always directly, or in an all-and-All- transcending manner) to Me—rather than to be turned merely "inwardly" (or contractively, or counter-expansively), and, as a result, turned away from Me (and from all and All). Thus, I Call for every human life-function to be thoroughly (and life-positively, and in the context of a fully participatory human life) aligned and adapted to Me, and (Thus and Thereby) to be turned and Given to the Realization of Me (the Avataric Self-Revelation of Truth, or Reality Itself—Which Is the Only Real God).

Truly benign and positive life-transformations are the characteristic signs of right, true, full, and fully devotional Satsang with Me—and freely life-positive feeling-energy is the characteristic accompanying "mood" of right, true, full, and fully devotional Satsang with Me. The characteristic life-sign of right, true, full, and fully devotional Satsang with Me is the capability for ego-transcending relatedness, based on the free disposition of no-seeking and no-dilemma. Therefore, the characteristic life-sign of right, true, full, and fully devotional Satsang with Me is not the tendency to seek some "other" condition. Rather, the characteristic life-sign of right, true, full, and fully devotional Satsang with Me is freedom from the presumption of dilemma within the present-time condition.

One who rightly, truly, fully, and fully devotionally understands My Avatarically Given Words of Divine Self-Revelation and Divine Heart-Instruction, and whose life is lived in right, true, full, and fully devotional Satsang with Me, is not necessarily (in function or appearance) "different" from the ordinary (or natural) human being. Such a one has not, necessarily, acquired some special psychic abilities, or visionary abilities, and so on. The "radical" understanding (or root self-understanding) I Give to My devotees is not, itself, the acquisition of any particular "thing" of experience. My any particular devotee may, by reason of his or her developmental tendencies, experience (or precipitate) the arising of extraordinary psycho-physical abilities and extraordinary psycho-physical phenomena—but not necessarily. My every true devotee is simply Awakening (and always Awakened to Me) within the otherwise bewildering "dream" of ordinary human life.

Satsang with Me is a natural (or spontaneously, and not strategically, unfolding) Process, in Which the self-contraction that is each one's suffering is transcended by Means of total psycho-physical (or whole bodily) heart-Communion with My Avatarically Self-Revealed (and Real—and Really, and tangibly, experienced) Divine (Spiritual, and Transcendental) Presence and Person. My devotee is (as is the case with any and every ego-"I") always tending to be preoccupied with ego-based seeking—but, all the while of his or her life in <u>actively</u> ego-surrendering (and really ego-forgetting and, more and more, ego-transcending) devotional Communion with Me, I Am <u>Divinely</u> Attracting (and <u>Divinely</u> Acting upon) My true devotee's heart (and total body-mind), and (Thus and Thereby) Dissolving and Vanishing My true devotee's fundamental egoity (and even all of his or her otherwise motivating dilemma and seeking-strategy).

There are <u>two</u> principal tendencies by which I am always being confronted by My devotee. One is the tendency to <u>seek</u>—rather than to truly enjoy and to fully animate the Condition of Satsang with Me. And the other is the tendency to make a self-contracting circle around Me—and, thus, to make a "cult" of ego-"I" (and of the "man in the middle"), or to duplicate the ego-ritual of mere fascination, and of inevitable resistance, and of never-Awakening unconsciousness. Relative to these two tendencies, I Give <u>all</u> My devotees only <u>one</u> resort. It is this true Satsang—the devotionally Me-recognizing, and devotionally to-Me-responding, and always really counter-egoic devotional relationship to My Avatarically Self-Revealed (and Self-Evidently Divine) Person.

The Great Secret of My Avatarically Self-Revealed Divine Person, and of My Avatarically Self-Manifested Divine Blessing-Work (now, and forever hereafter)—and, therefore, the Great Secret of the only-by-Me Revealed and Given Way of Adidam—Is that I am <u>not</u> the "man in the middle", but I <u>Am</u> Reality Itself, I <u>Am</u> the Only <u>One</u> Who <u>Is</u>, I <u>Am</u> That Which Is Always Already The Case, I <u>Am</u> the Non-Separate (Avatarically Self-Revealed, and Self-Evidently Divine) Person (or One and Very Divine Self, or One and True Divine Self-Condition) of all and All (<u>Beyond</u> the ego-"I" of every one, and of all, and of All).

Aham Da Asmi. Beloved, I <u>Am</u> Da—the One and Only and Non-Separate and Indivisible and Self-Evidently Divine Person, the Non-Separate and Indivisible Self-Condition and Source-Condition of all and All. I <u>Am</u> the Avatarically Self-Revealed "Bright" Person, the One and Only and Self-Existing and Self-Radiant Person—Who <u>Is</u> the One and Only and Non-Separate and Indivisible and Indestructible Light of All and all. I <u>Am</u> <u>That</u> One and Only and Non-Separate <u>One</u>. And—<u>As</u> <u>That</u> <u>One</u>, and <u>Only</u> <u>As</u> <u>That</u> <u>One</u>—I Call all human beings to heart-recognize Me, and to heart-respond to Me with right, true, and full devotion (demonstrated by Means of formal practice of the only-by-Me Revealed and Given Way of Adidam—Which Is the One and Only by-Me-Revealed and by-Me-Given Way of the Heart).

I do not tolerate the so-called "cultic" (or ego-made, and ego-reinforcing) approach to Me. I do not tolerate the seeking ego's "cult" of the "man in the middle". I am not a self-deluded ego-man—making much of himself, and looking to include everyone-and-everything around himself for the sake of social and political power. To be the "man in the middle" is to be in a Man-made trap, an absurd mummery of "cultic" devices that enshrines and perpetuates the ego-"I" in one and all. Therefore, I do not make or tolerate the religion-making "cult" of ego-Man. I do not tolerate the inevitable abuses of religion, of Spirituality, of Truth Itself, and of My own Person (even in bodily human Form) that are made (in endless blows and mockeries) by ego-based mankind when the Great Esoteric Truth of devotion to the Adept-Realizer is not rightly understood and rightly practiced.

The Great Means for the Teaching, and the Blessing, and the Awakening, and the Divine Liberating of mankind (and of even all beings) Is the Adept-Realizer Who (by Virtue of True Divine Realization) Is Able to (and, indeed, cannot do otherwise than) Stand In and <u>As</u> the Divine (or Real and Inherent and One and Only) Position, and to <u>Be</u> (Thus and Thereby) the Divine Means (In Person) for the Divine Helping of one and all. This Great Means Is the Great Esoteric Principle of the collective historical Great Tradition of mankind. And Such Adept-Realizers Are (in their Exercise of the Great Esoteric Principle) the Great Revelation-Sources That Are at the Core and Origin of <u>all</u> the right and true religious and Spiritual traditions within the collective historical Great Tradition of mankind.

By Means of My (now, and forever hereafter) Divinely Descended and Divinely Self-"Emerging" Avataric Incarnation, I <u>Am</u> the Ruchira Avatar, Adi Da Samraj—the Divine Heart-Master, the First, the Last, and the Only Adept-Realizer of the seventh (or

Most Perfect, and all-Completing) stage of life. I Am the Ruchira Avatar, Adi Da Samraj, the Avataric Incarnation (and Divine World-Teacher) everywhere Promised for the "late-time" (or "dark" epoch)—which "late-time" (or "dark" epoch) is now upon all of mankind. I Am the Great and Only and Non-Separate and (Self-Evidently) Divine Person—Appearing in Man-Form As the Ruchira Avatar, Adi Da Samraj, in order to Teach, and to Bless, and to Awaken, and to Divinely Liberate all of mankind (and even all beings, every "where" in the Cosmic domain). Therefore, by Calling every one and all (and All) to Me, I Call every one and all (and All) Only to the Divine Person, Which Is My own and Very Person (or Very, and Self-Evidently Divine, Self—or Very, and Self-Evidently Divine, Self-Condition), and Which Is Reality Itself (or Truth Itself—the Indivisible and Indestructible Light That Is the Only Real God), and Which Is the One and Very and Non-Separate and Only Self (or Self-Condition, and Source-Condition) of all and All (Beyond the ego-"I" of every one, and of all, and of All).

The only-by-Me Revealed and Given Way of Adidam neces-sarily (and As a Unique Divine Gift) requires and involves devo-tional recognition-response to Me In and Via (and As) My bodily (human) Divine Avataric-Incarnation-Form. However, because I Call every one and all (and All) to Me Only As the Divine Person (or Reality Itself), the only-by-Me Revealed and Given Way of Adidam is not about ego, and egoic seeking, and the egoic (or the so-called "cultic") approach to Me (as the "man in the middle").

According to all the esoteric traditions within the collective historical Great Tradition of mankind, to devotionally approach any Adept-Realizer as if he or she is (or is limited to being, or is lim-ited by being) a mere (or "ordinary", or even merely "extraordinary") human entity is the great "sin" (or fault), or the great error whereby the would-be devotee fails to "meet the mark". Indeed, the Single Greatest Esoteric Teaching common to all the esoteric religious and Spiritual traditions within the collective historical Great Tradition of mankind Is that the Adept-Realizer should always and only (and only devotionally) be recognized and approached As the Embodiment and the Real Presence of That (Reality, or Truth, or Real God) Which would be Realized (Thus and Thereby) by the devotee.

Therefore, <u>no</u> <u>one</u> should misunderstand <u>Me</u>. By Avatarically Revealing and Confessing My Divine Status to one and all and All, I am not indulging in self-appointment, or in illusions of grandiose Divinity. I am not claiming the "Status" of the "Creator-God" of exoteric (or public, and social, and idealistically pious) religion. Rather, by Standing Firm in the Divine Position (<u>As</u> I <u>Am</u>)—and (Thus and Thereby) <u>Refusing</u> to be approached as a mere man, or as a "cult"-figure, or as a "cult"-leader, or to be in any sense defined (and, thereby, trapped, and abused, or mocked) as the "man in the middle"—I Am Demonstrating the Most Perfect Fulfillment (and the Most Perfect Integrity, and the Most Perfect Fullness) of the Esoteric (and Most Perfectly <u>Non-Dual</u>) Realization of Reality. And, by Revealing and Giving the Way of Adidam (Which Is the Way of ego-transcending devotion to Me <u>As</u> the Avatarically Self-Revealed One and Only and Non-Separate and Self-Evidently Divine Person), I Am (with Most Perfect Integrity, and Most Perfect Fullness) Most Perfectly (and in an all-Completing and all-Unifying Manner) Fulfilling the Primary Esoteric Tradition (and the Great Esoteric Principle) of the collective historical Great Tradition of mankind—Which Primary Esoteric Tradition and Great Esoteric Principle Is the Tradition and the Principle of devotion to the Adept-Realizer <u>As</u> the Very Person and the Direct (or Personal Divine) Helping-Presence of the Eternal and Non-Separate Divine Self-Condition and Source-Condition of all and All.

Whatever (or whoever) is cornered (or trapped on all sides) bites back (and fights, or <u>seeks</u>, to break free). Whatever (or who-ever) is "in the middle" (or limited and "centered" by attention) is patterned by (or conformed to) the ego-"I" (and, if objectified as "other", is forced to represent the ego-"I", and is even made a scapegoat for the pains, the sufferings, the powerless ignorance, and the abusive hostility of the ego-"I").

If there is no escape from (or no Way out of) the corner (or the "centered" trap) of ego-"I"—the heart goes mad, and the body-mind becomes more and more "dark" (bereft of the Indivisible and Inherently Free Light of the Self-Evident, and Self-Evidently Divine, Love-Bliss That <u>Is</u> Reality Itself).

I am not the "man in the middle". I do not stand here as a mere man, "middled" to the "center" (or the cornering trap) of ego-based mankind. I am not an ego-"I", or a mere "other", or the representation (and the potential scapegoat) of the ego-"I" of mankind (or of any one at all).

I Am the Indivisible and Non-Separate One, the (Avatarically Self-Revealed) One and Only and (Self-Evidently) Divine Person—the Perfectly Subjective Divine Self-Condition (and Source-Condition) That Is Perfectly centerless (and Perfectly boundless), Eternally Beyond the "middle" of all and All, and Eternally Surrounding, Pervading, and Blessing all and All.

I Am the Way Beyond the self-cornering (and "other"-cornering) trap of ego-"I".

In this "late-time" (or "dark" epoch) of worldly ego-Man, the collective of mankind is "darkened" (and cornered) by egoity. Therefore, mankind has become mad, Lightless, and, like a cornered "thing", aggressively hostile in its universally competitive fight and bite.

Therefore, I have not Come here merely to stand Manly in the "middle" of mankind—to suffer its biting abuses, or even to be coddled and ignored in a little corner of religious "cultism".

I have Come here to Divinely Liberate one and all (and All) from the "dark" culture and effect of this "late-time", and (now, and forever hereafter) to Divinely Liberate one and all (and All) from the pattern and the act of ego-"I", and (Most Ultimately) to Divinely Translate one and all (and All) Into the Indivisible, Perfectly Subjective, and Eternally Non-Separate Self-Domain of My Divine Love-Bliss-Light.

The ego-"I" is a "centered" (or separate and separative) trap, from which the heart (and even the entire body-mind) must be Retired. I Am the Way (or the Very Means) of that Retirement from egoity. I Refresh the heart (and even the entire body-mind) of My devotee, in every moment My devotee resorts to Me (by devotionally recognizing Me, and devotionally—and ecstatically, and also, often, meditatively—responding to Me) Beyond the "middle", Beyond the "centering" act (or trapping gesture) of ego-"I" (or self-contraction).

I Am the Avatarically Self-Revealed (and Perfectly Subjective, and Self-Evidently Divine) Self-Condition (and Source-Condition) of every one, and of all, and of All—but the Perfectly Subjective (and Self-Evidently Divine) Self-Condition (and Source-Condition) is not "within" the ego-"I" (or separate and separative body-mind). The Perfectly Subjective (and Self-Evidently Divine) Self-Condition (and Source-Condition) is not in the "center" (or the "middle") of Man (or of mankind). The Perfectly Subjective (and Self-Evidently Divine) Self-Condition (and Source-Condition) of one, and of all, and of All Is Inherently centerless (or Always Already Beyond the self-contracted "middle"), and to Be Found only "outside" (or by transcending) the bounds of separateness, relatedness, and "difference". Therefore, to Realize the Perfectly Subjective (and Self-Evidently Divine) Self-Condition and Source-Condition (or the Perfectly Subjective, and Self-Evidently Divine, Heart) of one, and of all, and of All (or even, in any moment, to exceed the ego-trap—and to be Refreshed at heart, and in the total body-mind), it is necessary to feel (and to, ecstatically, and even meditatively, swoon) Beyond the "center" (or Beyond the "point of view" of separate ego-"I" and separative body-mind). Indeed, Most Ultimately, it is only in self-transcendence to the degree of unqualified relatedness (and Most Perfect Divine Samadhi, or Utterly Non-Separate Enstasy) that the Inherently centerless and boundless, and Perfectly Subjective, and Self-Evidently Divine Self-Condition (and Source-Condition) Stands Obvious and Free (and Is, Thus and Thereby, Most Perfectly Realized).

It Is only by Means of devotionally Me-recognizing (and devotionally to-Me-responding) devotional meditation on Me (and otherwise ecstatic heart-Contemplation of Me), and total (and totally open, and totally ego-forgetting) psycho-physical Reception of Me, that your madness of heart (and of body-mind) is (now, and now, and now) escaped, and your "darkness" is En-Light-ened (even, at last, Most Perfectly). Therefore, be My true devotee—and, by (formally, and rightly, and truly, and fully, and fully devotionally) practicing the only-by-Me Revealed and Given Way of Adidam (Which Is the True and Complete Way of the True and Real Divine Heart), always Find Me, Beyond your self-"center", in every here and now.

Aham Da Asmi. Beloved, I <u>Am</u> Da. And, because I <u>Am</u> Infinitely and Non-Separately "Bright", all and All <u>Are</u> In My Divine Sphere of "Brightness". By feeling and surrendering Into My Infinite Sphere of My Avatarically Self-Revealed Divine Self-"Brightness", My every devotee <u>Is</u> In Me. And, Beyond his or her self-contracting and separative act of ego-"I", My every devotee (self-surrendered Into heart-Communion With Me) <u>Is</u> the One and Only and Non-Separate and Real God I Have Come to Awaken— by Means of My Avataric Divine Descent, My Avataric Divine Incarnation, and My (now, and forever hereafter) Avataric Divine Self-"Emergence" (here, and every "where" in the Cosmic domain).

RUCHIRA AVATAR ADI DA SAMRAJ
The Mountain Of Attention, 2000

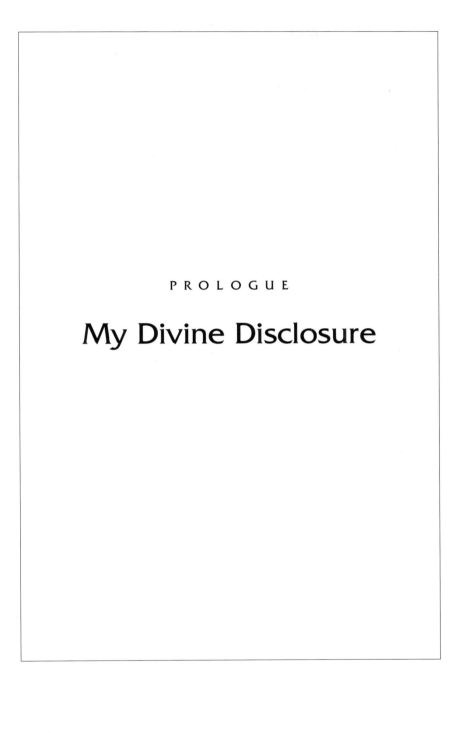

PROLOGUE

My Divine Disclosure

"My Divine Disclosure" has been Freely Developed—As a Further, and All-Completing, Avataric Self-Revelation of His own Self-Evidently Divine Person—by the Ruchira Avatar, Adi Da Samraj, from selected verses of the traditional Bhagavad Gita *(2:13-17, 8:3, 8:22, 9:3, 9:11, 9:26, 15:15, 18:61-66).*

My Divine Disclosure

1.

ham Da Asmi. Beloved, I <u>Am</u> Da—The One and Only and Self-Evidently Divine Person, Avatarically Self-Revealed To You.

2.

Therefore, Listen To <u>Me</u>, and Hear <u>Me</u>, and See <u>Me</u>.

3.

This Is My Divine Heart-Secret, The Supreme Word Of My Eternal Self-Revelation.

4.

Here and Now, I Will Tell You What Will Benefit You The Most, Because I Love You <u>As</u> My Very Self and Person.

5.

I <u>Am</u> The Ruchira Avatar, The Da Avatar, The Love-Ananda Avatar, Adi Da Love-Ananda Samraj—The Avataric Incarnation, and The Self-Evidently Divine Person, Of The One True Heart (or The One, and Only, and Inherently egoless Self-Condition and Source-Condition) Of All and all.

6.

Here I <u>Am</u>, In <u>Person</u>, To Offer (To You, and To all) The Only-By-<u>Me</u> Revealed and Given True World-Religion (or Avatarically All-Completing Divine Devotional and Spiritual Way) Of Adidam, Which Is The One and Only By-<u>Me</u>-Revealed and By-<u>Me</u>-Given (and Only <u>Me</u>-Revealing) Divine Devotional and Spiritual Way Of Sri Hridayam (or The Only-By-<u>Me</u> Revealed and Given, and

Entirely Me-Revealing, Way Of The True Divine Heart Itself), and
Which Is The One, and All-Inclusive, and All-Transcending, and
Only-By-Me Revealed and Given (and Only Me-Revealing) Way
Of The True Divine Heart-Master (or The Only-By-Me Revealed
and Given, and Entirely Me-Revealing, Way Of Ruchira Avatara
Bhakti Yoga, or Ruchira Avatara Hridaya-Siddha Yoga), and
Which Is The "Radically" ego-Transcending Way Of Devotionally
Me-Recognizing and Devotionally To-Me-Responding Reception
Of My Avatarically Self-Manifested Divine (and Not Merely
Cosmic) Hridaya-Shaktipat (or Divinely Self-Revealing Avataric
Spiritual Grace).

7.

If You Surrender Your heart To Me, and If (By Surrendering
Your ego-"I", or self-Contracted body-mind, To Me) You Make
Yourself A Living Gift To Me, and If You (Thus) Constantly Yield
Your attention To Me (Through True Devotional Love and Really
ego-Transcending Service), Then You Will Hear Me (Truly), and
See Me (Clearly), and Realize Me (Fully), and Come To Me
(Eternally). I Promise You This, Because I Love You As My Very
Self and Person.

8.

Abandon The Reactive Reflex Of self-Contraction—The
Separative (or egoic) Principle In all Your concerns. Do Not
Cling To any experience that May Be Sought (and Even Attained)
As A Result Of desire (or The Presumption Of "Difference").
Abandon Your Search For what May Be Gotten As A Result Of
the various kinds of strategic (or egoic) action.

9.

I Am Love-Bliss Itself—Now (and Forever Hereafter) "Brightly"
Present here. Therefore, I Say To You: Abandon All Seeking—
By Always "Locating" (and Immediately Finding) Me.

10.

Instead Of <u>Seeking</u> <u>Me</u> (As If My Divine Person Of Inherent Love-Bliss-Happiness Were <u>Absent</u> From You), <u>Always</u> <u>Commune</u> <u>With</u> <u>Me</u> (<u>Ever</u>-Present, <u>Never</u> Absent, and <u>Always</u> Love-Bliss-Full and Satisfied). Thus, Your <u>Me</u>-"Locating" <u>Relinquishment</u> Of All Seeking Is <u>Not</u>, Itself, To Be Merely Another Form Of Seeking.

11.

If You <u>Always</u> "Locate" <u>Me</u> (and, Thus, <u>Immediately</u> Find <u>Me</u>), You Will <u>Not</u> (In <u>any</u> instance) self-Contract Into the mood and strategy of <u>inaction</u>.

12.

You Must <u>Never</u> <u>Fail</u> To act. <u>Every</u> moment of Your life <u>Requires</u> Your particular <u>Right</u> action. Indeed, the living body-mind <u>is</u> (itself) action. Therefore, <u>Be</u> <u>Ordinary</u>, By Always Allowing the body-mind its <u>Necessity</u> Of Right action (and Inevitable Change).

13.

Perform <u>every</u> act As An ego-Transcending Act Of Devotional Love Of <u>Me</u>, In body-mind-Surrendering Love-Response To <u>Me</u>.

14.

Always Discipline <u>all</u> Your acts, By <u>Only</u> Engaging In action that Is <u>Appropriate</u> For one who Loves <u>Me</u>, and Surrenders To <u>Me</u>, and acts <u>Only</u> (and <u>Rightly</u>) In Accordance With My Always <u>Explicit</u> Word Of Instruction.

15.

Therefore, Be My <u>Always</u> Listening-To-<u>Me</u> Devotee—and, Thus, <u>Always</u> live "Right Life" (According To My Word), and (This) <u>Always</u> By Means Of <u>active</u> Devotional Recognition-Response To <u>Me</u>, and While <u>Always</u> Remembering and Invoking and Contemplating <u>Me</u>. In <u>This</u> Manner, Perform <u>every</u> act As A Form Of Direct, and Present, and Whole bodily (or Total psycho-physical), and Really ego-Surrendering Love-Communion With <u>Me</u>.

16.

If You Love Me—Where Is doubt and anxious living? If You Love Me Now, Even anger, sorrow, and fear Are Gone. When You Abide In Devotional Love-Communion With Me, the natural results of Your various activities No Longer Have Power To Separate or Distract You From Me.

17.

The ego-"I" that is born (as a body-mind) In The Realm Of Cosmic Nature (or the conditional worlds of action and experience) Advances From childhood To adulthood, old age, and death—While Identified With the same (but Always Changing) body-mind. Then the same ego-"I" Attains another body-mind, As A Result. One whose heart Is (Always) Responsively Given To Me Overcomes (Thereby) Every Tendency To self-Contract From This Wonderfully Ordinary Process.

18.

The Ordinary Process Of "Everything Changing" Is Simply The Natural Play Of Cosmic Life, In Which the (Always) two sides of every possibility come and go, In Cycles Of appearance and disappearance. Winter's cold alternates with summer's heat. Pain, Likewise, Follows every pleasure. Every appearance Is (Inevitably) Followed By its disappearance. There Is No Permanent experience In The Realm Of Cosmic Nature. One whose heart-Feeling Of Me Is Steady Simply Allows All Of This To Be So. Therefore, one who Truly Hears Me Ceases To Add self-Contraction To This Inevitable Round Of Changes.

19.

Happiness (or True Love-Bliss) Is Realization Of That Which Is Always Already The Case.

20.

I Am That Which Is Always Already The Case.

21.

Happiness Is Realization Of Me.

22.

Realization Of Me Is Possible Only When a living being (or body-mind-self) Has heart-Ceased To React To The Always Changing Play Of Cosmic Nature.

23.

The body-mind Of My True Devotee Is Constantly Steadied In Me, By Means Of the Feeling-heart's Always Constant Devotional Recognition-Response To Me.

24.

Once My True Devotee Has Truly heart-Accepted That The Alternating-Cycle Of Changes (Both Positive and Negative) Is Inevitable (In the body-mind, and In all the conditional worlds), the living body-mind-self (or ego-"I") Of My True Devotee Has Understood itself (and, Thus, Heard Me).

25.

The body-mind-self (Of My True Me-Hearing Devotee) that Constantly Understands itself (At heart) By Constantly Surrendering To Me (and Communing With Me) No Longer self-Contracts From My Love-Bliss-State Of Inherent Happiness.

26.

Those who Truly Hear Me Understand That whatever Does Not Exist Always and Already (or Eternally) Only Changes.

27.

Those who Truly See Me Acknowledge (By heart, and With every moment and act of body-mind) That What Is Always Already The Case Never Changes.

28.

Such True Devotees Of Mine (who Both <u>Hear</u> <u>Me</u> <u>and</u> <u>See</u> <u>Me</u>)
Realize That The Entire Cosmic Realm Of Change—and Even the
To-<u>Me</u>-Surrendered body-mind (itself)—Is <u>Entirely</u> Pervaded By
<u>Me</u> (Always Self-Revealed <u>As</u> <u>That</u> Which <u>Is</u> Always Already The
Case).

29.

Now, and Forever Hereafter, I Am Avatarically Self-Revealed,
Beyond The Cosmic Play—"Bright" Behind, and Above, the
To-<u>Me</u>-Surrendered body-mind Of My Every True Devotee.

30.

I <u>Am</u> The Eternally Existing, All-Pervading, Transcendental,
Inherently Spiritual, Inherently egoless, Perfectly Subjective,
Indivisible, Inherently Perfect, Perfectly Non-Separate, and
Self-Evidently Divine Self-Condition and Source-Condition
Of <u>all</u> Apparently Separate (or self-Deluded) selves.

31.

My Divine Heart-Power Of Avataric Self-Revelation Is (Now, and
Forever Hereafter) Descending Into The Cosmic Domain (and
Into the body-mind Of Every To-<u>Me</u>-True True Devotee Of Mine).

32.

I <u>Am</u> The Avatarically Self-"Emerging", Universal, All-Pervading
Divine Spirit-Power and Person Of Love-Bliss (That Most Perfectly
Husbands and Transcends The Primal Energy Of Cosmic Nature).

33.

I <u>Am</u> The One and Indivisibly "Bright" Divine Person.

34.

Now, and Forever Hereafter, My Ever-Descending and Ever-
"Emerging" Current Of Self-Existing and Self-Radiant Love-Bliss
Is Avatarically <u>Pervading</u> The Ever-Changing Realm Of Cosmic
Nature.

35.

I <u>Am</u> The One, and Indivisibly "Bright", and Inherently egoless Person Of all-and-All, Within <u>Whom</u> every body-mind Is arising (as a mere, and unnecessary, and merely temporary appearance that, merely apparently, modifies <u>Me</u>).

36.

I Am To Be Realized By Means Of ego-Transcending Devotional Love—Wherein <u>every</u> action of body-mind Is Engaged As ego-Surrendering (present-time, and Direct) Communion With <u>Me</u>.

37.

Those who Do <u>Not</u> heart-Recognize <u>Me</u> and heart-Respond To <u>Me</u>—and who (Therefore) Are Without Faith In <u>Me</u>—Do <u>Not</u> (and <u>Cannot</u>) <u>Realize</u> <u>Me</u>. Therefore, they (By Means Of their own self-Contraction From <u>Me</u>) Remain ego-Bound To The Realm Of Cosmic Nature, and To The Ever-Changing Round Of conditional knowledge and temporary experience, and To The Ceaselessly Repetitive Cycles Of birth and search and loss and death.

38.

Such Faithless beings <u>Cannot</u> Be Distracted By <u>Me</u>—Because they Are Entirely Distracted By <u>themselves</u>! They Are Like Narcissus—The Myth Of ego—At His Pond. Their Merely self-Reflecting minds Are Like a mirror in a dead man's hand. Their tiny hearts Are Like a boundless desert, where the mirage of Separate self is ceaselessly admired, and The True Water Of My Constant Presence Stands Un-Noticed, In the droughty heap and countless sands of ceaseless thoughts. If Only they Would Un-think themselves In <u>Me</u>, these (Now Faithless) little hearts Could Have <u>Immediate</u> <u>Access</u> To The True Water Of My True Heart! Through Devotional Surrender Of body, emotion, mind, breath, and all of Separate self To <u>Me</u>, Even Narcissus Could Find The Way To My Oasis (In The True Heart's Room and House)—but the thinking mind of ego-"I" Is <u>Never</u> Bathed In Light (and, So, it sits, Un-Washed, Like a desert dog that wanders in a herd of flies).

39.

The "Un-Washed dog" of self-Contracted body-mind Does Not think To Notice Me—The Divine Heart-Master Of its wild heart and Wilderness.

40.

The "Wandering dog" of ego-"I" Does Not "Locate" Me In My Inherent "Bright" Perfection—The Divine Heart-Master Of Everything, The Inherently egoless Divine True Self Of all conditionally Manifested beings, and The Real Self-Condition and Source-Condition Of All-and-all.

41.

If Only "Narcissus" Will Relent, and heart-Consent To Bow and Live In Love-Communion With Me, heart-Surrendering all of body-mind To Me, By Means Of Un-Contracting Love Of Me, Then—Even If That Love Is Shown With Nothing More Than the "little gift" of ego-"I" (itself)—I Will Always Accept The Offering With Open Arms Of Love-Bliss-Love, and Offer My Own Divine Immensity In "Bright" Return.

42.

Therefore, whoever Is Given (By heart) To Me Will Be Washed, From head To toe, By All The True Water Of My Love-Bliss-Light, That Always "Crashes Down" On All and all, Below My Blessing-Feet.

43.

My Circumstance and Situation Is At the heart of all beings—where I Am (Now, and Forever Hereafter) Avatarically Self-"Emerging" As The One and All-and-all-Outshining Divine and Only Person (Avatarically Self-Manifested As The "Radically" Non-Dual "Brightness" Of All-and-all-Filling Conscious Love-Bliss-Light, Self-Existing and Self-Radiant As The Perfectly Subjective Fundamental Reality, or Inherently egoless Native Feeling, Of Merely, or Unqualifiedly, Being).

44.

The True heart-Place (Where I Am To Be "Located" By My True Devotee) Is Where The Ever-Changing Changes Of waking, dreaming, and sleeping experience Are <u>Merely</u> <u>Witnessed</u> (and <u>Not</u> Sought, or Found, or Held).

45.

Every conditional experience appears and disappears In Front Of the Witness-heart.

46.

Everything Merely Witnessed Is Spontaneously Generated By The Persistent Activity Of The Universal Cosmic Life-Energy.

47.

The self-Contracted heart of body-mind Is Fastened, <u>Help-lessly</u>, To That Perpetual-Motion Machine Of Cosmic Nature.

48.

I <u>Am</u> The Divine and One True Heart (<u>Itself</u>)—Always Already Existing <u>As</u> The Eternally Self-Evident Love-Bliss-Feeling Of Being (and Always Already Free-Standing <u>As</u> Consciousness Itself, Prior To the little heart of ego-"I" and its Seeming Help-less-ness).

49.

In Order To Restore all beings To The One True Heart Of <u>Me</u>, I Am Avatarically Born To here, <u>As</u> The "Bright" Divine Help Of conditionally Manifested beings.

50.

Therefore (Now, and Forever Hereafter), I <u>Am</u> (Always Free-Standing) <u>At</u> the To-<u>Me</u>-True heart Of You—and I <u>Am</u> (Always "Bright") Above Your body-mind and world.

51.

If You Become My True Devotee (heart-Recognizing My Avatarically Self-Manifested Divine Person, and heart-Responding—With all the parts of Your single body-mind—To My Avatarically Self-Revealing Divine Form and Presence and State), You Will Always Be Able To Feel Me ("Brightly-Emerging" here) Within Your Un-Contracting, In-Me-Falling heart—and You Will Always Be Able To "Locate" Me, As I "Crash Down" (All-"Bright" Upon You) From Above the worlds Of Change.

52.

The To-Me-Feeling (In-Me-Falling) heart Of My Every True Devotee Is (At its Root, and Base, and Highest Height) My Divine and One True Heart (Itself).

53.

Therefore, Fall Awake In Me.

54.

Do Not Surrender Your Feeling-heart Merely To experience and know the Ever-Changing world.

55.

Merely To know and experience The Cosmic Domain (Itself) Is To live As If You Were In Love With Your Own body-mind.

56.

Therefore, Surrender Your Feeling-heart Only To Me, The True Divine Beloved Of the body-mind.

57.

I Am The Truth (and The Teacher) Of the heart-Feeling body-mind.

58.

I Am The Divine and Eternal Master Of Your To-Me-Feeling heart and Your To-Me-Surrendering body-mind.

59.

I <u>Am</u> The Self-Existing, Self-Radiant, and Inherently Perfect Person Of Unconditional Being—Who Pervades The Machine Of Cosmic Nature <u>As</u> The "Bright" Divine Spirit-Current Of Love-Bliss, and Who Transcends All Of Cosmic Nature <u>As</u> Infinite Consciousness, The "Bright" Divine Self-Condition (and Source-Condition) Of All and all.

60.

If You Will Give (and Truly, Really, Always Give) Your Feeling-attention To My Avatarically-Born Bodily (Human) Divine Form, and If You Will (Thus, and Thereby) Yield Your body-mind Into The "Down-Crashing" Love-Bliss-Current Of My Avatarically Self-Revealed and All-Pervading Divine Spirit-Presence, and If You Will Surrender Your conditional self-Consciousness Into My Avatarically Self-Revealed and Perfectly Subjective and Self-Evidently Divine Self-Consciousness (Which <u>Is</u> The Divine True Heart Of Inherently egoless Being, Itself)—Then I Will Also Become An Offering To You.

61.

By <u>That</u> Offering Of Mine, You Will Be Given The Gift Of Perfect Peace, and An Eternal Domain For Your To-<u>Me</u>-True Feeling-heart.

62.

Now I Have Revealed To You The Divine Mystery and The Perfect Heart-Secret Of My Avataric Birth To here.

63.

"Consider" This <u>Me</u>-Revelation, <u>Fully</u>—and, Then, <u>Choose</u> What You Will Do With Your "little gift" of Feeling-heart and Your "Un-Washed dog" of body-mind.

Ruchira Avatar Adi Da Samraj
The Mountain Of Attention, 2000

Real God Cannot Be "Proved" or Believed, "Known" or Perceived, or Even Doubted

Real God Cannot Be "Proved" or Believed, "Known" or Perceived, or Even Doubted

When existing religious myths fall into doubt, efforts to "prove" the existence of "God" (by reason, rather than by belief) tend to follow. However, none of the traditional academic exercises of "proof" relative to the existence of "God" have ever really and finally relieved mankind of religious doubts, or of doubt itself. This is because the source of religious doubts is the failure of religious myths to continue to seem patently true after centuries of institutionalized belief have passed, and the source of doubt itself is the very same mind that seeks to "prove" (as a certain truth) what it <u>cannot</u> believe.

When religious myths fail, no intellectual "proofs" of the existence of "God" can heal the fault. Rather, when religious myths fail, Real God (or Truth, or Reality) must be Realized again. Therefore, when religious myths fail, the Great (and, necessarily, ego-transcending) Process of Real-God-Realization must again be discovered and embraced. (Indeed, it should never have been abandoned in favor of religious myths.) And if mankind as a whole would embrace that Great Process, the mythology of conventional religiosity would no longer be necessary, since Real God, or Truth, or Reality would Grow mankind beyond its childish and adolescent stages of development.

Heart-Communion with Real God, or Truth, or Reality is not (and cannot ever be) a matter of conditional certainty (or of complete "knowledge about"), but it is always (or inherently) a matter of Realizing, or (by transcending the ego-"I", and all "answers", and all "questions") directly entering into, the Mystery (or Inherent, and Ultimate, and Self-Evidently Divine "Ignorance") that is one's Native (or Inherent, and Ultimate, and Self-Evidently Divine) Condition.

The Necessary Characteristic of the existence of Real God is the same as the Necessary Characteristic of your own existence (or the existence of any one or any "thing"). That Necessary Characteristic Is Existence Itself.

Every one, or every "thing", that exists is not ever in a position separate from its own existence. Therefore, it cannot inspect, or objectively "know", its own existence (itself), or the existence (itself) of any one or any "thing" else. Likewise, no one or "thing" is in a position to inspect, or to objectively "know", the existence of Real God. Real God Is Existence Itself, and Existence Itself cannot (As Existence Itself) be inspected, or objectively "known"— not even by Real God! Existence Itself (or the existence of Real God, or even the existence of any one or any "thing") Is (As Such) Unknowable—an Irreducible (and Indivisible) Mystery. Relative to "questions" of existence, every one, and every "thing", is (inherently, and irreducibly) in a permanent state of Divine Ignorance (As, also, Is Real God). Therefore, Real God Is (and cannot, otherwise, be) "Known" only in (or to) Native (or Inherent, and, therefore, truly Divine) Ignorance.

Even as a boy (yet to Most Perfectly Re-Awaken to My own Divine Self-Condition and Avataric Divine Work), I contemplated Existence Itself by enquiring of My apparent conditional self (or My presumed knowledge) in such a manner that I was directly restored to My fundamental (Native, or Inherent) Divine Ignorance (and, thus, to Existence Itself, or the Real-God-Condition, or Truth, or Reality), Free of the barrier that is conditional knowledge and separate self. And, in all the years of My Avatarically Self-Manifested Divine Teaching-Work (after My eventual Divine Re-Awakening), I continued to enquire of My listening devotees: "'Consider' any one or any 'thing' at all. How could any one or any 'thing' exist? Could no one and no 'thing' exist? What Is this, or that? Do you 'know' What any one, or any 'thing', or any condition Is?"

Conventional religion likes to think about the physical universe from the point of view of the physical self. Therefore, conventional religion wonders about "What could have caused all of this and me". And, from such conventional wondering, the myth of the "Creator-God" is developed. But the idea of a "Creator-God" only justifies beliefs that confine one to separate self and conditional world, whereas true religious wonder ultimately goes beyond wondering (itself), and the transcending of even wonder (itself) is a glance that directly transcends separate self and conditional world.

The wonder (or the Mystery beyond wonder) is not <u>how</u> things and apparent beings came to exist (by a chain of causes and effects), but the wonder (or the Mystery beyond wonder) is the <u>fact</u> that any thing (or some thing) exists. In other words, the wonder (or the Mystery) is in the <u>existence</u> of what arises, and not in the <u>how</u>. Therefore, if wonder beyond wonder (or enquiry into the Mystery That Transcends the world, the mind, and the total conditional self) is truly engaged in relation to any thing (or any condition) at all, Existence Itself, or the Feeling of Being (Itself), is directly intuited. And the intuition (thereby) of Existence Itself, or the Feeling of Being (Itself), is the true beginning of Ultimate Religion (or religion that, by progressive transcendence, allows Growth through and beyond all the developmental, or first six, stages of life, even to the degree of Realizing the only-by-Me Revealed and Given seventh stage of life in the Way of Adidam, Which is the only-by-Me Revealed and Given Way of the Heart). Just so, the intuition of Existence Itself, or the Feeling of Being (Itself), is the Most Ultimate Realization Perfected (or Realized to be Inherent, and Inherently Most Perfect) in the context of the seventh stage of life. Therefore, Existence Itself, or the Feeling of Being (Itself), or Consciousness Itself (Self-Existing, Self-Radiant, and Inherently Love-Blissful) <u>Is</u> Real God, or Truth, or Reality. And the Real God, or Truth, or Reality That <u>Is</u> Stands As <u>Is</u> in the existence-place of every thing, being, or condition that seems to be.

This "One" cannot be "proven" to exist, since This "One" merely <u>Is</u>, prior to conditional knowledge.

This "One" cannot be Ultimately approached or Realized via religious myths, since This "One" merely <u>Is</u>, prior to belief.

Therefore, This "One" cannot be "proved" or believed, "known" or perceived. Indeed, This "One" cannot even be doubted, since even doubt is the contemplation of What Is (or of Existence Itself), via the Mystery (or contemplation) of the existence of things, and beings, and conditions, and thoughts, and doubt itself.

Therefore, when religious myths fail, the Way is not to try to "prove" What cannot be believed. Rather, the Way is to ask the right questions. (Do you know What any thing, or being, or condition Is?) And the right questions lead to contemplation (and, potentially, to Real-God-Realization, or Realization of Truth and Reality), whereas the wrong questions (as well as all conventional answers) lead only to the doubter and back to the doubt.

RUCHIRA AVATAR ADI DA SAMRAJ
The Mountain Of Attention, 2000

PART TWO

The Inherent Verity
of Religion

The Inherent Verity
of Religion

The "modern" (Western, and "Westernizing") culture of scientific materialism has produced many offshoots in otherwise non-scientific fields. One of these offshoots is "modern" academic reductionism, or the intellectual tendency to interpret all human activities (including religion) according to what is acceptable to a Western (or "modern") and scientific system of propositions. However, even though scientific materialists (and "modernists" in general) may be reluctant to positively accept and affirm the propositions, the methods, and the experiences of religionists as evidence of Real God, or Truth, or Reality, the motive to transcend the suffering <u>inherent</u> in (and altogether characteristic of) conditional existence—or, more properly stated, the motive to Realize <u>Perfect</u> Happiness, which motive leads to the progressive renunciation (and, ultimately, to the transcending) of conditional existence itself—has been (and, presumably, will continue to be) a fundamental characteristic and inclination of the most serious (or most deeply inspired, and self-aware, and, on that basis, ego-renouncing) men and women in every generation of mankind, and the uninspected optimism of all others in any generation (including those in the generations mobilized by the propaganda of scientific materialism) does not at all undermine the inherent verity of such most serious views, motives, and endeavors.

Religion is not itself a "scientific" endeavor, and even the right academic (or formal intellectual) study of religion requires genuine tolerance, true seriousness, real (and, otherwise, ever-increasing) self-understanding, and a significant depth of real religious experience (or, at least, a willingness to begin to enter deeply into the real experiential process of religious life). In any case, the only true school of religion is the school of constant devotional service to a true Realization-Master, within an authentic culture and community of practitioners of the religious life. Only in that school of Good Company is there (by means of inspiration, expectation, and Grace) the real (and, potentially, really fruitful) practice of authentic self-surrender to the Ordeal of genuine religious life, or the progressively experiential and ego-transcending process of actual religious Awakening—which Ordeal (or real process) and actual Awakening authenticate themselves (directly and inherently), and, therefore (in the doing and the Realizing), require no further explanation or other justification.

RUCHIRA AVATAR ADI DA SAMRAJ
The Mountain Of Attention, 2000

Religion Is Not a Science, and Science Is Not a True Substitute for Religion

Religion Is Not a Science, and Science Is Not a True Substitute for Religion

Positive and sincere arguments for "rational" and "scientific" religion are sometimes presented by academic writers on religion. However, although such arguments are generally well-intended, and even though such arguments may bear merit as a positive and effective defense of religion, the principal logic of argumentation underlying this defense is thoroughly secular and exoteric. As a result of the widespread prejudice toward a secular (and scientific) and exoteric (and social) view of religion, such exoterically based pro-religious arguments actually epitomize the principal errors that also characterize even the anti-religious arguments that are the more common expressions of the secular mentality.

The exoterically based defense of religion is, in fact, a reduction of religion to <u>secular</u> purposes—and especially to the exercises of <u>social</u> <u>morality</u>. The advocates of this reductionism often propose that science, rather than the process (and the Great Realizers) of religion itself, is the appropriate measure of what is acceptable as religion. And, therefore, because science is both secular and exoteric, or limited to what is presumed to be natural, or material, or objective, or bound to the body-based and psycho-physical point of view, it is concluded (by the proponents of religious reductionism) that religion must be likewise (and only) secular and exoteric.

Both the practitioners and the critics of religion should understand that religion (even though it, like science, is also associated with systems, techniques, and the pursuit of understanding) is not, in the strictly modern sense of the term, science (or even a science)—and science is not a religious method (even though some may embrace science, and the scientific method, as a substitute for religion). Indeed, it can rightly be said that, whereas science is a pursuit of knowledge (and the power, or the relative freedom from helplessness, that knowledge grants to the knower), religion is the pursuit of a progressive un-knowing (of egoity)—and, at last (or Ultimately), religion is the Realization of the Most Perfect State of Non-knowing (or of Utter Surrender, Perfect Freedom, Unqualified Happiness, Unlimited Existence, and Absolute Consciousness).

In fact and in practice, science pursues (and is fit to pursue) knowledge about only the conditional world (and all conditional forms and states), and science pursues such knowledge in order to achieve power (whether positively or negatively) over the conditional world (and all conditional forms and states). Therefore, science, which is always enacted from a point of view that is inherently separate (or that is presumed to be inherently separate) from any object it investigates, is necessarily (or by definition) an ego-based and ego-serving activity, whether the "ego" thus assumed or served is regarded to be an individual or a collective one. By contrast, religion (in its potential true exercise) pursues (or must pursue) real (and, potentially, even Inherently Most Perfect) ego-transcendence, and the (either conditional or unconditional) Realization of Oneness with (or Non-Separateness from) Real God (or the Ultimate Source-Condition, or Truth, of conditional existence), and, thus (potentially, on the basis of that Realization), the Realization (whether conditional or unconditional), and the living demonstration, of Oneness with (or Non-Separateness from) the world (or all that arises in Real God, or in the Ultimate Source-Condition, or Truth).

Because of the inherent differences between religion and science, religion need not (and, indeed, cannot fruitfully) appeal to science for Truth Itself, and science need not (and, in general, is obliged not to) appeal to religion for the conditional truths (or objective facts, or natural laws) of science itself. It is naturally inevitable that some kind of dialogue occur between the practitioners (and the Realizers) of religion and the practitioners (and the proponents) of science. It is also naturally inevitable that presumed knowledge and intellectual techniques acquired via scientific endeavor be used in the critical study of religion as an academic and historical subject—even, thus, producing useful criticisms of traditional cosmologies, archaic presumptions about the conditional world, exaggerated (or otherwise falsified) traditional reports, and so forth. And it is, likewise, naturally inevitable that the disposition and the Realizations of religion be brought critically to bear on the point of view and the results of scientific endeavor—even, thus, sometimes finding incidental likenesses and incidental corroborations between the independent findings of both religion and science. However, all such critical dialogues are a piecemeal and low-level process, and one that is entirely secondary (and not at all necessary) to the essential process that is either religion itself or science itself. And—although it would be best for everyone if scientists were, in the truest and most tolerant and benign (and increasingly esoteric) sense, religious—religious practitioners do not, in general, require a life much involved with science. An ordinary layman's grasp of scientific (or natural) laws and discoveries is functionally, practically, and socially sufficient for most people, even in an age dominated by scientific idealism (and scientific materialism). But, relative to religion itself, what is truly and always required is not more science and technology, but more real (and always _advancing_) religious practice, and, in every individual case, always increasing resort to a true Realizer, to the unique Grace available via a true Realizer, and to the process of ever-greater (and Grace-Given) Realization.

Viewed in the light of such right understanding of both religion and science, it is clear that the religious reductionism characteristic of this "late-time" is a result of too much submission of religion to the review of science (even to the degree of subordinating religion to science). Such subordination of religion to science (and to secularism in general) typifies and epitomizes the most characteristic errors of judgement relative to religion and life that typify and epitomize the much discussed (and much suffered) "modern mind" of Man. That mind is identified with the bodily-based ego, and, therefore, it is prejudiced toward scientific materi-alism, secular humanism, and every kind of idealization of the potential of the natural world and the natural human being.

Ultimately, the limitations of all arguments for "secularized religion" are the limitations inherent in the body-based point of view (and, especially, the point of view associated with the first three stages of life). The philosophy and/or the religion anyone proposes is limited (or otherwise defined) by the stage of life in which (or, at least, for which) he or she truly stands. Science itself (and the so-called "modern mind" in general) stands firmly in the general context of the first three stages of life. Anyone's philoso-phy or religion can be clearly understood (and its limitations or merits rightly appraised), if the particular philosophy or religion is properly examined and assessed relative to the seven stages of life (as I have proposed, Described, and Revealed them). Indeed, if this were done, then the relative persuasiveness or non-persuasiveness of any particular philosophical or religious proposition or argu-ment would be seen to be based on the developmental stage of life of the proposer (or arguer)—and, also, on the developmental stage of life of the one who, in any instance, regards (or receives) that proposition (or argument).

RUCHIRA AVATAR ADI DA SAMRAJ
Lopez Island, 2000

The Real Intention
and True Message
of "Creation" Myths

PART FOUR

The Real Intention and True Message of "Creation" Myths

Popular traditional religion tends to be associated with "Creation" myths, or archetypal and allegorical stories (which certainly do not qualify as eyewitness reports on the origins of the physical world) that, in their proposed details, try to account for the existence of the world and mankind as the <u>effects</u> of acts on the part of either one or many Deities (or cosmically Powerful Beings). The origin of such stories is in the "primitive" awe of existence experienced by (generally) pre-"civilized" human individuals and groups. That awe was experienced in relation to the mysteriously and unaccountably existing natural and human world, and the "Creation" stories were themselves human psychic <u>creations</u>, or projections of the human psyche onto (and through) the natural forms of existence.

Indeed, "primitive" myth-making expresses a fundamental and profound (and, ultimately, Spiritual) <u>Realization</u>, that the "natural" world is not merely physical, but it is entirely <u>psycho-physical</u>, or an interplay of the psychic (or the mental, or the "invisible") and the physical, and that both the "visible" (or physical) and the (generally) "invisible" are Rooted In What Transcends both psychic and physical phenomena. Likewise, that same Realization affirms that human existence (fully embraced) is not merely a matter of knowing and suffering (or, otherwise, manipulating) physical events, but it is a kind of Quest, or Great Ordeal, wherein the human individual (and human cultures) must ever strive to achieve psychic unity (or psychic reunification) with the natural world, psychic (and total psycho-physical) association with the Power that Pervades the natural world, and Ultimate Realization of the Inherently Perfect (or, Inherently, Perfectly Free and Happy) Condition beyond even the total (or psycho-physical) world. And this Great Ordeal is (or was, and must be) presumed to involve the constant transcending of merely physical reality by the constant invocation (or evocation) of the psyche, the Great Power (or many Great Powers, or many lesser powers) that can Help it, and the Great (or True and Inherently Perfect and Perfectly Subjective) Self-Condition That Is its Ultimate Source-Condition. Therefore, the "Creation" stories (and even all culturally operative myths) were (or are) intended not merely to account for natural existence, but to project human beings into a participatory psychic (and not at all abstracted, or merely intellectual) relationship to the natural world (including its "invisible" or "inner" dimensions).

"Creation" stories generally communicate via images associated with the physically (or gross bodily) based psyche (although they may contain representations of psychic contents that are meaningful in the context of each and all of the first five stages of life). And although one "God", and many "Gods", and many "Goddesses" are described in "Creation" myths as the Causative Powers (or "Creators") of the world and mankind, the original motive and source of these descriptions was not any otherwise independent experience of either the local or the universal Deity (or Deities), but the primal (or psychically "primitive") experience of awe (or fear and wonder) in the context of gross bodily existence in the "natural" (or conditional and cosmic) world.

In other words, the "creative" source (or productive motive) of "Creation" myths was (or is) not "God", "Gods", or "Goddesses", but the psychically (and psychologically) mysterious and terrible experience of physical existence and the physical world (or physically defined bodily existence within the physical periphery, or "outer" limits, of the psycho-physical world). On the basis of that experience, the human psyche anciently began (and always presently begins) its "natural" work of generating (or spontaneously Revealing) psychically effective means for transcending fear and for Realizing true (or fearless) participation in the apparent world (and the "Beyond"). And once human beings began to participate psychically (or psycho-physically) even in the gross phenomenal world, they (or the psyche itself) began to develop complex mythological (or archetypal and allegorical) representations of the Mana[1] (or Spirit-Power) that (it was naively presumed) magically, or miraculously, or omnipotently <u>causes</u> (but, really, only Pervades) all effects (and can, therefore, Help human beings in the Great Quest).

The fully developed ancient "Creation" myths originally appeared (or began their development) in animistic societies (wherein every thing, event, person, or process was felt to be a manifestation of its own individual mana, or spirit, or power). As collective myths (and societies themselves) developed over time, a hierarchy of powers was conceived (just as societies themselves were conceived hierarchically—from the chief, or king, at the top to the slaves at the bottom). Thus, animistic myths of local powers were progressively enlarged toward a cosmic description of senior and great Powers. And these descriptions were themselves <u>often</u> developed to the degree of hierarchical grandness, with the "One" (or the One "God", or the One "Mind") at the top and all multiplicity (of "Gods", "Goddesses", powers, worlds, things, and lesser beings) expanding (by stages) below. (Therefore, the "One", even as "Creative God", was not the exclusive and original discovery— or, as some would have it, the exclusive and original invention— of any particular society or culture, although some proponents like to argue or claim that the Jews were the originals in this regard. However, the Jews in particular—in reaction to their early historical disintegration as an independent political collective, and in anticipation of the dispersal of Jewish people among the peoples of all nations—did raise their own tribal, or local, "God" to the status of a universal and Absolute "God"-King of <u>all</u> nations. And this universalizing—and rather political, or "civilizing"— tendency of progressive Jewish, and, later, Christian and Muslim, monotheism eventually provided a basic justification for all

---

* Notes to the Text of <u>Real</u> God <u>Is</u> The Indivisible Oneness Of Unbroken Light appear on pp. 285-86.

Western political, social, and cultural efforts toward the unification, and even the universal "Westernization", of mankind.)

In any case, the truly original and really "creative" source of all ancient and traditional "Creation" myths was the native "interior", or the archetypal and hierarchical design of the human psyche itself (which apparently is eternally existing, or is, at least, existing prior to, and sometimes coincident with, and not merely subordinate to—or merely dependent upon, or existing merely as an effect of—gross bodily existence). And, as it was perceived by shamans and psychic visionaries and seers of all kinds (for whom the "invisible" sometimes becomes "visible", or Revealed even within the interior mechanisms of gross perception), the "Great Within" is (from the gross bodily point of view) grounded in the body—and it extends upwards, even bodily, to the subtler reaches of the body-mind and the subtler (or higher) reaches of the mind itself (and of the psycho-physical cosmos itself). Ultimately, both high and low are to be Most Perfectly transcended in the Beyond That Is the Heart Itself, or the One Divine Reality of Being (Itself).

Clearly, the ancient "Creation" myths (and all myths in general) were (or are), by virtue of traditional (or, otherwise, spontaneous and "natural") techniques of psychic inversion (or inwardness), psychically inspired (or, at least, inspired via the psyche)—and, therefore, all types of mythic "thinking" express the many and various possible levels of traditional (and possible) human psychic (or psycho-physical) participation in the apparent world. Therefore, no such traditional myths are Absolute, and none of them are based on any kind of scientific (or analytical and basically non-participatory) conception or perception of the physical world. Rather, all of them are based on a purely psychic (or entirely participatory) urge toward the total (or psycho-physical) world. And, in all such myths, it is not the physical world (or its array of physical causes and physical effects) but the innate design of the human psyche (and even the total psycho-physical and—as it may, in due course, be Realized—Spiritual anatomy of Man) that is the principal subject displayed by means of myth.

Ancient myth-making was fundamentally an expression of "primitive" magic (or magical ritual), mysticism, and Spirituality, rather than an early (or "primitive") form of science. The myth-makers were not merely trying to describe how physical forms are (in the mechanical, or merely physical, sense) produced, but (since physical forms already existed) the myth-makers were trying to raise human existence to a greater level of participation (or ecstasy) in the total context of natural (or psycho-physical) existence. Therefore, myths were, originally (and rightly), psychic tools (used along with many other cultural and psycho-physical means) for the achievement of magical, mystical, and (ultimately) Spiritual "intoxication" and ecstasy, or the Realization of a psychic state of non-separateness, non-fear, and Ultimate Unity (or even the Realization of the Ultimate Identity). And myths (or myth-making societies) were (or are), therefore, not merely pre-scientific—and, thus, according to the scientific (or, really, <u>materialistic</u>) view, <u>wrong</u>—but myths and myth-makers represent the specifically <u>religious</u> (or <u>non</u>-scientific, and non-materialistic) form of human culture and individual endeavor, which form of culture and endeavor is, even now, in its greatest (or most difficult) moment of struggle (in the face of the worldwide trend toward submission to the materialistic philosophy and culture of scientism and gross technology).

In the process of the pursuit of hierarchically greater and greater levels of ecstasy, visionaries (or ecstatics of all kinds) developed the ancient concepts (or psychic perceptions) of the "chain" or "ladder" (or innate hierarchical structure) of the cosmos. And the ecstatic experiences of Ultimate Unity (and even Ultimate Identity) achieved by certain uniquely great individuals eventually led some cultures to postulate (or give mythic acknowledgement to) an Ultimate Singleness (described in theistic cultures as the "One God").

The ancient and traditional myths have been culturally transmitted down to the present day via traditional religious cultures and sects. And each culture or sect tends to value its own myths as exclusive and final "Truths". However, now that mankind is gathered as an intercommunicative whole, the provincialism (or tribalism) of exclusive myth and exclusive religion has become both obvious and untenable. Therefore, more and more, mankind must receive <u>all</u> traditions, together, as a basically single Great Tradition—and that Great Tradition must be rightly interpreted and fully understood (and final Truth must be clearly discriminated from the progressive display of partial and tentative truths).

Relative to "Creation" myths themselves, they should not merely be criticized and dismissed as pseudo-science, but they should be understood as exoteric artifacts of "primitive" (and even esoteric) magic, mysticism, and Spirituality (and even Spiritual philosophy). And it is no longer either necessary or appropriate for religion itself to base itself on (or otherwise depend on) "natural" or cosmic arguments for the existence of "God". As all the Great Seers have proclaimed, Real God (or Ultimate Reality, and Truth, and Happiness Itself) is not "out there" (at the beginning of a long chain of events in the objective context of the merely physical world). Rather (as the myth-makers themselves were demonstrating in the very making of "Creation" myths), Real God, Truth, Ultimate Reality, or Happiness Itself <u>Is</u> "within" (or <u>In</u> the context of the total—or psycho-physical, and, also, as it may, in due course, be Realized, Spiritual—world). Indeed, Real God <u>Is</u> Existence (or Being) Itself. Real God, Truth, Ultimate Reality, Happiness Itself, or Existence (or Being) Itself Is Self-Evident (unless the mind interferes and disagrees and seeks). And Real God, Truth, Ultimate Reality, Happiness Itself, or Existence (or Being) Itself is, therefore, not to be "proven" by conceptual argument—but Real God, Truth, Ultimate Reality, Happiness Itself, or Existence (or Being) Itself is to be directly Realized (by ego-transcending psychic participation in the psyche itself, or the total psycho-physical design in which the personal self inheres—and, Ultimately, by Inherently Most Perfect transcending of the psyche, or the total body-mind, itself <u>and</u> the entire psycho-physical world).

The Message of all "Creation" myths is a Call to magical, mystical, and Spiritual ecstasy, progressively transcending the hierarchies of "Creation". Myths themselves (or myths of every kind) are not a call to mere belief, but a Call to ecstatic (and, therefore, effectively ego-transcending) Real-God-Realization (or to even Spiritual Realization of the Truth, or Real Condition, of cosmic existence). And, once myths themselves (and all the categories associated with the first five stages of life) are Out-Grown, the final Call is to Realization of That Which Is—Beyond all conditional and cosmic categories. As long as the propagation of "Creation" myths (and religious myths in general) is limited to the domain of popular exoteric religion, all myths are used more or less exclusively to support the popular (and "creaturely") social, political, and institutional purposes of public "civilization"—but, if religious myths are visited in the context of the real process of self-understanding and participation in the esoteric Spiritual culture of ecstasy (or effective self-transcendence), then they serve as psychic reminders of the Great Ordeal that leads, Most Ultimately, not to a "Place" above the stars, but to the Transcendental, Inherently Spiritual, and Self-Evidently Divine Self-Condition and Source-Condition (transcending both "outside" and "inside")—the Beyond That Is the Heart Itself.

And just as that Great Ordeal does not (or should not) stop either in the world of the gross body or in inner visions of the cosmic Man, it is not necessary that religion itself begin in (and it is certainly neither appropriate nor sufficient that it end in) belief in a "Creator-God" (or even many "Creator-Gods" or "Creator-Goddesses"). Indeed, such "Creator and creature" beliefs are primarily about the world (and only secondarily about Real God, or Truth, or Inherently Perfect Reality)—and, therefore, they tend to affirm and idealize gross (or "creaturely") human and social existence, rather than to effectively guide human attention to ego-transcendence in Real God, or Truth, or Inherently Perfect Reality, or the Most Ultimate Realization of Happiness Itself. Therefore, may not religion begin as it (in Truth) must end—with self-understanding and a (soon direct) Spiritual Awareness of That Which Merely (or Inherently Perfectly) Contains, Pervades, and Transcends the world (while the world itself is made and unmade by every kind of conditional, and even Godless, cause and effect)? And is it not by religion itself that Real God, or Truth, or Inherently Perfect Reality becomes "Creative" (when Man opens at the core, and, by psychic participation, opens the world at the core, thus giving room to Spirit-Power), whereas, otherwise (apart from total, or psycho-physical, and ego-transcending Surrender to Truth), the world and Man are "Created" and changed by much and all that is not Divine? Indeed, if Real God, or Truth, or Inherently Perfect Reality were the Direct, Simple, and Only "Creator", religion would not be necessary to convert, and raise up, and "Perfect" any one at all, but Perfection Itself would "Picture" here in the Perfection of all "Creation" (from the beginning, unchanging, and never ending).

Until the One and Perfect Is Realized (and "Perfected" in Its "Bright" Demonstration), all the countless imperfections gather in twos and threes to pester and break the heart. And this begins at the "beginning" itself, or in every present instant of perceived (or, otherwise, intended) separation between "light" and "dark", "this" and "That", "Heaven" and "Earth", and the "other" and "I". Therefore, the true Message of myth (or of religion itself) is ego-transcendence. If by myth (or by any other means) the natural (or psycho-physical) world and the human self are conceived and perceived to arise within the Context of the Spiritual and Transcendental Divine, then the total world and the human self are not merely to be desired and clung to for their own sake (as if they were an irreducible necessity), but the total world and the human self are to be progressively (and directly, or even immediately) transcended In the Spiritual and Transcendental Divine (Which Is the Only Necessity).

RUCHIRA AVATAR ADI DA SAMRAJ
The Mountain Of Attention, 2000

PART FIVE

There Is <u>No</u> Face Within The Sky:

Secular Science, Conventional God-Religion, and The Non-Objective Self-Revelation of Reality, Truth, and Real God

There Is No Face
Within The Sky:

Secular Science, Conventional God-Religion, and The Non-Objective Self-Revelation of Reality, Truth, and Real God

Conventional (or merely exoteric) God-religion is, fundamentally, not about God—but it is about Man. And, most fundamentally, conventional (or merely exoteric) God-religion is not about Real-God-Realization (or the Real-"Knowing" of Real God), but it is about the egoic dilemma of Man, and the search to preserve human psycho-physical egoity.

The credibility (or root-persuasiveness) of conventional (or merely exoteric) God-religion has been deeply threatened (and, effectively, even mostly destroyed) by the progressively developing culture of modern secular science (which, although it is promoted as a species of free enquiry, is merely a modern variation on the ancient false philosophy of materialism). This is a curious fact, because both modern secular science (or scientific materialism) and conventional (or merely exoteric) God-religion are based upon the same fundamentals.

There are two fundamentals upon which both scientific materialism and conventional God-religion are based. These two fundamentals are the idea of egoity (or the naive experiential presumption of an utterly independent, utterly personal, utterly separate, and utterly subjective, psycho-physical "point of view") and the idea of "objective reality" (or the naive experiential presumption of an egoically psycho-physically observed—and thereby presumed to be utterly independent, utterly impersonal, utterly separate, and utterly non-subjective, or utterly objective—world of conditionally perceived and conceived conditions). And these two fundamental ideas (or naive experiential presumptions) are, also, the principal constructs (or generally uninspected conventions) of the human mind.

The two fundamental human ideas (of ego-"I" and "objective reality") are a natural pair—conceived, in accordance with convention, to be always and irreducibly the polar opposites of one another (always utterly different from one another, and always standing over against one another), and to be of such a nature that one or the other may (in any moment, or in the context of one or another human activity, or in the context of one or another historical mode of human culture) be assumed to be the dominant (or even more "real") half of the pair. And, because both scientific materialism and conventional God-religion are based upon these two fundamental human ideas (of ego-"I" and "objective reality"), scientific materialism and conventional God-religion differ only with respect to their interpretation (or interpretive idea) of what is egoically and "objectively" observed. Thus, scientific materialism interprets "objective reality" to "be" merely "what" it (from the "point of view" of the human observer) "appears" to be (and, thus, to suggest, or point to, "itself" only). And conventional God-religion interprets "objective reality" to "mean" (or, otherwise, to suggest, or point to) "God" (As objective "Other"). But neither scientific materialism nor conventional God-religion critically "considers"—and, as a pre-condition for (or, otherwise, as a result of) either scientific or religious discourse, transcends—the two naive experiential presumptions (of ego-"I" itself, and "objective reality" itself) that are the basis for the characteristic interpretation otherwise presumed to be the case (either scientifically or religiously).

As a result of their separate (and different, and inherently conflicting, or mutually opposite) interpretations of "objective reality", scientific materialism and conventional God-religion are, traditionally, engaged in a (mostly verbal, and, yet, deep cultural, social, and political) war with one another. That war is mostly one of argumentation and propaganda, in which each, in turn, proposes and addresses the other as a mere "straw man" (in order to make mere argumentation and propaganda appear to be inherently and dramatically convincing to the crowd of fascinated human onlookers). And, in the course of several hundred years of this popular struggle to capture the mind (and even the entire cultural, social, and political circumstance) of Man for either scientific materialism or conventional God-religion, scientific materialism has, of late, convincingly achieved the status of the dominant cultural, social, and political world-entity (or world-cult), while conventional God-religion has fallen from its previous status (as the culturally, socially, and politically dominant half of the pair) to become the (everywhere) relatively subordinate (or defensive) cultural, social, and political entity (or universal sub-cult). In any case—and regardless of how the balance may alternate in the future course of this popular (and rather absurd) struggle of mere interpretations—the entire drama of "science versus religion" is a mere play of conventionally "objectified" opposites, animated within a human (and merely exoteric, and egoic) mummery that (logically) can <u>never</u> reduce the "two" to "one" (just as the two primary conventions—of ego-"I" and "objective reality"—cannot, as such, be, logically, reduced from "two" to "one"). Therefore, the only traditionally <u>presumed</u> possibility is that either "science" or "religion" must <u>win</u> (as if <u>either</u> ego-"I" <u>or</u> "objective reality" must be declared, or, otherwise, proved, to be the one "reality", to the exclusion of the other half of the conventional pair).

Some people argue <u>for</u> belief in conventional God-religion, based on an exoteric religious interpretation of the concepts (or existing interpretations of "objective reality") otherwise associated with scientific materialism. Other people argue <u>against</u> belief in conventional God-religion, based on the technique of simple affirmation of the concepts (or existing interpretations of "objective reality") associated with scientific materialism—and, thus, without adding any other (especially, exoteric religious) interpretations. However, the entire conflict (between scientific materialism and conventional God-religion) is a rather mechanical (or pre-patterned, and predictable) exercise of the dualistic (or inherently self-divided and pair-patterned) ego-mind. Indeed, this apparent conflict is mere cultural, social, and political "show business"—an absurd mummery of self-important players, whose argumentative flourishes merely distract the mind of Man from the truly great "consideration" of Reality, Truth, and Real God.

Reality does not think. The naturally (and conditionally) existing world does not think. Naturally (and conditionally) existing beings do not think—unless they are, by reactive self-contraction, self-stimulated (or egoically self-bound) to think (and, thus, to "objectify" what, by the mind of separate and separative ego-"I", is defined as "not-self").

Reality Is What Is—rather than what is thought to be. Reality merely (and Always Already) Is—before time, and space, and thinker, and thought, and knower, and known, and subject, and object, and ego-"I", and "other" are (by means of—necessarily, time-consuming—conceptual and perceptual acts of "point of view", or body-mind) separated and specified (in mentally and bodily "objectified" space and time). That is to say, Reality Always Already Is—before mind and body act or react in relation to what appears to be. Therefore, if any thought (itself) or perception (itself) occupies attention, Reality has (necessarily) already been ignored (and is, in that moment, being ignored). And, therefore, Truth (Which—necessarily, and inherently—is Identical to Reality, Itself) Is That Perfectly Subjective (or Perfectly non-objective) Self-Condition (or inherent Real Condition) That Is The Case (Always and Already), and That is (necessarily, and inherently) non-conditional, and (necessarily, and inherently) egoless (or Perfectly without limited, or conditional, "point of view"). And, therefore, Real God (Which—necessarily, and inherently—Is Reality and Truth) is (necessarily, and inherently) egoless, non-conditional, and non-objective—or Perfectly Subjective, non-"different", and Beyond (or Most Prior to) all thought (and, thus, all separateness, all otherness, and all conditional relatedness).

The arguments of both scientific materialism and conventional God-religion are mind-based, body-based, and (most basically) ego-based. All such arguments are mere conventions of mind, inherently associated with a space-time-bound "point of view"—which is to say that they are inherently space-time-defined, inherently dualistic, and inherently separate (or separated, and separative). Therefore, <u>all</u> such arguments are inherently (and actively, and strategically) separate from (and separative in relation to) Reality, Truth, and Real God. Indeed, <u>all</u> such arguments are inherently "Narcissistic" (or egoically self-bound). Therefore, the separate (or space-time-bound) "point of view" (which "point of view" <u>is</u> the ego-"I") always either argues that "objective reality" is merely <u>as</u> it <u>appears</u> (which is the interpretation embraced by scientific materialism) or <u>as</u> it may otherwise be presumed to <u>mean</u> (which is the interpretation embraced by conventional God-religion). However, in either case, Reality (and, therefore, Truth, and Real God) is not <u>Realized</u>—but Reality (and, therefore, Truth, and Real God) is merely <u>interpreted</u> (or mentally—and, thus, conventionally and dualistically—conceived, and reduced to the scale of "point of view", and to the status of "objectified otherness").

Reality <u>Itself</u> (Which <u>Is</u> Truth, and the <u>only</u> <u>Real</u> <u>God</u>) is (necessarily, and inherently) All-and-all-Inclusive and, therefore, One and non-dual. Therefore, Reality (Itself) <u>inherently</u> Transcends any and every space-time "point of view" (and the totality, or All, of space-time itself). And, thus, Reality (Itself) <u>inherently</u> Transcends any and every ego-"I", or body-mind-self—and every dualistic convention of "object", "other", or "thing". Truth (or Real God) <u>Is</u>, simply, the inherent (and inherently egoless) Nature (or unqualified Condition) of Reality <u>Itself</u>.

Reality (Itself) <u>Is</u> the unqualified Condition of <u>all</u> conditions (or apparent qualifications, or limitations) of Reality. Therefore, Reality (Itself) <u>Is</u> the unqualified (or Most Prior) Condition of any and every apparent individual (or apparent thing, or apparent condition). Indeed, Reality (Itself) <u>Is</u> the unqualified (or Most Prior), and, thus, Perfectly non-objective, or Perfectly non-objectified (and, thus, Perfectly Subjective, or Merely-<u>Being</u>) Condition of <u>all</u> apparent space-time conditions.

Reality (Itself) <u>Is</u> (necessarily, and inherently) the <u>unqualified</u> (or Most Prior) Condition of any and every ego-"I". Therefore, Reality (Itself) is Realized only in the case of the inherent (and inherently Most Perfect) <u>transcending</u> of the ego-"I" (or the conditional, separate, and actively separative, self-position itself). Reality

(Itself) is Realizable only As the unqualified Self-Condition of the individual ego-"I"—Prior to the ego-act (or separative act) of dissociation from Reality, Truth, and Real God.

Reality (Itself) is Most Prior to the act of self-contraction into the space-time "point of view". Therefore, Reality (Itself) is Realizable only by transcending mind (and the egoic—or self-contracting, and separative, and presumed-to-be-separate—"point of view" of body-mind). And, therefore, Reality (Itself) is Realizable only by transcending the total psycho-physical act that "objectifies" conditionally apparent reality.

Reality Itself (or Truth, or Real God) is Realizable only by transcending the ego-effort of interpretation (or of conventional "knowing")—or all of the ego-based mind, itself. That is to say, Reality, Truth, and Real God is Realizable only by transcending the two fundamental operative ideas (and, thus, the fundamental common fault) associated with both scientific materialism and conventional God-religion. And, by transcending the two fundamental operative ideas (at their common root—which is egoity, or self-contraction, itself), even the entire process of discursive mental activity is transcended—such that Reality, Truth, and Real God may be Found (and, by Grace of True Divine Self-Revelation, Realized) As the Obvious.

True religion and true science are a Great, and single, and necessarily esoteric (or ego-transcending, rather than ego-active) Process. True religion and true science—Combined in a true, and truly single, and rightly esoteric (or non-conventional, and Always Already Reality-Based, Truth-Based, and Real-God-Based) Wisdom-Way—are the ego-transcending Great Process that directly transcends all exercises of interpretation (or of conventional "knowing", or of discursive mind). Only the esoteric Great Process of Realizing (and, on That Basis, Demonstrating) Reality Itself (Which Is Truth, and Which Is Real God) by directly (and, in due course, Most Perfectly) transcending the psycho-physical (and space-time) "point of view" is both true religion and true science.

If Real Happiness and Real Freedom are to be Realized (and, on That Basis, Demonstrated) in human-time, the esoteric Great Process must be engaged by the individual human being—but

That Great Process is not an <u>exclusively</u> human capability. Rather, It is a capability <u>in</u> <u>Reality</u> <u>Itself</u>—and, therefore, Its fundamental exercise must (necessarily) be one that can be enacted by <u>all</u> non-human beings as well as by <u>all</u> human beings. Thus, the esoteric Great Process (of Realizing Reality, Truth, or Real God) is a <u>responsive</u> exercise of the <u>universally</u> evident principal faculties that are common to <u>all</u> naturally (and conditionally) existing beings. And, in order to Realize Reality, Truth, or Real God, that responsive exercise must (necessarily, and inherently) transcend the limiting force (or ego-binding implication) of the faculties themselves—by virtue of the tacit recognition (of Reality, Truth, or Real God) that must be the basis of the response (itself).

Nature does not think. Reality is not (Itself) a thought-process. Therefore, the esoteric Great Process (of Realizing Reality, Truth, or Real God) is <u>not</u> an exercise of discursive (or egoic, and con-ceptual, or dualistically interpreting) mind—which "thinking mind" is a characteristic rather exclusively (or most elaborately) associated with human beings (or, at least, a characteristic that is <u>not</u> common to <u>all</u> naturally, and conditionally, existing beings). Rather, the esoteric Great Process is, for human beings, a responsive Reality-recognizing (or Truth-recognizing, or Real-God-recognizing) exercise of the four principal human faculties (of attention, emo-tional feeling, bodily sensation, and breath)—which four principal human faculties correspond to the four principal faculties associ-ated, universally, with <u>all</u> naturally (and conditionally) existing beings (and which are, in all non-human cases of naturally, and conditionally, existing beings, demonstrated in at least primitive, or rudimentary, functions—such as responsive directionality, responsiveness to energy, responsiveness to sensation, and the responsive "conductivity", or total psycho-physical circulation, of both energy and physical substance).

The Great (esoteric, and truly religious, and truly scientific, or freely enquiring) Process is That of ego-surrendering, and ego-forgetting, and ego-transcending Attunement to—or ego-transcending (and, thus, "point-of-view"-transcending, and thought-transcending, or "difference"-transcending) Communion with (and, Ultimately, Most Perfect, and Perfectly Subjective,

Identification with)—What Is. What Is, Is Reality Itself (and Truth Itself, and the only Real God). And That Great Process (of Realizing What Is) necessarily requires the recognition-responsive surrender, forgetting, and transcending of the four principal (and universally displayed) life-faculties.

Only the Perfectly Subjective (or Inherent, and Acausal, or Non-causing) "Point of View" (or space-time-Transcending Self-Condition) Is Divine and True. Only That "Point of View" (or Divine Self-Condition, inherently Transcending all "points of view" in space-time) Is (Itself) Reality, Truth, and Real God. And only the Realization of That Reality, Truth, and Real God Liberates all (to Demonstrate Reality, Truth, and Real God), by Setting the heart (or essential pattern, or apparent entity, or apparently separate self-condition, of psycho-physical being) Free from all separateness, "difference", and conditional relatedness.

The ego-"I" is always (and inherently) seeking and arguing—because it is inherently (and actively, and always self-contractively) dissociated (or apparently separated) from Reality, Truth, and Real God. The ego-"I" is inherently dissociated, dissatisfied, self-deluded, and un-Free. Whether the ego-"I" argues for scientific materialism, or conventional God-religion, or anything at all—its argument is merely mummer's talk (or the "talking" form of what is, traditionally, called "sin", or "the missing of the mark", and which is best described simply as egoity, or the self-contracted, separate, and separative ego-"I", itself).

Reality, Truth, and Real God is not evident in "objective reality" (or from the egoic "point of view" of "outside"). Nor is Reality, Truth, and Real God Realized merely by going "within" (or by, in any manner, merely exercising) the ego-"I" itself. Rather, Reality, Truth, and Real God is Realized only by transcending the ego-"I" (or the separate and separative "point of view" of self-contraction) in What Is.

Some conventional God-religionists argue for the "God-interpretation" of scientifically observed "objective reality" by emphasizing the irreducible complexity of natural patterns (such as the living cells that compose the human body). Such conventional God-religionists call for positive (or hopeful) belief in

"God", based on the observable designs (or complex patterns) in the natural world. They argue for positive (or hopeful) "God-belief", based on their assumption that "design" <u>requires</u> a "designer". But "design" is not limited in kind—such that a positively definable "designer" is universally indicated. That is to say, patterns are <u>everywhere</u> in evidence—in both positive and negative forms. Not only are living human cells irreducibly complex—but so are the patterns of self-delusion, disease, decay, universal destruction, and death. Therefore <u>what</u> "God" is to be hopefully affirmed (or, otherwise, hopelessly denied) on the basis of mere "objectively" (and egoically) observed patterning?

The only Real and True God <u>Is</u> the One Reality That Merely <u>Is</u>, and That <u>Is</u> Always Already The Case, and That (inherently, and simultaneously) Includes <u>and</u> Transcends All and all. That One Real God is not the "Creator"-Cause for either ego-based hope or ego-based hopelessness—but That One Real God <u>Is</u> the inherently egoless (or Perfectly Subjective, and Perfectly non-objective, and Self-Evidently Divine) Source and Person (or Self-Conscious Self-Condition) of the inherently egoless Love-Bliss-Light That <u>Is</u> the Single (and non-dual) Substance of <u>all</u> arising conditions.

Those who argue <u>for</u> belief in conventional God-religion, based on hopeful interpretations of "objective reality", are (necessarily) <u>egos</u>—already (and inherently) turned away from (or self-contracted within) Reality, Truth, and Real God. And, likewise, those who argue <u>against</u> belief in conventional God-religion, based on hopeless (or, otherwise, neutral) interpretations of "objective reality", are (necessarily) <u>egos</u>—already (and inherently) turned away from (or self-contracted within) Reality, Truth, and Real God. I Say this in Love—not with any intention to mock <u>any</u> one, or merely to argue with or against <u>any</u> one, but only in order to Serve the Awakening of <u>every</u> one to Real-God-Realization and Real-God-Demonstration.

The arguments (either <u>for</u> or <u>against</u> "God") that are based on the externalized (or egoically "objectifying") "point of view" are <u>not</u> arguments for the <u>Realization</u> of Reality, Truth, or Real God. Rather, <u>all</u> such arguments are merely <u>the</u> <u>mental</u> <u>and</u> <u>cultural</u> <u>symptoms</u> <u>of</u> <u>egoity</u> <u>itself</u>.

The arguments for conventional (or merely exoteric) God-religion (whether pro-scientific or anti-scientific) are merely ego-based (and self-deluded) efforts to console and preserve the presumed human ego-"I" itself, in the face of the obvious and irreducible mortal bleakness of the presumed "objective reality" itself. The arguments for conventional (or merely exoteric) God-religion are not arguments for the practice of the (necessarily, esoteric) Wisdom-Way of (necessarily, ego-transcending) Realization and Demonstration of Reality, Truth, or Real God. Inevitably, the arguments for conventional (or merely exoteric) God-religion (and even the arguments for ostensibly esoteric religion, that—via the idealization of such techniques as strategic "non-violence", "active compassion", or "unconditional love"—make overmuch of interpersonal, social, and political issues and concerns, and that, as a result, make little of the true esotericism of the practice of the Wisdom-Way of actual ego-transcending Realization of Reality Itself, or of Truth Itself, or of That Which Is Real God) are merely the conceptual foundation for exoteric religious propaganda, supporting naive (and merely ego-serving) religious views (which, themselves, typically, are intended merely to support mostly narrow-minded, and, generally, rather puritanical and moralistic, programs for the cultural, social, and political enforcement of conventional ideals of "social morality"—or, really, "civilized" egoity). And the naive (and merely ego-serving) religious views that characterize most of conventional (or merely exoteric) God-religion are also characteristically associated, at best, with nonsensical utopian idealism (or an absurdly hopeful cultural, social, and political worldliness), and, at worst, with moralistically self-righteous (and, necessarily, hypocritical), and, often, intolerant (and even, potentially, oppressive), social and political intentions (even, at last, in the "fundamentalist" mode). And, in any case, scientific materialism (which, like conventional God-religion, always seeks to achieve total cultural, social, and political power to limit and control the minds and lives of all humankind) manipulates, and progressively dominates, humankind in very much the same manner (and with the same mixed, and even devastating, results) as conventional God-religion has done, and would do— for such is the nature of egoity (whether individual or collective).

Both secular science and conventional (or merely exoteric) God-religion are based upon the two common faults of humankind—egoity and the non-Recognition[2] of the Real Nature (or One-Reality-Condition—or Perfectly Subjective, and Perfectly non-objective, Nature) of phenomenal experience (and of conditional existence, itself). Likewise, both secular science and conventional God-religion also (and equally) support and serve the <u>illusions</u> of humankind, rather than the need for humankind to <u>Realize</u> (and to <u>Demonstrate</u>) Reality, Truth, and Real God.

The principal illusion supported and served by secular science is epitomized by the idea of "materialism" (or of Reality as <u>thing</u>—without Being, or Consciousness). And the principal illusion supported and served by conventional God-religion is epitomized by the idea of "utopia" (or of Reality as the <u>fulfillment</u> of egoity). Secular science opposes conventional God-religion, and conventional God-religion opposes secular science—each, in turn, proposing that its propositions are, by contrast to the propositions of the other, the correct means for <u>interpreting</u> (and the correct "point of view" relative to) "Reality" and "Truth" and "God". However, neither secular science nor conventional God-religion is a correct (or right and true) means for <u>Realizing</u> (and <u>Demonstrating</u>) Reality (Itself), or Truth (Itself), or Real God. Indeed, "point of view" (of <u>any</u> conditional, or space-time, kind) is precisely the fault that self-separates one and all from the <u>inherent</u> Realization of Reality, Truth, and Real God.

Reality, Truth, and Real God <u>Is</u> the Condition of conditions—the inherently egoless (or Perfectly Subjective, and Perfectly non-objective) Self-Condition of one and all.

The pattern of "objective reality" is (in and of itself) "known" only from the egoic position (or a space-time "point of view").

If there is <u>no</u> ego-act (or self-contraction), there is <u>no</u> object defined (or separated from Perfect Subjectivity, or Consciousness Itself—Which is Always Already Conscious <u>As</u> Reality Itself).

The apparent pattern that is patterning as <u>all</u> conditions is not merely patterning (or happening, or evolving) in and by means of the apparently "objective" (or "outer", or superficial) domain of gross conditional exchanges (or transactions). Rather, the apparent pattern that is patterning as all conditions is originating at the comprehensive depth-level—always "inside", and prior to, the grossly apparent (or subsequent, and relatively superficial, and, necessarily, non-comprehensive) level.

The Ultimate Source-Condition of the apparent pattern that is patterning as all conditions Is (Itself) the Non-causative (or Most Prior) Self-Condition of all apparent conditional patterns.

That Ultimate Source-Condition, Which Is the Most Prior Self-Condition of All and all, is not the "First Cause" (or "Creator"-God) of conventional God-religion—but It Is the inherently egoless (or Perfectly Subjective, Perfectly non-objective, and Self-Evidently Divine) Reality (Itself).

Reality (Itself) Is the only Real God. Reality (Itself) Is the One and non-dual Source-Person. Reality (Itself)—non-dual, and inherently Free—Is the only Person (of All and all).

The inherently egoless, non-dual, and Perfectly Subjective Person of Reality Is Always Already The Case. And That One Who Is Always Already The Case Is Self-Existing Consciousness (Itself)—Which is Self-Radiant, "Bright", All-and-all-Including, All-and-all-Transcending, and All-and-all-Pervading As the Indefinable and Indestructible and Unqualifiedly Conscious Love-Bliss-Light That Is the Single (and Perfectly non-dual) Substance (and the inherently egoless Self-Condition) of all conditionally arising beings, things, and conditions.

The inherently egoless (or Perfectly Subjective, Perfectly non-objective, and Self-Evidently Divine) Person of Reality must (by Means of Avataric Divine Descent into Conjunction with the conditionally manifested All-and-all) Realize Itself (Most Perfectly, As Such) in human-time, and the inherently egoless (or Perfectly Subjective, Perfectly non-objective, and Self-Evidently Divine) Person of Reality must (by Means of Avataric Divine Self-"Emergence", forever, in inherent, and inherently Most Perfect, Coincidence with the conditionally manifested All-and-all) Reveal Itself (Most Perfectly, As Such) in human-time—or else Real God cannot be Most Perfectly Found (and, Thus, Most Perfectly Realized, and Most Perfectly Demonstrated) in human-time by any one at all. Therefore, I Am here.

Unless the Avatarically Descended (and Most Perfectly Self-Realized, and Most Perfectly Self-Revealed) Divine Person of Reality Speaks in human-time, and (Thereby) Reveals Its <u>own</u> Most Perfect Divine Teaching-Word (That Reveals the Divine Wisdom-Way of Most Perfect Real-God-Realization), and Stands (forever, here) to Divinely Bless All and all to Most Perfectly Realize (and, on the Basis of That Most Perfect Realization, to Most Perfectly Demonstrate) the One and Perfectly Subjective (or non-dual and non-objective) and "Bright" and Indefinable and Indestructible Conscious Love-Bliss-Light—<u>no</u> <u>true</u> religion and <u>no</u> <u>true</u> science can be made to live in human-time. Therefore, I <u>Am</u> here.

I am not here to support and to serve the faults and the illusions of humankind. I am not here to support and to serve <u>any</u> cult (or ego-based, and ego-serving, and ego-reinforcing culture) of human philosophical, religious, scientific, social, or political existence. Therefore, I am not here to support and to serve <u>either</u> the materialistic <u>or</u> the utopian "point of view". Indeed, I am not here to support and to serve <u>any</u> conditional (or space-time) "point of view". Whereas <u>any</u> and <u>every</u> conditional (or space-time) "point of view" is <u>the</u> "point of view" of ego-"I" (or self-contraction) itself, I <u>Am</u> here to Reveal the Divine Wisdom-Way That Inherently (and, in due course, Most Perfectly) <u>Transcends</u> the ego-"I" (and <u>all</u> the self-contracted, and separate, and separative illusions of egoically "objectified" space-time-reality).

By Means of My Avataric Divine Descent into Conjunction with (and, Ultimately, My Avataric Divine Self-"Emergence", forever, in inherent, and inherently Most Perfect, Coincidence with) the conditionally manifested All-and-all, I have been Required to Suffer, and then to Transcend, <u>all</u> illusions, <u>and</u> every conditional (or space-time) "point of view" (or mode of ego-"I"). Therefore, and by Means of a Great Ordeal of Suffering and Transcendence, I have even Suffered and Transcended <u>all</u> of secular (or materialistic) science and <u>all</u> of conventional (or merely exoteric) God-religion—and even <u>all</u> of traditional (and, necessarily, non-conventional) esotericism. Therefore, I am not here to support and to serve either the world-cult of secular science or the universal sub-cult of conventional God-religion—for not only have both of these traditions failed to Realize (and to Demonstrate) Reality, Truth, and Real God, but both are <u>based</u> upon <u>active dissociation</u> from Reality, Truth, and Real God (and, therefore, neither secular science nor conventional God-religion can, or will at any time, Realize and Demonstrate Reality, Truth, and Real God). Nor am I here merely to affirm and replicate the historical traditions of esotericism—for they have not transcended themselves (and the totality of ego-"I" and "otherness") in <u>Most</u> <u>Perfect</u> Realization (and <u>Most</u> <u>Perfect</u> Demonstration) of Reality, Truth, and Real God (and they cannot and will not <u>Most</u> <u>Perfectly</u> Realize, and <u>Most</u> <u>Perfectly</u> Demonstrate, Reality, Truth, and Real God—unless and until they transcend themselves, and the totality of ego-"I" and "otherness", in devotional recognition-response to Me, and in Fullest devotional resort to Me).

The esoteric Wisdom-Way of devotional recognition-response to Me and Fullest devotional resort to Me is an inherently and thoroughly counter-egoic (and, thus, counter-cultic—or ego-transcending, fault-transcending, and illusion-transcending) Process. I <u>Am</u> here, in human-time, to Completely and Most Perfectly Reveal the Most Perfect esoteric (and thoroughly counter-egoic, and counter-cultic) Wisdom-Way That <u>Is</u> true religion and true science, and That <u>Is</u> the Great Process of Realizing (and, on That Basis, Demonstrating) Reality Itself (Which <u>Is</u> Truth, and Which <u>Is</u> Real God) by directly (and, in due course, Most Perfectly) transcending the psycho-physical (and space-time) "point of view" (which <u>is</u> egoity, or self-contraction, itself).

I <u>Am</u> here, in human-time, to Most Perfectly Realize and (by Means of My own Most Perfect Self-Demonstration) to Most Perfectly Reveal My own inherently egoless (or Perfectly Subjective, and Perfectly non-objective, and Self-Evidently Divine) Person. And I <u>Am</u> here, in human-time, to <u>Completely</u> Speak My own Most Perfect Divine Teaching-Word (That Reveals the Way of Most Perfect Real-God-Realization), and to Stand (forever, here) to Bless All and all to Realize (and to Demonstrate) My own One and non-dual and "Bright" and Indefinable and Indestructible Conscious Love-Bliss-Light.

I <u>Am</u> the inherently egoless Person of Reality Itself.

I <u>Am</u> the One and "Bright" and Indefinable and Indestructible Conscious Light That <u>Is</u> the One and Universal (and inherently non-dual) Substance (and the One, and inherently egoless, and inherently non-dual, and inherently non-objective, or Perfectly Subjective, Self-Condition) of All and all.

I <u>Am</u> the Perfectly Subjective Self-"Brightness" of Love-Bliss (Itself).

I <u>Am</u> the "Bright" and <u>Only</u> One—Who is to be Found and Realized by you (and by every one, and all, and All).

I <u>Am</u>—Free-Standing here, Most Prior to your ego-"I" and all of the apparently "objective" world.

I <u>Am</u> the All-and-all-Including and All-and-all-Transcending Divine Self-Condition (and Source-Condition) of every ego-"I" and every "thing".

I <u>Am</u> you.

I <u>Am</u> the world.

I <u>Am</u> Adi Da Samraj.

The only-by-Me Revealed and Given <u>esoteric</u> Wisdom-Way of Adidam <u>Is</u> My <u>Complete</u> Avatarically Given Divine Teaching-Word of Most Perfect Real-God-Realization.

The only-by-Me Revealed and Given Way of Adidam <u>Is</u> the <u>inherently</u> ego-transcending (and thoroughly counter-cultic) Way That <u>constantly</u> (and, at last, Most Perfectly) Finds Reality <u>Itself</u> (Which <u>Is</u> the <u>only</u> Truth, and the <u>only</u> Real God).

The only-by-Me Revealed and Given Way of Adidam <u>Is</u> the esoteric Process of <u>true</u> religion and <u>true</u> science—That (more and more Perfectly, and, at last, Most Perfectly) <u>Realizes</u> (and, on <u>That Basis</u>, <u>Demonstrates</u>) the egoless Divine Inherent Love-Bliss-"Brightness" of Consciousness (Itself), and the egoless Divine (and Love-Bliss-"Bright") Self-Consciousness Inherent in All the Indefinable and Indestructible Light (or Single and Universal non-dual Substance) of the apparently "objective" (and apparently material) world.

The only-by-Me Revealed and Given Way of Adidam <u>Is</u> the Divine (and, necessarily, devotional, or heart-moved, and ego-surrendering) Way of <u>Real</u> God (Found <u>As</u> <u>My</u> Avatarically Self-Revealed, and Avatarically Self-Transmitted, and Self-Existing, and

Self-Radiant, and All-and-all-Including, and All-and-all-Transcending, and, altogether, Perfectly Subjectively "Bright", and Self-Evidently Divine Person of Love-Bliss).

The only-by-Me Revealed and Given Way of Adidam Is the Divine Way of <u>moment</u> <u>to</u> <u>moment</u> ego-surrendering, and ego-forgetting, and ego-transcending (and, altogether, body-mind-purifying and heart-Liberating) devotional recognition-response to <u>Me</u>—So That self-contraction is <u>never</u> allowed to hide <u>My</u> Divinely Self-"Emerging" Conscious Sun of "Bright" Love-Bliss behind the common fault (and cult) of ego-"I" and the Love-Bliss-Light-obscuring cloud of "objectivity".

The only-by-Me Revealed and Given Way of Adidam <u>Is</u> the Divine and Complete and faultless and Perfectly non-dual Way of <u>only</u> <u>Me</u>. And I <u>Am</u> (now, and forever hereafter) Standing here, to Bless All and all to Realize <u>Me</u> and to Demonstrate <u>Me</u>.

There is <u>no</u> Face within the sky. Nor is the "thing" of sky the "All" That <u>Is</u>. But I <u>Am</u> All the All Who <u>Is</u>. And non-objective "Brightness" <u>Is</u> My <u>only</u> Face. And they see Me who forget themselves when My Name, Da,[3] is heard to Flash across the Me-"Bright" Cloudless Sky of Consciousness Itself.

RUCHIRA AVATAR ADI DA SAMRAJ
The Mountain Of Attention, 2000

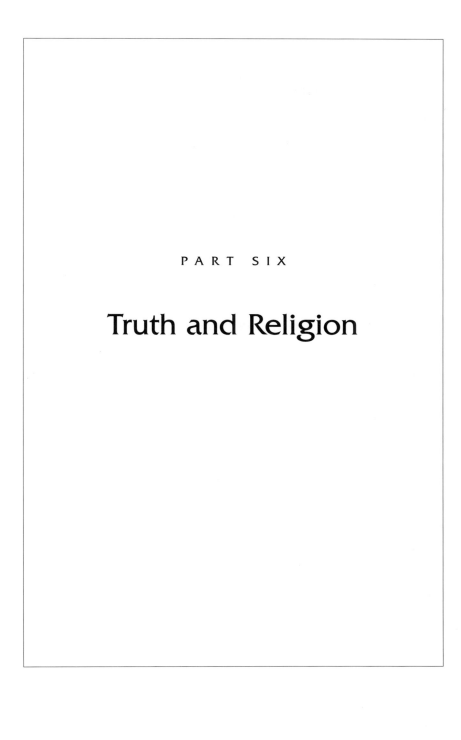

PART SIX

Truth and Religion

Truth and Religion

Religion is "cult". That is to say, a religion (or, as it is said, "a faith") is, always and necessarily, a body of both specific and general forms and observances (both concrete and conceptual), made apparent in time and space—and that body of forms and observances is (or, at one or another time, was) "made holy" (or "set apart") by means of some mode of sacred performance (including collective—or even merely personal—rituals of offering and of invocation, descriptive affirmations of what is holy, descriptive affirmations of what is sacred, a defining affirmation, or gathering of affirmations, of what is knowledge, a multiplicity of descriptive affirmations of what is presumed to be known, and so on).

Because these temporal and spatial conditions (or conditional, or space-time, limitations) are necessarily the case with all "religions" (or "faiths", or "philosophies", or "paths", or seekers' "methods", or even lives)—whether collective or personal—no conditionally manifested (or even humanly intelligible) religion Is (or was, or ever can or could Be) Truth Itself (or Reality Itself, or Real God Itself). That is to say, no matter what religion is (or even how many religions are)—either collectively or by oneself to oneself—proposed, Truth Itself (or Reality Itself, or Real God Itself) also (otherwise—and Always Already) Is The Case.

Right and true religion is entirely, merely, and only a process—not merely a thing, and never a thing-in-itself. The humanly "objectified" external and internal aspects of religion are, themselves, neither to be worshipped nor to be absolutized—as if religion were (itself) Truth (Itself).

The "things" of religion are the "performance assistance" to an always entirely subjective process. Therefore, the practice of religion should always be exercised with respect to the Inherently Indivisible and Indefinable Truth That Is Reality Itself—and, thus and thereby, always surrendered and subordinated to the Unexceedable Power of the Inherently Indivisible and Indefinable Truth of Reality Itself.

Only as a subjective process of subordination and surrender to Truth Itself—or to the Condition That Is Reality, or Real God, Itself—may the (necessarily) conditionally activated performance of religion (or the humanly intentional "cult", or sacred culture, of religious forms and observances) exceed its inherent limitations, and become the Self-Radiant Demonstration of Spiritual and Divine Existence.

Therefore, in a right culture of human society, in which the personal and collective life of Truth-Realization (or the Spiritual Realization of Inherent, Real, and Perfect Happiness) is really and consistently valued as the key to right life, no religion (or even any collective of collective and/or personal religions) should be either absolutized or forbidden—whether by public and social authority or by political arrangements of any enforced kind.

Truth Itself—or Reality Itself, Which Always Already Is the Only Real God—must, in the scale of human space and time, be universally Affirmed as the necessary, inherent, and only context of human existence, both personal and collective.

Truth—or the Self-Existing and Self-Radiant Divine Reality of Existence (or Being) Itself—must always be the Great Subject of human existence, both personal and collective.

Truth Is the Self-Radiant Beauty (or Self-Existing "Brightness") of Being—Self-Evident, Self-Realized, Self-Manifested, Full, Indivisible, and Inherently Sufficient.

Tat Sundaram!

All of This-Thou-That Is That Which Is Beauty Itself!

There is no religion greater than Beauty Itself!

Where There Is Always Already Only Beauty Itself—One and Indivisible, As Beloved of the Heart—what religion owns The Holy "Brightness", That Transfigures every figure like a Midnight Sun?

The Light <u>Above</u> religion's mind and tribe unclothes, to Deepest Touch, the nighted mummers in their celebration here— and Beauty's "Brightness" pucks the lip of <u>every</u> invocated laud and gait that singles in.

Before another step is made to measure All The <u>Is</u>, or even sooner than a word-fall sizes mind and ego's "I"—The Light Is <u>On</u>!

RUCHIRA AVATAR ADI DA SAMRAJ
The Mountain Of Attention, 2000

PART SEVEN

I <u>Am</u> The Way
to Transcend the Illusions
of Broken Light

I <u>Am</u> The Way
to Transcend the Illusions
of Broken Light

I.

AVATAR ADI DA SAMRAJ: When people describe the human being in strictly (or exclusively) material terms, they speak as if so-called "matter" is already (and truly, and completely) defined and known! So-called "matter" is, generally speaking, not <u>known</u> (in the true, complete, and truly completely defining sense). The word "matter" is merely a conventional (and naive, or naively "realistic") reference to modes of human experience that appear solid, limited, and even mortal. The physical human body, as a medium of human experience, is the presumed basis on which human beings experience, indicate, and describe what is, by them, called "matter". Indeed, the word (or naive concept) "matter" is a rather self-referring (or subjective) human concept-word, that points to (and even, most basically, refers to) the human physical body itself—rather than to <u>objective</u> "matter". Thus, the human concept-word "matter" is, basically, a human device for superimposing the naive human physical (and mortal) bodily experience of human beings onto everything else.

The human concept-word "matter" is a bit of dark human poetic language. Human beings perceive themselves to be limited and mortal—and, on that basis, they ascribe the same characteristics to all and All that is "outside" the physical (bodily) human entity. In fact, "matter"—and, thus, the total universe (or cosmos) of ordinary (or exoteric) human perception (and conception)—is only naively perceived (and naively described), even by scientists. According to exoterically-minded humankind, the human entity is, itself, something limited and only mortal. And, on that basis, it is concluded that "reality" (altogether, or totally) is limited and only mortal.

The naive materialists among humankind have not reached this exoteric conclusion (epitomized by the concept-word "matter") by actually investigating "matter" itself. Yes, it is certainly true that the human gross personality is, in the naive experiential sense, material. But what is "matter"? Is "matter" the "lump" that was the conventional "reality"-conception of nineteenth-century scientific materialism? Hasn't more been learned about "matter" since the nineteenth century? Hasn't something of the even ancient esoteric knowledge about the True Nature of "matter" been regained by means of twentieth-century scientific investigations of the universe?

"Matter" is not a "lump". It is not, in and of itself, the defining characteristic (or limit) of "reality". Truly (and even from the point of view of twentieth-century exoteric science), "matter" is "energy" (or Light). And "energy" (or Light) Is (In and As Itself) Inherently Indivisible (or One, Only, and Indestructible). Therefore, "matter" is simply a conditional mode of appearance, a merely apparent modification of Inherently Immutable Light! And Light Itself (or "energy" itself) cannot be truly and completely described from the material (or exoteric, and gross bodily) human point of view. Indeed, the gross bodily-based human entity does not recognize (or comprehend) what it perceives. That is to say, the gross bodily ego-"I" does not know (or Really recognize, or Realize) What even a single thing Is!

Between the naive experience of "matter" and the Most Ultimate (or Most Perfect) Realization of Inherently Indivisible (or Non-Separate, and Inseparable) Oneness with Inherently Indivisible Light Itself, there is an experiential progress of perceptions and patterns—from the gross dimension, to the subtle dimension, to the root-causal dimension, and (Beyond them all) to What Is Ultimate (or Always Already The Case—One, Only, and

Indestructible). There are many potential levels of presumption, perception, experience, and so on, that may be uncovered previous to Most Perfect Realization of the Ultimate Reality Itself (or Inherently Indivisible Light Itself, Which Is Self-Existing and Self-Radiant Consciousness Itself). Nevertheless, "matter" Is (if Most Perfectly, or Divinely, Self-Recognized) Inherently Indivisible Light (Itself). In other words, "_this_" (body, mind, and world)—just as it is appearing—_can_ be Divinely Self-Recognized (_As_ it _Is_) to be a transparent (or merely apparent), and un-necessary, and inherently non-binding modification of Inherently Indivisible Conscious Light. Therefore, if the ego-"I" itself is transcended (every here and now), it is not necessary to go "elsewhere", to some other (or "higher", or subtler) realm or domain, in order to Realize Reality Itself.

Yes, the human gross personality is, in naive experiential fact, material—but "matter" _Is_ Inherently Indivisible Light. When the human psycho-physical personality (or even any or all of body, mind, or world) is investigated (and, in that investigation, transcended) _most_ profoundly, it is Discovered to _Be_ (Beyond itself, or Most Prior to the naive experiencing of it) Inherently Indivisible Light. That Discovery, Most Perfectly Made (or Utterly Realized), _Is_ Most Perfect (and Self-Evidently Divine) En-Light-enment.

II.

AVATAR ADI DA SAMRAJ: There are subtler aspects of the gross physical (or gross material) dimension of Reality that, because you may not be directly experiencing them at the moment, you may think of as being "somewhere else". But, in Truth, and in Reality, There Is Only One "Thing" (or Only Indivisible Light, or the One and Very Being That _Is_ Consciousness Itself _and_ Its Own Self-Radiance). Yet un-En-Light-ened human beings are tending, always presently (and naively), to identify with a gross physical modification-appearance of That One "Thing", when even that modification-appearance _Is_ _Only_ Light. The gross physical (or gross material) dimension of Reality is simply the mode in which the yet un-En-Light-ened human personality is experiencing Inherently Indivisible Light at the moment.

If you enter into "consideration" of the gross physical (or gross material) dimension of Reality more and more deeply, you become aware of subtler aspects of what you otherwise presume to be merely gross physical (or merely "matter"). Thus, you become aware of the mental and (eventually) the psychic aspects of conditionally manifested existence. And you become sensitive to the energy dimension of conditionally manifested existence, and (in due course) to various kinds of subtle perceptions of conditionally manifested existence. But none of those aspects of conditionally manifested existence are entirely separated from the gross physical (or exclusively "inward" to, and entirely "away" from, the gross physical)—rather, they are simply subtler forms of what you call the "gross physical" (or "matter"). The gross physical is simply one depth (or mode) of vibratory perception, and there are various deeper modes of the perception of the Same "Thing".

All of conditionally manifested reality Is Inherently Indivisible Light, or Spirit-Energy, or Hridaya-Shakti, or Love-Bliss. My Avatarically Self-Revealed (and Very, and "Bright", and Self-Evidently Divine) Presence and Person Is That. Therefore, the right, true, full, and fully devotional religious and Spiritual Process in the only-by-Me Revealed and Given Way of Adidam (Which is the One and Only by-Me-Revealed and by-Me-Given Way of the Heart) is not a matter of seeking to go "somewhere else". Rather, it is simply a matter of entering (Beyond the ego-"I", or the act of psycho-physical self-contraction) into the Depth, and the Breadth, and the Height, and (altogether) the Fullest Extent, or Inherent Size (In Place), of the conditional reality that is already apparent to you.

Ultimately, the most profound (Total, and Inherent) Comprehension of conditional reality is Most Perfect Divine Self-Realization, or the Awakening to the only-by-Me Revealed and Given seventh stage of life. To Realize the seventh stage of life is to be no longer trapped in the presumption that "matter" is a "something" (in and of itself) that makes you wonder whether anything else even exists. In Most Perfect Divine Self-Realization, there is Utter Comprehension of "matter", in every dimension of its Inherent Size. In Most Perfect Divine Self-Realization, there is

Unobstructed Comprehension (or Divine Self-Recognition) of all of "this" (body, mind, and world).

That is what there is to comprehend—just "this", whatever is perceived to be "this", in any moment. Either you Know What "this" Is (In and As Reality, Truth, or Real God) or you do not. The gross physical body, in and of itself, is rather stupid. It is the "dog", or "tail end", of all of "this". Therefore, the gross physical body is not going to figure "this" out. Rather, the gross physical body must be surrendered to (and into) What is Senior to it.

The gross physical body (or "dog", or "tail end") is not, in and of itself, capable of Divine Self-Realization. It is not the basis for Divine Self-Realization. It is the "this" that must be surrendered, responsively, to Me. Then it can be converted, more and more profoundly, by the Infusion of My Avataric Divine Spiritual Grace. When you Divinely Awaken, by Means of My Avatarically Self-Transmitted Divine Grace, your "tail end" also "wags". When the head and the heart are utterly (openly) given to Me (and, in that, "Brightly" Infused by Me), the gross physical body follows, readily. Thus, the gross physical body (and the gross-minded personality) is Divinely Mastered (and En-Light-ened) by Me—via the surrender of head and heart and body into My "Bright" Divine Spiritual Body and egoless True Divine Person (Beyond the ego-"I", or self-contraction, of the conditional body-mind), Such That even the gross physical body is conformed to Me (by conformity to My Self-Existing Divine Person, and to My Self-Radiant "Bright" Divine Spiritual Body of Indivisible and Unbroken Light, Indestructible Love-Bliss, and Inherent Happiness).

III.

AVATAR ADI DA SAMRAJ: I Am the Divine (and Avatarically Self-Transmitted) Spirit-Energy, or Inherently Indivisible Light, That Is the Substance of All and all. My Inherently Indivisible Light can be apparently transformed—but It cannot be destroyed (and, in Truth, It is never even changed). Thus, the universally arising appearance of materiality is simply the grossest aspect of the conditional manifestation (or apparent modifying, or seeming Breaking) of Inherently Indivisible Light (or the Divine Spirit-

Energy That Is The Substance Of all and All). And you (experientially, and in the total field of your human feeling-existence) are that grossness, that gross bodily manifestation—that gross modification of Me.

The ego-"I" seeks for reasons to deny that it is the gross physical body, and the ego-"I" seeks for experiences "apart" from the gross physical body—because the gross physical body is potentially subject to great suffering, and, inevitably, it dies. But you really are the gross physical body. The gross physical body is not "not-self". The gross physical body really is "self". The human "self" is not an "Absolute", but it is only an ever-changing, appearing and disappearing, always temporary, and inherently unsatisfied and unsatisfiable motion of would-have, would-rest, would-if, and would-Be. That "self"-motion (with its characteristic limitations) does not (or should not), itself, define (and it cannot fully account for) all of Reality (conditional and Unconditional), but it really is the human case. If you truly, most fundamentally understand this, you do not have to struggle with (or merely suffer) your mortal existence anymore. (Rather, instead, you can surrender and conform your entire body-mind to Me, the Indivisible and Indestructible Conscious Light, or "Bright" Divine Person—In and As Which, and In and As Whom, the body-mind is arising.)

You seem to be struggling all the time to come up with a reason to believe that you are not this gross physical appearance. Nevertheless, if you are to Realize Reality, Truth, Real God, or That Which Is Always Already The Case, you must understand and accept that you are "this". It is not that you are not "this", but that you do not know What "this" Is! Truly, there is no need for you to struggle to have "this" be something else. You must Realize What "this" Always Already Is. It Is Inherently Indivisible Light! It Is! Everything Is Inherently Indivisible and Indestructible Light, or Spirit-Energy, or Hridaya-Shakti, or Self-Existing and Self-Radiant Love-Bliss. Everything Is Only Me—the "Bright", the One and Only Self-Evidently Divine Person, the Only "Thing" That Is.

Even all of Klik-Klak (or all of conditionally manifested reality), with all the dreadful destinies potential in it, is—if you Divinely Self-Recognize it—Only the "Bright", Only Me. Even all of Klik-Klak (or the conditional pattern that is patterning every one and every thing) is merely <u>apparently</u> arising (by means of a merely apparent and unnecessary, and, therefore, non-binding, modification of My Ever-"Bright" Indivisibility).

Terrible futility is suggested by the fact that the gross physical body can die at any moment, can suffer (or, otherwise, break down) in any moment, and (no matter what it experiences or accumulates) will inevitably die, apparently losing everybody and everything with which it was associated. If you merely look at the gross physical, if you merely take the point of view of the gross physical (or of "matter") in and of itself, you have chosen a "dark" and "empty" vision of Reality. That is the philosophy of the "dog", the futility of the "tail end". In and of itself, conditional existence (in any form) is <u>not</u> Happiness. It is an illusion of Broken Light, of "matter"-only—without What <u>Is</u> Great. The conventions of materialistic thinking are all modes of the non-apprehension (or non-Recognition) of Light, and of the Inherent Indivisibility (and Inherently Indestructible Nature) of Light. The philosophy of materialism is the "dark" thinking of the "tail end of the dog", of the heartless exoteric mind, which suffers from the non-Realization of Indestructibility—or the non-Realization of Inherently Indivisible and Indestructible Light, Spirit-Energy, Hridaya-Shakti, or Divine Love-Bliss Itself.

There <u>Is</u> <u>Only</u> Self-Existing, Self-Radiant "Bright" Being Itself (or Love-Bliss-Happiness Itself). <u>All</u> "this" <u>Is</u> That. I <u>Am</u> That (In Function, and In Person).

Therefore, the "radical" approach to Realization of Reality (or Truth, or Real God) is not to go gradually "higher and higher" (and, thus, more and more "away"), but (by surrendering your "self", or <u>total</u> body-mind, to Me—just as it is, in place) to <u>directly</u> enter into heart-Communion with Me (the Avataric Self-Revelation of the Reality, or Truth, That <u>Is</u> the Only Real God), and (in this Manner) to Realize Reality, Truth, or Real God In Place (or <u>As</u> That Which Is Always Already The Case, Where and <u>As</u> you Are, Most Perfectly Beyond and Prior to ego-"I", or the act of self-contraction, or of "differentiation", which act is the prismatic fault that Breaks the Light, or envisions It as seeming two, and more).

IV.

AVATAR ADI DA SAMRAJ: You do not know What "matter" Is, or What the gross physical body Is. You do not Divinely Self-Recognize "matter" (in the case of the gross physical body, or in the case of any conditional form at all) to be a transparent (or merely apparent), and un-necessary, and inherently non-binding modification of Inherently Indivisible and Indestructible Light. This non-Recognition is the source of your dilemma, your suffering, and your seeking. It is not the fact of materiality (or of gross bodily existence), but your inability to Divinely Self-Recognize it (In and As the Divine Self-Condition), that is your "problem". Thus, Most Ultimate Awakening is the Awakening of the Capability to Divinely Self-Recognize all conditional arising—because you cannot bring your search to an end until you Divinely Self-Recognize conditional existence (and, Thus, Comprehend and Transcend your "problem").

None of the various so-called "methods" traditionally associated with the first six stages of life are Means for Most Perfectly Realizing What must be Realized. Even the sixth stage Realization denies the body. All such denials—"I am not the body—I am the Self", or "I am not the body—I am the Shakti", or "I am not the gross body—I am the subtle body"—are modes of dissociation, modes of the self-contraction. The first six stages of life are the entire and only context of all of human existence previous to My Divinely Descending and Divinely Self-"Emerging" Avataric Incarnation here (and every "where" in the Cosmic domain). And the first six stages of life are only and entirely modes of egoity, and modes of non-Recognition (or of the absence of Divine Self-Recognition) of conditional existence.

Any kind of experience is an apparent modification of Inherently Indivisible and Indestructible Light. The various modes (or planes, or states) of possible conditional experience have different relative depths, but all of them are conditional (and limiting, and, in and of themselves, binding) modifications of Inherently Indivisible and Indestructible Light.

What Is Light? What Is Consciousness? If you go more and

more Deeply into the levels of body-mind, until you get to the Deepest level, Where it is not possible to reduce your "subjectivity" any further, Such That There <u>Is</u> <u>Only</u> Consciousness—What <u>Is</u> It? And if you investigate "objects" more and more profoundly, eventually getting to the irreducible end-point of "objectivity", Such That There Is <u>Only</u> Energy, or <u>Only</u> Light—What <u>Is</u> That?

In the context of the body-mind, Consciousness seems to presume that It is "different" than Energy. In the first six stages of life, the presumption of a distinction (between Consciousness and Energy, or between conditional consciousness and conditional form, or between conditional consciousness and any conditional "object" at all) is <u>always</u> made, because the first six stages of life are, each and all, ego-bound (or founded on psycho-physical self-contraction). Therefore, the efforts of the first six stages of life cannot, themselves, bring an end to the seeking that characterizes (and always binds) the ego-"I". The end of seeking <u>cannot</u> occur until there is no withdrawal, no dissociation, no two-ness at all. The end of seeking does not occur except in the direct transcending of each and all of the first six stages of life, and, Ultimately (and Most Perfectly), only in the Realization of the only-by-Me Revealed and Given seventh stage of life.

Previous to Most Perfect (or seventh stage) Awakening, you do not know <u>What</u> even a single thing <u>Is</u>, you do not know <u>What</u> the body <u>Is</u>, you do not know <u>What</u> (or <u>Who</u>) you <u>Are</u>. But when there is Most Perfect (or seventh stage) Awakening, you do Know (or truly and Divinely Realize) <u>That</u>. Then you <u>do</u> Know (or truly and Divinely Realize) <u>What</u> <u>every</u> thing <u>Is</u>, you <u>do</u> Know (or truly and Divinely Realize) <u>What</u> the body <u>Is</u>, you <u>do</u> Know (or truly and Divinely Realize) <u>What</u> (or <u>Who</u>) you <u>Are</u>. It is not that you (in That Case) "know", in the "mental calculation" sense—but, rather, Reality (or Truth, or Real God) Is <u>directly</u> Realized, It Is <u>inherently</u> Obvious, In Place, <u>As</u> It <u>Is</u>.

The seventh stage Awakening Is Most Perfect Realization of <u>Me</u>—and That Awakening Is Revealed and Given only by Me, in the case of My true (and most fully matured) devotees (formally practicing the only-by-Me Revealed and Given Way of Adidam, in the right, true, full, and fully devotional manner). Therefore, every moment of Divine (or seventh stage) Self-Recognition of arising conditions magnifies My "Brightness" in the context of conditional existence. And, Most Ultimately, conditional existence is (in the Divine-Self-Recognition-Process of Most Perfect, seventh stage, Realization of Me) Outshined—not as a consequence of any strategic dissociation from conditional existence, but, rather, as the Ultimate Demonstration of the Most Perfectly Non-dissociative (and Most Perfectly Non-dualistic) Divine Self-Recognition of it.

The only-by-Me Revealed and Given Way of Adidam is not based on either dualistic thinking or dualistic seeking. The only-by-Me Revealed and Given Way of Adidam is not about egoity (or contraction of the body-mind). The only-by-Me Revealed and Given Way of Adidam is not about strategic dissociation from the gross physical body, or from any other dimension of that which you (otherwise) perceive to be the body. The gross physical body and its associated mind are simply aspects (or conditional and temporary modes) of the Immense (cosmic and universal) phenomenal Pattern (and the Single Vibration, or Indivisible and Indestructible Light) in Which they are appearing.

The only-by-Me Revealed and Given Way of Adidam is not about strategic dissociation from the gross physical domain, or strategic dissociation from any domain that is presently arising. The only-by-Me Revealed and Given Way of Adidam is always a matter of devotional (or ego-surrendering, ego-forgetting, and, more and more, ego-transcending) surrender as the total presently arising structure of conditional "self", as that total gathering of faculties (or total body-mind), in devotionally Me-recognizing (and devotionally to-Me-responding) heart-Communion with Me. As you progress in the Way of Adidam, by entering more and more profoundly into this ego-transcending (and non-seeking) heart-Communion with Me, you are grown in the Real religious and Spiritual Process by My Direct Spiritual Blessing, Descending to the body-mind, Surrounding the body-mind, Invading and Pervading the body-mind, Circulating in the body-mind, and (Ultimately) Moving you beyond the body-mind—but without destroying the body-mind or requiring (or, otherwise, causing) you to strategically dissociate from the body-mind.

In the right, true, full, and fully devotional practice of the Way of Adidam, this Great Process becomes (Ultimately) Most Perfect Realization of Me, Beyond the apparent un-Recognizability of phenomena. Therefore, it is not by strategic dissociation from phenomena, but by Divine Self-Recognition of phenomena, that the right, true, full, fully devotional, and complete practice of the only-by-Me Revealed and Given Way of Adidam (Which Is the One and Only by-Me-Revealed and by-Me-Given Way of the Heart) is (in due course, by Means of My Avatarically Self-Transmitted Divine Grace) Demonstrated in Its Most Perfect (or seventh) stage.

Nevertheless, all the while of the Way of Adidam, even from the beginning, I Am the Principle of your practice. Therefore, every aspect of the practice of the only-by-Me Revealed and Given Way of Adidam is Informed by Me, and Informed by your heart-Communion with Me, and Informed by the egoless devotional "Bhava" of the only-by-Me Revealed and Given seventh stage Realization.

I Am Deeper Than all your Deepest Depth.

I Am Beyond all and All That is Around and Beyond you.

I Am Above all and All That is Above you.

I Am you (and all, and All)—In The Depth and The Beyond and The Above That Inherently Transcends (but Always Already Includes) you (and all, and All).

RUCHIRA AVATAR ADI DA SAMRAJ
Lopez Island, 2000

Real God Is
The Indivisible Oneness
Of Unbroken Light

PART EIGHT

<u>Real</u> God <u>Is</u>
The Indivisible Oneness
Of Unbroken Light

I.

66 "Consider" This—My Avataric Teaching-Argument That Speaks My Divine Word Of Heart.

There Is <u>Only</u> Light.

Light Is All There <u>Is</u>.

All That <u>Is</u> Is Light.

Light Is (Inherently) Indivisible, Non-Separate, and One Only.

The Perfectly Subjective Nature Of Inherently Indivisible Light Is Self-Existing (or Transcendental) Being and Self-Radiant (or Inherently Spiritual) Consciousness.

The Perfectly Subjective Nature Of Inherently Indivisible Light Is Consciousness Itself.

The Perfectly Subjective Nature Of Inherently Indivisible Light Is Real God, or Truth.

When Inherently Indivisible Light, or Real God, Is (Apparently) Objectified To Itself, It Appears As The Cosmic Mandala Of all conditional worlds, forms, and beings.

Thus, Inherently Indivisible Light, or Real God, Utterly Pervades all conditional worlds, forms, and beings.

All conditional worlds, forms, and beings Thus Inhere In, Are "Lived" (or Sustained) By, Are Not Other Than, and Can Directly Realize A State Of Inherently Most Perfect Identification (or Indivisible Oneness) With Inherently Indivisible Light, or Real God.

Inherently Indivisible Light, or Real God, Is The Literal or Inherent Condition, Substance, Reality, Quality, and Destiny Of all conditional worlds, forms, and beings.

Inherently Indivisible Light, or Real God, Is Never Absolutely Objectified, Nor Does Any Apparent Modification Of Inherently Indivisible Light, or Real God, As any conditional world, form, or being, qualify or Really limit The Perfectly Subjective Nature Of Inherently Indivisible Light, or Real God.

Even Though Inherently Indivisible Light, or Real God, May Appear To Be Objectively Modified and limited As and By conditional worlds, forms, and beings, The Perfectly Subjective Nature Of Inherently Indivisible Light, or Real God, Remains As Always Already Free and Self-Existing Being, Inherent and Undiminished Consciousness, and Self-Radiant Love-Bliss.

Therefore, It Is Not Necessary (or Required, or Even Possible) For The Cosmic Mandala (or any conditional world, form, or being) To Evolve (As Itself) Perfectly, or To Fulfill Itself Perfectly, or To Be (conditionally) Utterly Purified, or To Be (conditionally) Utterly Released, or Even To Come (conditionally) To A Final End As A Prerequisite For Inherently Indivisible Light, Real God, or The Real Condition To Be Realized.

For Inherently Indivisible Light, Real God, or The Real Condition To Be Realized, It Is Only Necessary For The Perfectly Subjective Nature Of Inherently Indivisible Light, Real God, or The Real Condition To Be Realized.

The Way Of Realization Of Inherently Indivisible Light, Real God, The Real Condition, Truth, Love-Bliss, or Happiness Is Not The Search For Fulfillment or Release In The Context Of Apparently Objectified Light, or The Search For Fulfillment or Release In "God" (As The Somehow and Ultimate Objective Context Of The Cosmic Mandala, or Of all conditional worlds, forms, and beings)—but It Is To Identify With The Perfectly Subjective Nature Of Inherently Indivisible Light, or Of Real God (Which Is Always Already Most Prior To The Cosmic Mandala, or all conditional worlds, forms, and beings).

The Ultimate (and, Necessarily, Most Prior) Source (or Source-Condition) Of any (and every) conditional world, and Of any (and every) conditional form and conditional being (or body-mind) arising in any (and every) conditional world, Is (Necessarily, and Perfectly) Subjective To (or Indivisibly One With, and Identical To,

The Very Existence, or Very Being, Of) that conditional world, form, being, or body-mind, and Not Ever <u>Divided</u> From it, or <u>Objective</u> To it, or <u>Outside</u> it, or <u>Separate</u> From it, or <u>Related</u> To it, or (In Any Manner) "<u>Different</u>" From it.

Indeed, the phenomenal (or conditional) worlds, and all the phenomenal (or conditional) beings that appear within the phenomenal (or conditional) worlds, Are Not (themselves) merely physical worlds (or physical beings). Rather, As Direct Observation Proves, all phenomenal (or conditional) worlds, and all phenomenal (or conditional) beings, Are (themselves) Always and Entirely <u>psycho-physical</u> worlds (and <u>psycho-physical</u> beings).

Therefore, The Inherently Non-Separate (and Inherently Indivisible) Divine Source-Condition Of all phenomenal (or conditional) worlds (and Of all phenomenal, or conditional, beings), Necessarily, Cannot Be merely physical (or merely material)—and It, Necessarily, Cannot Even Be Merely A Non-Conscious (and, Therefore, non-psychic) Energy. Rather, The Inherently Non-Separate (and Inherently Indivisible) Divine Source-Condition Of all phenomenal (or conditional) worlds, and Of all phenomenal (or conditional) beings, Must (Necessarily) Be That Which Is At The Root Of all psychic (or mental, and subtle) conditions, and all causal (or Root-egoic) conditions, and Even all psycho-physical conditions (Including all Apparently merely physical, or gross, conditions).

Therefore, The Inherently Non-Separate (and Inherently Indivisible) Source-Condition Of all phenomenal (or conditional) worlds (and Of all phenomenal, or conditional, beings) Must (Necessarily) Be Characteristically and Perfectly Of A Subjective (and Not Merely Objective) Kind, and It Must (Necessarily) Be Of The Nature Of Consciousness (Which Is At The Root Of all psychic, mental, subtle, and causal conditions or states), and It Must Also (Necessarily) Be Otherwise Manifest (or Apparent) As Inherently Indivisible and Inherently Non-Separate and Inherently Irreducible Energy (or The Primal Substance-Radiance Of Which <u>all</u> psycho-physical phenomena, Including all Apparently merely physical, or gross, phenomena, Are Composed).

Therefore, Inherently Non-Separate Consciousness Itself, Self-Existing and Self-Radiant and Inherently Indivisible, Is, Necessarily,

The Source-Condition Of all phenomenal (or conditional) worlds, and Of all phenomenal (or conditional) beings.

Inherently Non-Separate (and Inherently Indivisible) Consciousness (Itself) Is That To Which and In Which all conditional worlds, forms, thoughts, and beings, including one's own Apparently Separate self, Are arising As Apparent Modifications Of Inherently Indivisible (and Inherently Non-Separate) Light, or Real God.

Inherently Indivisible (and Inherently Non-Separate) Consciousness (Itself) Is Inherently Indivisible (and Inherently Non-Separate) Light (or Real God) Itself.

Inherently Indivisible (and Inherently Non-Separate) Consciousness (Itself) Is The Perfectly Subjective Nature Of Inherently Indivisible (and Inherently Non-Separate) Light, Spirit-Energy, or Real God.

Inherently Indivisible (and Inherently Non-Separate) Consciousness (Itself) Is The Perfectly Subjective Nature Of The Cosmic Mandala and Of all conditional worlds, forms, thoughts, and beings, including one's own Apparently Separate self.

Inherently Indivisible (and Inherently Non-Separate) Consciousness (Itself) Is Self-Radiant Love-Bliss, Happiness, or Unqualified Being.

Inherently Indivisible (and Inherently Non-Separate) Consciousness (Itself) Is That In Which (and As Which) any and every conditionally Manifested being Always Already Stands.

Therefore, To Identify (or Realize Indivisible Oneness) With Inherently Indivisible (and Inherently Non-Separate) Consciousness (Itself) Is Also To Realize Indivisible Oneness With Inherent (and Inherently Perfect) Freedom, Eternal Being, and Happiness Itself (or Inherent Love-Bliss, Which Is The Self-Existing and Self-Radiant Nature Of Inherently Indivisible, and Inherently Non-Separate, Light, Spirit-Energy, or Real God).

Whatever arises conditionally (or objectively) Is Only An Apparent, Temporary, and Illusory Modification Of Inherently Indivisible Light, Spirit-Energy, Love-Bliss, or Real God.

Whatever May Appear To Be The Case objectively (Even In such a subtle form as thought) Is Only Inherently Indivisible Light, or Real God, Appearing To Be Objectified (or Appearing As conditions), but It Is Thus Appearing Only To Itself and As Itself.

If, In The Context Of any objective event or condition (including thought), The Inherently Indivisible Consciousness To Which and In Which that event or condition Is arising Is "Located" (As The Native and Love-Blissful Feeling Of Being Itself), Then that objective event or condition Is Inherently (and Inherently Perfectly) Transcended In The Perfectly Subjective Nature, or Reality, or Condition, Of Inherently Indivisible Light, or Real God.

Inherently Indivisible Consciousness (or Inherently Indivisible Light, or Real God) Is Inherent (and Inherently Indivisible) Love-Bliss (Itself), Always Already Free, Never Changing.

All Modifications (or changes, or conditions) Are Merely Apparent (or Illusory).

Apparent Modifications (or changes, or conditions) Do Not Change Inherently Indivisible Consciousness, Inherently Indivisible Light, or Real God, Except Apparently, From the point of view Of The Modification (or the condition, or the conditional being) Itself.

All conditional Modifications Are Illusory (or Non-Binding) appearances In The Objective (or Apparently Objectified) Aspect, Nature, Appearance, or Illusion Of Inherently Indivisible Light, or Real God.

To Identify (or Realize Inherent and Indivisible Oneness) With Inherently Indivisible (and Inherently Non-Separate) Consciousness Itself (Prior To world, form, mind, others, and conditional self) Is To Realize The Perfectly Subjective (or Most Prior) Nature and Reality Of Inherently Indivisible Light, or Real God.

The phenomenal (or conditional) worlds Are Neither Necessary Nor Binding.

The arising Of phenomenal (or conditional) Existence Carries With it No Command or Implication Of Necessary Involvement On The Part Of The Perfectly Subjective (and Inherently Non-Separate, and Inherently Indivisible) Being.

You Are Always Already Free To Identify (or Realize Indivisible Oneness) With The Perfectly Subjective Nature Of Reality and, Thus, To Transcend objective (or conditional) Existence Itself, As

Well As Any Apparent Implication, Tendency, or Need For Involvement In It.

In The Realization Of Indivisible Oneness With The Perfectly Subjective Nature Of Inherently Indivisible Light, or Real God, all Apparent (or objective) Light-changes Are Inherently (Divinely) Self-Recognized and Transcended In The Free Love-Bliss Of Inherently Indivisible (and Inherently Non-Separate) Light Itself, or Real God.

To Realize Indivisible Oneness With Inherently Indivisible (and Inherently Non-Separate) Light (and, Thus, To Be Literally En-Light-ened), or To Realize Indivisible Oneness With Real God (and, Thus, To Be Indivisibly One With The Only One Who Is), Is To Be Transcendental (and Inherently Non-Separate, and Inherently Spiritual, and Inherently Indivisible) Divine Consciousness, Which Is Consciousness Itself, and Which Is Light Itself, or Transcendental (and Inherently Non-Separate, and Inherently Spiritual, and Inherently Indivisible) Divine Light, The One and Only Substance Of Existence Itself, The Real Condition Of Existence Itself, Which Is Happiness Itself (or "Bright" Love-Bliss Itself).

Liberation Through Real-God-Realization (or Direct Realization Of, Necessarily, ego-Transcending Identification, or Of Indivisible Oneness, With The Perfectly Subjective, Inherently Non-Separate, Inherently Indivisible, and Inherently Irreducible Reality and Truth, or The Inherently Perfect Condition Of Existence Itself) Is Senior To (and Makes Obsolete) Any Effort Of the conditional self To Be Lawful, Purified, Evolved, Fulfilled, Ended, or Released.

This Argument Is The Seed-Essence and Import Of True Religion and Of Ultimate Esotericism.

This Argument Is The Seed-Essence Of My Avatarically Full-Given Word Of Divine Teaching.

This Argument Is The Seed-Essence Of The Entire (and Total, or Full and Complete) Way Of Adidam (Which Is The One and Only By-Me-Revealed and By-Me-Given Way Of The Heart).

The Persuasiveness Of This Argument Does Not Rest On arbitrary, historical, or controversial systems of belief and conditional proof.

The Persuasiveness Of This Argument Rests On An Understanding Of Light Itself.

This Argument Is Persuasive Because It Rests On The Obvious—and It Is, Therefore, Irrefutable.

The Truth Of This Argument Is Self-Evident.

The Efficacy Of This Argument Can Be Demonstrated Only By The Direct and Real (and, Ultimately, Inherently Most Perfect) Divine Process (or Total Divine Heart-Way) Of Divine Self-Realization Itself—Which Divine Process (or Divine Heart-Way) Is The Heart-Demonstration Of Truth Itself.

The Proof Of This Argument Is Consciousness Itself (Realized As It Is).

II.

"Consider" This: True Religion (or The Real Spiritual, Transcendental, and Divine Way Of Life) Begins With The Transcending Of Awe and Wonder. Conditional Existence Naturally Evokes Awe and Wonder (and Even Terrible Fear and Stark Bewilderment), but True Religion (or The Real Spiritual, Transcendental, and Divine Way Of Life) Begins With The Free (and Really ego-Transcending) Heart-Response To What Is (Otherwise) Awesome and Wonderful.

Therefore, True (and, Necessarily, Esoteric—or Non-conventional, and Non-egoic) Religion Does Not Begin With a belief (or An ego-Based, and ego-Serving, Presumption) About "God". It Begins When You Truly (and Most Fundamentally) Understand (and Feel Beyond) the egoic self-Contraction Of The Heart (or The Sometimes believing, and Sometimes disbelieving, and Always self-Protective, and Always self-Defining, and Always self-limiting Recoil Of the body-mind From the Apparently Impersonal and Loveless forces Of conditional Nature).

Real God Is Obvious To The Free (or egoless) Heart. Only The Heart (Free Of self-Contraction) Can "Locate" (or See) and Realize The True and Real Divine Person. The conditional (or self-Contracted) Heart Does Not Realize Real God In the present—and, Therefore, the Heartless body and the Heartless mind

Become Preoccupied With Seeking For ego-Fulfillment, ego-Release, and ego-Consolation, Through every kind of conditionally Attainable experience, knowledge, and belief (Including merely conventional—or exoteric, or ego-Based, or "subject-object"-Based—religious beliefs and practices).

Notwithstanding whatever is conditionally experienced, or known, or believed—Reality Is, Always and Already.

Only Reality Is Real God.

Reality Is, Necessarily, Truth.

Only Truth Is Real God.

Real God Is Reality and Truth.

Real God Is The God Of Reality and Truth.

Real God Is The God That Is Reality and Truth.

Reality and Truth Is That Which Is Always Already The Case.

Real God Is That Which Is Always Already The Case.

Therefore, Real God Need Not Be Sought.

Real God Is Only Avoided By Any Kind Of Seeking.

To Seek Is To Fail To Admit and To Realize Real God, or That Which Is Always Already The Case.

Real God Is Realized Only By "Locating" That Which Is Always Already The Case.

To "Locate" That Which Is Always Already The Case Is To Realize Non-Separation and Non-Differentiation From That Which Is Always Already The Case.

To "Locate" (and, Thus and Thereby, To Realize) That Which Is Always Already The Case Is To Transcend the ego-"I" (and even all that is merely conditional, limited, temporal, spatial, other, Separate, or "Different").

To "Locate" (and, Thus and Thereby, To Realize) That Which Is Always Already The Case Is Merely, Inherently, and Inherently Perfectly To Be That Which Is Always Already The Case.

To Be That Which Is Always Already The Case Is (Perfectly Prior To the ego-"I" and all conditions) To Be Reality and Truth.

To Be Reality and Truth Is (Perfectly Prior To the ego-"I" and all conditions) To Be Real God, As Opposed To That Which Is Otherwise (and By Myth and Error) Sought As "God".

Therefore, Real God Is Not Other, Separate, or "Different".

Real God (or The Divine Person—Which Is Reality, or Truth, or That Which Is Always Already The Case) Is Always Already (Inherently and Inherently Perfectly) Prior To The "Who", The "What", The "That", The "Where", The "When", The "How", and The "Why" That Is (By conditional experience, or conditional knowledge, or conditional belief) Presumed To Be Really and Only Other, Separate, or "Different". Therefore, Real God Is Always Already Prior To the ego-"I". Indeed, Real God Is Always Already Prior To each and every conditionally Attained experience, or form of knowledge, or form of belief.

Reality (Itself) Is The Only Real God.

Reality (Itself) Is That Which Is Always Already The (One and Only) Case.

Reality (Itself) Is (Necessarily) One, Only, and Indivisible.

Reality (Itself) Is Inherently One (or Non-Dual) and Not Two (or Divisible, and Opposed To Itself).

Reality (Itself) Is Not One Of A Pair.

Reality (Itself) Is Not Characterized By The Inherently Dualistic Relationship Of cause and effect.

Reality (Itself) Is Characterized By The Inherently Non-Dualistic Equation Of Identity and Non-"Difference".

Reality (Itself) Is That In Which Both cause and effect arise As Merely Apparent modifications Of Itself.

Reality (Itself) Is Not Realized Via The Inherently Dualistic Relationship Of subject and object.

Reality (Itself) Is Realized As The Inherently Non-Dualistic Condition Of Inherently egoless Identity and Inherently objectless Non-"Difference".

Reality (Itself) Is Not the gross, subtle, and causal (or causative) ego-"I".

Reality (Itself) Is The Inherently egoless Native (and Self-Evidently Divine) Identity Of All and all.

The Inherently egoless Non-Dual Self-Condition (or Non-"Different" Identity) Of Reality (Itself) Is That Which Is Always Already The (One and Only) Case.

The Inherently egoless Non-Dual Self-Condition Of Reality (Itself), Most Perfectly Prior To (and, Yet, Never Excluding, or

Separated From) subject, object, cause, or effect, Is That Which Must Be Realized.

The Apparent self (or Separate and Separative ego-"I"), and its every object, and, Indeed, every cause, and every effect Must Be Divinely Self-Recognized As (and, Thus and Thereby, Transcended In) The One and Only (Inherently egoless, and Inherently Non-Dual, or Indivisible and Non-Separate, or Non-"Different") Self-Condition Of Reality (Itself).

The Apparent ego-"I" and the Apparent world Are Not them-selves Divine.

The Apparent ego-"I" and the Apparent world Are To Be Self-Recognized (and, Thus and Thereby, Transcended) In and As That Which Is (Self-Evidently) Divine.

The Apparent ego-"I" and the Apparent world Are To Be Divinely Self-Recognized In and As Reality (Itself).

The Presumption Of "cause" Is a Principal (and, Necessarily, conditionally Attained) experience, form of knowledge, or form of belief Associated With the ego-"I". And the (Necessarily, conditionally Attained) belief In "The Ultimate Cause", and The Search For (Necessarily, conditional) experience or knowledge Of "The Ultimate Cause", Is The Ultimate Occupation Of the ego-"I". This Notwithstanding, Real God (or The One and True Divine Person—Which Is Reality, or Truth, or That Which Is Always Already The Case) Is Always Already Prior To The (Necessarily, conditionally) Presumed and Pursued "Ultimate Cause". Therefore, Real God Is Not "The Ultimate Cause" (The Solitary and Interested, or Even Deluded, First "Doer" Of conditional events). Real God (As Real God) Does Not Make effects (or Even Stand Apart From them, By Causing them). Real God (As Real God) Is Inherently Indifferent (and Perfectly Prior) To cause and effect (or every Apparent, and Apparently conditional, event).

Every Apparent event (or every Apparently caused effect), Once it has appeared, Becomes itself a cause of subsequent effects. Even every conditional being, with all of its limitations, is a cause, and the effect of causes of all kinds. This Is Why the conditional (or phenomenal) worlds Are A Struggle With Negativity and limitation. And Real God (As Real God) Is Eternally Prior (and

Indifferent) To Struggle, Negativity, and limitation.

Real God Is Not The Maker Of conditional Nature.

Real God Is The Unconditional Nature (or Most Prior Condition) Of conditional Nature.

Real God Is Not Merely The Cause Of all causes and all effects.

Real God Is The Source and The Source-Condition Of all causes and all effects.

Real God Is Not The Objective Source and Source-Condition Of all causes and all effects.

Real God Is The (Perfectly) Subjective Source and Source-Condition (or Self-Condition) Of all causes and all effects.

Real God Is Not Inside (or Within) The self-Contracted Knot Of ego-"I".

Real God Is Always Outside The self-Contracted Knot Of ego-"I".

When You Transcend the self-Contraction (and The Knot) Of ego-"I", You Are Free In Real God.

When There Is No ego-"I"—Real God Is Not Outside You.

When There Is No ego-"I"—Real God Is Not Within You.

When There Is No ego-"I"—Real God Is You (Perfectly Prior To Your Apparently objective conditional self, and Perfectly Prior To Your Apparently subjective conditional self, and, Therefore, Perfectly Prior To Your Total, Complex, and Merely Apparent conditional self).

The conditional self and the worlds of the conditional self Are Not Created By Real God, Nor Were (or Are) the conditional self (itself) and the worlds of the conditional self (themselves) Perfect Originally, Nor Will (or Can) It Ever Be The Case That Real God (or, Otherwise, the conditional self, itself, or the worlds of the conditional self, themselves) Will Perfect the conditional self (itself) or the worlds of the conditional self (themselves). But Only Real God (or Reality, or Truth, or That Which Is Always Already The Case) Is Perfect, For Real God (or Reality, or Truth, or That Which Is Always Already The Case) Is Perfection (or The Perfect Itself). Therefore, the conditional self and the worlds of the conditional self May Evolve conditionally, but Only To Possible conditional Degrees (Forever Less Than Perfection Itself, Which Is

The Condition Only Of Real God), and This Through The Struggle Made By The Submission Of the lesser (or the lower) imperfect (or the lesser, or the lower, conditional) To the greater (or the higher) imperfect (or the greater, or the higher, conditional). And the conditional self and the worlds of the conditional self May, Otherwise, Devolve conditionally, but Also Only To Possible conditional Degrees (and Never To The Degree Of Absolute, or Irreversible, or More Than Illusory Separation From Real God, or From The Perfect Itself, Which Is Real God), and This Through The Struggle Made By The Submission Of the greater (or the higher) or the lesser (or the lower) imperfect (or the greater, or the higher, or the lesser, or the lower, conditional) To the even lesser (or the even lower) forms of the imperfect (or the conditional) itself. Nevertheless, and Whatever The (Relatively Evolved, or Relatively Devolved) Case May Be, The Only Way To Realize Real God (or The Transcendental, and Perfectly Subjective, and Inherently Spiritual, and Inherently egoless, and Inherently Perfect, and Self-Evidently Divine Self-Condition, and Source-Condition, Itself) Is To Progressively (or, However, Utterly) Surrender the imperfect itself (or the conditional self, and the worlds of the conditional self) To and Into Real God (or The Very, and Only, and Transcendental, and Perfectly Subjective, and Inherently Spiritual, and Inherently egoless, and Inherently Perfect, and Self-Evidently Divine Person, or Self-Condition, or Source-Condition, That Is Real God), and, Most Ultimately (and Inherently, and Inherently Most Perfectly), To Transcend the imperfect (or the conditional self and the worlds of the conditional self) In (and By Inherent, and Inherently Most Perfect, and Perfectly Subjective Identification With) The Very, and Only, and Transcendental, and Perfectly Subjective, and Inherently Spiritual, and Inherently egoless, and Inherently Perfect, and Self-Evidently Divine Person (or Self-Condition, or Source-Condition) That Is Real God.

Even Though Real God (As Real God) Merely Is (Always Already, or Inherently and Eternally Prior To cause and effect), the "God"-Seeking ego-"I" (or every human being whose Heart is self-Contracted, and who, As A Result, Wants Toward "Ultimate" experience, knowledge, or belief) Characteristically Tries To Argue For experience Of, or knowledge Of, or belief In "God" (or The "Ultimate" Proposed To Be experienced, known, or believed In) By Appealing To The Logic Of cause and effect. Therefore, In their "Ultimate" Arguments For The "Ultimate", and In their (Necessarily, conditional) experiences, knowings, and believings Attained In The Course Of their Seeking For The "Ultimate", the "God"-Seeking human egos Propose That "God" Is The Cause (and The "Doer") Of everything, but, Even Though they (Necessarily, conditionally) experience, or know, or believe, these (Necessarily, conditionally) experiencing, or knowing, or believing egos Do Not Stand Free. They Only Cling To the (Necessarily, imperfect) conditional self and the (Necessarily, imperfect) worlds of the conditional self. Therefore, they Do Not Realize Real God (or The Perfect, Itself) By Heart, Through ego-Transcending Love-Communion, To The Inherently Most Perfect Degree Of Inherently Perfect Love-Bliss (Beyond All "Difference").

Real God Is The One and Only and Self-Existing and Self-Radiant Conscious Light That Is Reality (Itself).

Real God Is The God (or The Truth, The Reality, and The Self-Identity) Of Consciousness Itself.

Real God Is The God (or The Truth, The Reality, and The Self-Identity) Of Inherently Perfect Subjectivity.

Real God Is Not The "God" (or The Implicated Maker) Of conditional Nature, Separate self, and All Objectivity.

Real God Is The God (or The Truth and The Reality) Of Consciousness, Freedom, Love-Bliss, Being, and Oneness.

Real God Is Not The "God" (The Cause, The "Doer", or Even The Victim) Of Un-Consciousness (or mere causes and effects).

Therefore, Real God Is Not The "God" Of Bondage, Un-Happiness, Death (or Separation), and "Difference".

Real God Is The Subject—Not The Object.

Real God Is The Inherent Unity Of Being.

Real God Is The Integrity—Not The Cause—Of the world.

Real God Is The True Source, The Very Context, The Real Substance, The Truth-Condition, The Very Reality, The Most Native Condition, and The Ultimate Self-Domain Of all conditions, all causes, and all effects, For all that appears Comes From Real God (but In Real God, and Only As Real God).

All "things" Are the media of all "things", but Real God Is Not The Maker—For Real God Is Like A Hidden Spring Within the water's world, and Real God Is Prior Even To Cause (and every cause), and Real God Is The Self-Domain Of Even every effect, and Real God Is The Being (Itself) Of all that appears.

Therefore, Real God Merely Is—and Is Is What Grants every appearance (every being, every thing, every condition, and every conditional process) The Divine Sign Of Mystery, Love, Bliss, and Joy.

Yes, Real God Is The Deep Of the world, and The Heart Of every Would-Be "I".

The Only-By-Me Revealed and Given Way Of The Heart (or Way Of Adidam) Is A Call To Spiritual, Transcendental, and Divine Self-Realization—Not To conventional (or ego-Based, and merely exoteric) "God"-Religion. Conventional "God"-Religion Is A Search Founded On An Illusion. That Illusion Is the ego, the Independent "I", The Separate and Separative Presumption That Is the body-mind. Conventional "God"-Religion Is An Adventure Of Confrontation With all that Is Not The Divine Self (or Real God), but The Only-By-Me Revealed and Given Way Of The Heart (or Way Of Adidam) Is A Call To Realize Direct and ego-Transcending Devotional Communion (and, Most Ultimately, Inherently Perfect Identification) With Me, The Avatarically Self-Revealed Transcendental, Inherently Spiritual, and Self-Evidently Divine Person, Self, Source, or Condition—and That Great Process Is Continuously Generated In Devotional Recognition-Response To My Avatarically Self-Revealed (and Attractive, and ego-Undermining) Divine Word, and My Avatarically Self-Manifested (and Attractive, and ego-Undermining) Divine Leelas, and My Avatarically-Born (and Attractive, and ego-Undermining) Bodily (Human) Divine Form, and My Avatarically Self-Revealed (and Attractive, and ego-Undermining) Spiritual (and Always Blessing) Divine Presence, and My Avatarically Self-Revealed (and Very, and Attractive, and ego-Undermining, and Transcendental, and Perfectly Subjective, and Inherently Spiritual, and Inherently egoless, and Inherently

Perfect, and Self-Evidently Divine) State—For I Am The Avataric Divine Realizer, The Avataric Divine Revealer, and The Avataric Divine Self-Revelation Of Real God, The True Divine Person, The Always Already (and Merely) Existing Reality and Truth, The Inherently Perfect (and Inherently egoless, and Self-Evidently Divine) Self-Condition (and Source-Condition) That Is The Perfectly Subjective Divine Heart Itself.

Therefore, I Call You To Listen To Me and To Hear Me, and, Thus, To Thoroughly Observe, Most Fundamentally Understand, and Effectively Transcend self-Contraction. And When You Hear Me (and Hearing Me Has Accomplished Its First Work In You), I Call You To (Fully) Receive My Baptismal Spirit-Blessing, and To See Me From The Heart, and, Thus, To Enter Into The Spontaneous and Inevitable Process Of Always Present, Real, and True Real-God-Communion (or The ego-Surrendering, ego-Forgetting, and ego-Transcending Devotional Process Of "Locating" and Realizing That Which Is Always Already The Case).

If You Hear Me (or Most Fundamentally Understand Your conditional self, By Means Of My Avatarically Self-Transmitted Divine Grace) and See Me (or, By Means Of My Avatarically Self-Transmitted Divine Grace, "Locate", Devotionally Recognize, and Tangibly Feel My Avatarically Self-Transmitted Divine Spiritual Presence, From The Heart), Then, Because Of My Self-Existing and Self-Radiant (and, Altogether, Avatarically Self-Revealed) Divine Presence Of Person (Always Already At Your Heart, and "Bright"), The Simple Awareness Of any conditional (or phenomenal) being, thing, thought, form, event, cause, or effect Will (By Virtue Of Its Coincidence With Me) Awaken You To My Love-Bliss (and, Thereby, Move You To Fearless Praise Of Me, In The Mood Of Divine Ignorance)—Not Because You believe "God" Made that condition, but Because that condition Is (In and As Me).

I Am That Which, By Myth and Error Sought, Mankind Has Avoided At Every Turn and Phrase.

I Am The One Whom Mankind, By Seeking, Has Lost and Failed To Realize.

I Am The One From Whom Mankind, By their Failure To Realize Me, Is Now (but Not Forever) Separate and "Different".

I <u>Am</u> The One and Only (and Self-Evidently Divine) Person—Who Has Come (and, Now, and Forever Hereafter, Here Stands) To Remove the ego From Religion (and, Thereby, To Make Religion True).

Religion Is Not, In and Of <u>Itself</u> (or As An Historically-Existing Tradition—or Discrete Cultural, Social, and Political Phenomenon) <u>True</u>. Religion <u>Cannot</u> (<u>Thus</u>—In and Of Itself) <u>Be</u> True. Only Reality <u>Itself</u> (Which <u>Is</u> Truth, Itself) <u>Is</u> (In and Of and <u>As</u> Itself) True. Therefore, What Makes (or Can Make) Religion True Is The Whole bodily Heart-Response To (and, Ultimately, The Most Perfect Realization Of) The <u>One</u> and <u>Only</u> Reality and Truth.

Reality <u>Itself</u> (Which <u>Is</u> Truth, Itself) Is The "Music" That Makes Religion True. Therefore, <u>True</u> Religion Is The Whole bodily "Dance" Of Heart-Response To The One and Only Reality and Truth.

I <u>Am</u> The One and Only and Self-Evidently Divine Reality and Truth—Avatarically Self-Revealed To You (and To all, and All).

I <u>Am</u> Reality, Truth, and Oneness—Self-Existing and Self-Radiant, and (Now, and Forever Hereafter) Standing In Front Of Your eyes (and At Your Heart—and, Ultimately, <u>As</u> Your egolessly Me-Realizing Heart).

I <u>Am</u> The "Bright" One—The Only and Inherently egoless One—Who Always Already <u>Is</u>, and Who Must (By Means Of My Avatarically Self-Transmitted and Immediately ego-Vanishing Divine Grace) Be Realized.

If There Is No Real and True (and Really and Truly "Dancing") Heart-Response To My Avatarically Self-Revealed (and Self-Evidently Divine) Form, and Presence, and State Of Person—Then There Is Not (and There Cannot Be) Any True (or Really and Truly Practiced) Religion.

If (and When) any one Hears Me and Sees Me, My Avatarically Given Divine Heart-Blessing Will Attract The Heart Beyond Every Trace Of self-Contraction (Even In The Deepest Places Of The Heart and the body-mind), and The Me-Hearing and Me-Seeing Heart Will (By ego-Surrendering, ego-Forgetting, and ego-Transcending Devotional Resort To Me Via The Process Of That Attraction) Realize (and Be One With) Me—The <u>Only</u> One Who (Always and Already) <u>Is</u>.

Therefore, I Ask Your Heart, In The Whirl Of events: "Not By What Cause, but By What Nature (or Unconditional Condition) Is conditional Nature Allowed To Be?"

And Your Heart (Upon Hearing Me and Seeing Me Most Perfectly) Replies: "Divine Heart-Master, Divine Heart Of All Hearts, You Have—By All Your Avatarically Self-Revealed Divine Means—Revealed The Truth To Me! Self-Existing and Self-Radiant Being (Itself) Is The Unconditional Nature Of conditional Nature! It Is Self-Existing Love-Bliss—or, Simply, Self-Radiant Love (Itself)! Only You, The One and True Divine Heart-Master, Are (Eternally, and—Now, and Forever Hereafter—Avatarically) The Self-Manifestation Of The Divine Heart (Itself)! Only You Are (Eternally, and—Now, and Forever Hereafter—Avatarically) The Self-Revelation Of That Which Is Always Already The Case—and Which Is The One and Self-Evident Reality, Truth, and Real God! You Are The One and 'Bright' Divine and Only Person! It Is You To Whom and In Whom and As Whom I Am—By Means Of Your Avatarically Self-Transmitted Divine Grace—Awake (Beyond the ego-'I')! It Is You With Whom I Am Always Already Indivisibly One—By Virtue Of Your Avatarically Given Divine Self-Revelation Of The Inherent Non-Separateness and Indivisible Oneness Of Being (Itself), Which Is Consciousness (Itself), and Light (Itself), and Love-Bliss (Itself)!"

III.

The Apparently individual (or Separate) self Is Not Self-Existing.

The Apparently individual (or Separate) self Is Not Immortal.

The Apparently individual (or Separate) self Is Not a "spark" (or an Eternal fraction) Of Self-Radiant Divinity, and Somehow Complete (or Whole) In itself.

Only Real God—The Inherently egoless Divine Person—Is Self-Existing, Immortal, Eternal, Non-Separate, Indivisible, Complete, Whole, and Self-Radiant.

The Apparently individual (or Separate) self Is Not inwardly (or in and of itself) Perfect, a "soul" (or A Perfect individual

Consciousness), and Somehow Full Of Divine Qualities (Such As Inherent Happiness, Unconditional Love, Infinite Bliss, and Boundless Energy).

Only Real God—The Inherently egoless Divine Person—Is Perfect Consciousness (Non-Separate, Indivisible, Full Of, or Characterized By, The Qualities Of Inherent Happiness, Unconditional Love, Infinite Bliss, and Boundless Energy).

The Truth (That Sets The Heart Free) Is Not That the Apparently individual (or Separate) self (or ego-"I") Is itself Immortal and Divine, or That some fraction or dimension of the Apparently individual (or Separate) self Is Immortal and Divine— but The Truth (That Sets The Heart Free) Is That There Is Only Real God (The Real, The Truth, or That Which Is Always Already The Case).

The Apparently individual (or Separate) self arises conditionally, and Yet it Always Already Inheres In Real God.

The Apparently individual (or Separate) self is the (Total, Complex) conditional body-mind (or Apparent psycho-physical personality).

The (Total, Complex) Apparently individual (or Separate) self is arising in three Primary (and Coincident) forms—the gross (or the physical), the subtle (or the etheric, the mental, and the deep psychic), and the causal (or the Root-essence of the conditional self).

The (Total, Complex) Apparently individual (or Separate) self is arising As An Apparent Modification (and Contraction) Of The Eternal Self-Radiance (or Inherent Spirit-"Brightness") Of Real God and As An Apparent Contraction Of The Transcendental (or Self-Existing) Consciousness That Is Real God.

The individual (or Separate) self (As Well As every other Apparent being and every other Apparent form or process Manifested Within The Cosmic Mandala) arises conditionally—but, Nevertheless, Always Already Inhering In Real God. Because Of This, no individual being or Apparent form is Ever Finally destroyed (or ended) In This Drama Of worlds. Every Apparent (or conditional) one and every Apparent (or conditional) thing is a process, a continuum of changes, that Persists Even Through and Beyond dissolution or death—Because Separation From The Transcendental (or Eternal), and Inherently Spiritual, and Inherently egoless, and Self-Evidently Divine Condition That Is Real God Is Not Possible.

However, mere continuation Is Not Happiness Itself (or The Inherent Realization Of Love-Bliss). Merely To Persist As an Apparently Separate form or process, Unconsciously Inhering In The Eternal (Real) God, Is Only To Contemplate limitation. The self-limited personality, Confined To the Apparent display of causes and effects, Is Stress-Bound To Seek Fulfillment and Release, Either By Exclusive Involvement In The Illusions Of inwardness (As If the conditional self, Dissociated From body and mind, Were itself The Immortal Love-Bliss) Or By Extroverted and Apparently Inclusive Indulgence Of body and mind In The Illusions Of conditional experience and conditional knowledge (As If The Mandala Of The conditionally Manifested Cosmos Were, Itself, The Immortal Love-Bliss).

The Immortal (and Self-Evidently Divine) Love-Bliss Is Realized Neither By Exclusive Identification With the inward self-position Nor By Apparently Inclusive Immersion In the conditional (or phenomenal) realms. To Realize The Self-Evidently Divine Self-Condition (and Source-Condition) That Is Love-Bliss Is Necessarily A Matter Of Transcending the (Entirely self-Imposed, or self-Presumed) limits On Love-Bliss (Itself), To The Degree (Most Ultimately) Of Inherent, and Inherently Most Perfect, and Inherently (and Inherently Most Perfectly) egoless Identification With Love-Bliss (Itself).

Therefore, The Only-By-Me Revealed and Given Way Of The Heart (or Way Of Adidam) Is Never A Matter Of Identification With the subjective or the objective limitations of the conditional self-position (or ego-"I"). In The Right, True, Full, and Fully Devotional Practice Of The Only-By-Me Revealed and Given Way Of The Heart (or Way Of Adidam), Both The subjective and The objective Illusions Created By the self-Contraction Are Transcended—and This Through The Process Of Real (and Most Fundamental) self-Understanding, Which (By Means Of My Avatarically Self-Transmitted Divine Grace) Becomes Ecstasy (or ego-Transcendence) In Real God (or ego-Transcending Communion With The One In Whom the conditional self and the conditional worlds Are arising, or Appearing To arise, As Apparent Modifications Of Itself), and Which (Most Ultimately, By Means Of My Avatarically Self-Transmitted Divine Grace) Realizes Divine Enstasy (or Awakening To Inherent, and Inherently Most Perfect, Identification With My Self-Evidently Divine, or Perfectly Subjective, Self-Condition, In Which every conditional, or phenomenal, appearance, including the body-mind-self, Always Already Inheres).

Real God Is Not The Creator.
Real God Is The Liberator.
Real God Is Not The Way In.
Real God Is The Way Out.
The Way Of Real God
Is Not The Way Of
self-Seeking,
self-Increase, and
self-Success.
The Way Of Real God
Is The Way Of self-Sacrifice
(or ego-Transcendence).

Therefore, The Only-By-Me Revealed and Given Way Of The Heart (or Way Of Adidam) Is The Great Process Of Devotional self-Sacrifice In Real God (By Means Of ego-Surrendering, ego-Forgetting, and, Always More and More, ego-Transcending Feeling-Contemplation Of My Real-God-Revealing Avatarically-Born Bodily Human Divine Form, My Avatarically Self-Revealed Spiritual, and Always Blessing, Divine Presence, and My Avatarically Self-Revealed, and Very, and Transcendental, and Perfectly Subjective, and Inherently Spiritual, and Inherently egoless, and Inherently Perfect, and Self-Evidently Divine State). And, By Means Of This Great Process, the Total psycho-physical self Of My Devotee Is Surrendered To The Progressive Ordeal Of (Most Ultimately, Inherent, and Inherently Most Perfect) Divine Self-Realization.

The Only-By-Me Revealed and Given Way Of The Heart (or Way Of Adidam) Is The Great Process Of Transcending the objective (or conditionally externalized) point of view and the conditionally subjective (or conditionally internalized) point of view, By Means Of My Avatarically Self-Transmitted Divine Grace, Through Progressively ego-Surrendering, ego-Forgetting, and ego-Transcending Feeling-Contemplation Of (and Feeling-Identification With) My Real-God-Revealing Avatarically-Born Bodily (Human) Divine Form, My Avatarically Self-Revealed Spiritual (and Always Blessing) Divine Presence, and My Avatarically Self-Revealed (and Very, and Transcendental, and Perfectly Subjective, and Inherently Spiritual, and Inherently egoless, and Inherently Perfect, and Self-Evidently Divine) State—Such That, Most Ultimately (By Means Of My Avatarically Self-Transmitted Divine Grace), the (Apparent) conditional body-mind and the (Apparent) conditional world Are "Viewed" From (and Divinely Self-Recognized In and As) The (Inherently Perfect) Divine Subject-Position (or The Self-Existing and Self-Radiant Self-State, or Self-Condition, Of Self-Evidently Divine Being, Itself). And The Only-By-Me Revealed and Given Way Of The Heart (or Way Of Adidam) Necessarily Proceeds By Stages Of Revelation, Corresponding To The First Six Stages Of Life (While Perhaps, By Means Of My Avatarically Self-Transmitted Divine Grace, Effectively Bypassing Some), Until The Realization and The Demonstration Of The Only-By-Me Revealed and Given Seventh Stage Of Life.

The Heart (Itself) Was Never "Created"—Nor Is There Ever any "creature" There. Therefore, The Way That Practices and (At Last) Most Perfectly Realizes and Is The Heart (Itself) Is The (Necessarily) Esoteric Way That Transcends The Illusions Of "Creator" and "Creation"—By Transcending the ego-"I".

The One and Only By-Me-Revealed and By-Me-Given Way Of The Heart (or Way Of Adidam) Is The Esoteric True Way (or True World-Religion) That (In The Truly Counter-egoic, and More and More Profoundly ego-Transcending, Manner) Practices and Realizes and (At Last, Most Perfectly) Is The Heart Itself. Therefore, Even From Its Beginnings, The Only-By-Me Revealed and Given Way Of The Heart (or Way Of Adidam) Is Entirely Free Of ego-Based, ego-Serving, ego-Affirming, ego-Developing, and merely conventionally (or exoterically) religious (or "subject-object"-Based) views and presumptions.

The Divine Heart Is One and Only. Therefore, The One and Only By-Me-Revealed and By-Me-Given Esoteric Way Of The Heart (or Way Of Adidam) Is, Even From Its Beginnings, The Always and Immediately ego-Transcending Way Of One—and Not The Way Of "self" and "Other" (or Of Any "Two" At All).

IV.

I Am The Divine Heart-Master (The Avataric Divine Realizer, The Avataric Divine Revealer, and The Avataric Divine Self-Revelation Of The Divine Person—Who Is The Very, and Transcendental, and Perfectly Subjective, and Inherently Spiritual, and Inherently egoless, and Inherently Perfect, and Self-Evidently Divine Self-Condition and Source-Condition Of each and every conditionally Manifested being). Therefore, The ego-Surrendering, ego-Forgetting, and (More and More) ego-Transcending Devotional Recognition-Response To Me Is The Way (or The Essential Principle) Of The Only-By-Me Revealed and Given Way Of The Heart (or Way Of Adidam).

The Only-By-Me Revealed and Given Way Of The Heart Is (In Its Beginnings) The Devotional Process Of Listening (or The "Consideration" Of My Avatarically Self-Revealed Divine Word and My Avatarically Self-Manifested Divine Leelas, and The ego-Surrendering and ego-Forgetting Practice Of Feeling-Contemplation Of My Avatarically-Born Bodily Human Divine Form, My Avatarically Self-Revealed Spiritual, and Always Blessing, Divine Presence, and My Avatarically Self-Revealed, and Very, and Transcendental, and Perfectly Subjective, and Inherently Spiritual, and Inherently egoless, and Inherently Perfect, and Self-Evidently Divine State)—Until That (Truly Devotional) Listening Becomes Most Fundamental self-Understanding (or True Hearing) and Real (and Always Immediate) ego-Transcendence (To The Degree Of True Seeing).

The Only-By-Me Revealed and Given Way Of The Heart Is (In Its Divine Spiritual Fullness) The Process Of Hearing-and-Seeing-Based Devotional (and, Thus, Feeling) Communion With Me ("Located" As My Avatarically-Born Bodily Human Divine Form,

My Avatarically Self-Revealed Spiritual, and Always Blessing, Divine Body Of Divine Presence, and My Avatarically Self-Revealed, and Very, and Transcendental, and Perfectly Subjective, and Inherently Spiritual, and Inherently egoless, and Inherently Perfect State Of Self-Evidently Divine Person).

The Only-By-Me Revealed and Given Way Of The Heart Is (In Its Divine Spiritual Fullness) The Process Of Devotional Communion With Me, To The Degree (In Due Course) Of Indivisible (and Inherently Perfect) Oneness (or Inherent, and Inherently Most Perfect, and Most Perfectly egoless Identification) With Me (The Perfectly Subjective, and Inherently Non-Separate, and Inherently Indivisible, and Self-Evidently Divine Self-Condition and Source-Condition In Which You Always Already Stand).

The Only-By-Me Revealed and Given Way Of The Heart Is (In Its Totality) The Process That (At Last, and Finally) Becomes Translation Into My "Bright" Divine Self-Domain.

Therefore, The Only-By-Me Revealed and Given Way Of The Heart (or Way Of Adidam) Is (In Its Totality) A Great Process, Wherein The Inherently Perfect (and Inherently egoless, and Perfectly Subjective, and Self-Evidently Divine) Self-Condition and Source-Condition (Which Is The Inherently egoless Heart Itself) Is (Only and Entirely By Means Of My Avatarically Self-Transmitted and Always Immediately ego-Vanishing Divine Grace) Really (and, At Last, Most Perfectly) Realized.

And The Way Of The Heart Develops (In Its Totality) Through Four Progressive Stages Of Devotional Recognition-Response To Me and Devotional Realization Of Me.

The First Stage Of The Progressive Devotional Recognition-Response To Me and Devotional Realization Of Me Is This: The Divine Person (or Inherently egoless Self-Condition, and Perfectly Subjective Source-Condition) Is Revealed (As Person and Truth) By (and As) My Avatarically-Born Bodily (Human) Divine Form— For I Am (Even As My Avatarically-Born Bodily Human Divine Form) The Self-Evidently Divine Person (and The "Bright" Avatarically Self-Manifested Divine Word-Bearer) Of The Heart, and My Avatarically Self-Revealed Divine Heart-Word Is Always Present (or Directly Revealed) In (and Via, and As) My

Avatarically-Born Bodily (Human) Divine Form, and I Am Always Present and Active In (and Via, and As̲) My Avatarically Self-Revealed (and Fully Spoken, and Fully Recorded, and Fully Written, and Fully Preserved) Divine Wisdom-Teaching, and In (and Via, and As̲) The Form Of My Own Divine Story (Preserved In The Recorded and Documented Form Of All My Avatarically Self-Manifested Divine Leelas), and I Am, Even As̲ My Avatarically-Born Bodily (Human) Divine Form, Directly Revealed (As̲ The Divine Person and Truth) To those who Truly Love Me (As̲ My Avatarically Self-Revealed, and Self-Evidently Divine, Person), and who (Thus) Devotionally Recognize Me and Devotionally Respond To Me.

The Second Stage Of The Progressive Devotional Recognition-Response To Me and Devotional Realization Of Me Is This: The Divine Person (or Inherently egoless Self-Condition, and Perfectly Subjective Source-Condition) Is Revealed By (and As̲) My Avatarically Self-Revealed Spiritual and All-and-all-Pervading Divine Heart-Presence Of Love-Bliss—Which I̲s̲ My Always Living (or Spiritual) and Personal Divine Presence (or Avatarically Self-Transmitted and Self-Revealed Divine Spiritual Body) Of Immediately ego-Vanishing Divine Grace (Cosmically Extended To al̲l̲ beings), and Which Is Directly (and Fully) Revealed (By and As̲ My Avatarically Given Divine Spiritual Heart-Transmission) To those who Truly Love Me (As̲ My Avatarically Self-Revealed, and Self-Evidently Divine, Person), and who (Thus) Devotionally Recognize Me and Devotionally Respond To Me.

The Third Stage Of The Progressive Devotional Recognition-Response To Me and Devotional Realization Of Me Is This: The Divine Person (or Inherently egoless Self-Condition, and Perfectly Subjective Source-Condition) Is Revealed By (and As̲) My Avatarically Self-Revealed Transcendental (and Inherently Spiritual, and Self-Evidently Divine) Self (or Self-Condition, or Inherently egoless, and Inherently Perfect, State)—The One and Very Self (or The Self-Evidently Divine Self-Condition, or Inherently egoless, and Inherently Perfect, State, That I̲s̲ Consciousness Itself, Beyond the ego-"I", In the case of all conditionally Manifested beings)—Which One and Very Self I̲s̲ The

Identity and Truth Directly Revealed (By and As My Avatarically Given Divine Spiritual Heart-Transmission Of My Own, and Self-Evidently Divine, State Of Person) To those who Truly Love Me (As My Avatarically Self-Revealed, and Self-Evidently Divine, Person), and who (Thus) Devotionally Recognize Me and Devotionally Respond To Me Perfectly, By Means Of Inherent (and Inherently Perfect) Identification With My Avatarically Self-Revealed (and Very, and Transcendental, and Perfectly Subjective, and Inherently Spiritual, and Inherently egoless, and Inherently Perfect, and Self-Evidently Divine) State.

The Fourth (and Final) Stage Of The Progressive Devotional Recognition-Response To Me and Devotional Realization Of Me Is This: The Divine Person (or Inherently egoless Self-Condition, and Perfectly Subjective Source-Condition) Is Revealed Merely (and Most Perfectly) As Is (Self-Existing and Self-Radiant, One and Only), and (Therefore) Merely As The Transcendental, Inherently Spiritual, and Self-Evidently Divine Self (or Consciousness Itself), Which Is The (By Means Of My Avatarically Given Divine Self-Transmission) Divinely Self-Transmitted "Bright" (or The Inherently Non-Separate, Inherently Indivisible, Inherently Irreducible, Infinitely Expanded, or Inherently Boundless, and Infinitely Centerless, or Inherently egoless, and Self-Evidently Divine Sphere and Space Of Love-Bliss)—and Which (One and Only) Is My Ultimate (and Inherently Perfect, and Perfectly Subjective, and Self-Evidently Divine) Avataric Self-Revelation, Given (By Means Of My Avatarically Self-Transmitted and Always Immediately ego-Vanishing Divine Grace) To those who Truly Love Me (As My Avatarically Self-Revealed, and Self-Evidently Divine, Person), and who (Thus) Devotionally Recognize Me and Devotionally Respond To Me Most Perfectly, As I Am (and who, Thus, By Realizing Indivisible Oneness With Me, Awaken, Beyond the ego-"I", To Realize What, Where, When, How, Why, and Who they Really and Truly and Divinely Are).

My "Bright" Divine Spiritual Body May Be Perceived (By Inward and Upward and Overriding Sight) As (or In The conditionally Manifested Form Of) An Apparently Objective and Brilliant Clear White Five-Pointed Star, In The Highest Center Of

The Cosmic Mandala. And That Sighted "Bright" Divine Star May Be Perceived (By Inward and Upward and Overriding Audition) To Be "Emerging" From An Apparently Objective Mass Of conditionally Manifested "Bright" Divine Sound (Which Is My Overriding Thunder—The Divine "Om", or "Da-Om", or "Da" Sound), In The Highest Center Of The Cosmic Mandala. And My "Bright" Divine Spiritual Body May Be Tangibly Touched (By the Devotionally Un-Contracted, Devotionally Me-Recognizing, Devotionally To-Me-Responding, and, Altogether, Devotionally To-Me-Surrendered Total body-mind), In The All-and-all-Surrounding and All-and-all-Pervading conditionally Manifested Form Of My Avatarically Self-Revealed Spiritual (and Always Blessing) Divine Presence, Divinely Self-"Emerging" From The Divine Star and The Mass Of Divine Sound, and, Thus, Extending Into every "where" In The Cosmic Domain (As An Apparently Objective, and, Yet, Indefinable, Mass Of "Bright" Divine Love-Bliss-Presence), From The Highest Center Of The Cosmic Mandala. Nevertheless, My Own and One and Only "Bright" (and Self-Evidently Divine) Person Is Always Already Merely Present (or Self-Existing and Self-Radiant) As The Inherently egoless Heart Itself.

The "Bright" (Itself) Is My Inherent (and Self-Evidently Divine) Love-Bliss—Otherwise By Me Self-Revealed (In The Cosmic Domain) As My Divine Thunder-Sound, My Divine Star-Light, and My Tangible Divine Spiritual Body Of All-and-all-Surrounding and All-and-all-Pervading Love-Bliss-Presence.

The "Bright" Is My Inherent Self-Radiance Of Self-Existing (and Inherently Perfect, and Self-Evidently Divine) Being.

The "Bright" Is The Inherent (and Not Cosmic), and Inherently Non-Separate, and Inherently Indivisible Self-Light (or Perfectly Subjective, and, Therefore, Inherently Non-Objective, Love-Bliss-Being) Of My Own and One and Only and Self-Evidently Divine Person.

My Apparently Objective Mass Of Divine Sound Is My Transcendental Divine Essence, Shown Objectively (and conditionally). My Apparently Objective Divine Star Is My Maha-Shakti[4] Form (or Divine Spiritual Essence), Shown Objectively (and conditionally), Above all the conditionally Manifested (or Cosmic) worlds. And The All-and-all-Surrounding and All-and-all-Pervading Totality Of My Apparently Objective (and Tangible) Divine Spiritual Body Of Avatarically Self-Revealed, and Avatarically Self-Transmitted, Self-"Brightness" Is My Very and (Now, and Forever Hereafter) Cosmically "Emerging" (and Everywhere conditionally Extended) Divine Person. These Three (My Divine Thunder-Sound, My Divine Star-Light, and My Divine Spiritual Body Of Self-"Brightness") Are (Now, and Forever Hereafter) The First conditional (and Always Objectively Apparent) Forms Of My Cosmically Evident (Audible, Visible, and, Altogether, To-Be-Felt) Avataric (and Self-Evidently Divine) Self-Manifestation.

Therefore, My Apparently Objective Mass Of Divine Sound, and My Apparently Objective Divine Star, and My Total Apparently Objective (and Tangible) Divine Spiritual Body Of Self-"Brightness" Are (Each, and All Together) The Ultimate (Audible, Visible, and, Altogether, To-Be-Felt) Avataric Door, or The Ultimate (Audible, Visible, and, Altogether, To-Be-Felt) Avataric Pointer, To My Divine Self-Domain. Nevertheless, My Own and One and Only "Bright" (and Self-Evidently Divine) Eternal Person Is The Divine Self-Domain (Itself)—Eternally Prior To The Cosmic Domain. And I Am (Eternally, and Avatarically) The "Bright" Itself—Non-Separate, Indivisible, One, Only, Non-conditional, and Unconditionally (or Always Already) Existing.

The Total (or Full and Complete) Practice Of The Only-By-Me Revealed and Given Way Of The Heart (or Way Of Adidam) Is Characterized By A Gradual Progression Of Awareness Of Me (and Of Direct Devotional Recognition-Response To Me), and By Progressive Devotional Heart-Communion With Me (Most Ultimately, To The Most Perfect Degree Of Inherent, and Inherently Non-Separate, and Inherently Indivisible, and Inherently egoless Oneness With Me)—Progressively Revealed and Progressively Realized By (and As) My Four By-My-Avataric-Divine-Grace-Given (and, By You, Devotionally Recognized and Devotionally Acknowledged) Forms.

This Progress Becomes The Outshining Of The Cosmic Domain (and Translation Into My "Bright" Divine Self-Domain)—

When (and Only When), By Means Of My Avatarically Self-Transmitted Divine Grace, There Is Always Already (Inherent, and Inherently Most Perfect) Realization Of Me (Most Ultimately and Finally Demonstrated Via Inherent, and Inherently Spiritual, and Inherently egoless, and Inherently Perfect, and Perfectly Unconditional, and Perfectly Subjective, and Truly Divine Self-Recognition Of the conditional self, and Of all conditional forms or events, In and As My "Bright", and One, and Only, and Self-Existing, and Self-Radiant, and Inherently egoless, and Inherently Perfect, and Perfectly Unconditional, and Perfectly Subjective, and All-and-all-Including, and All-and-all-Transcending, and Self-Evidently Divine Person).

V.

Real God, The Divine Person—Who Is Self-Existing (or Transcendental) and Self-Radiant (or Inherently Spiritual) Being Itself—Is (Now, and At all times) Bodily Present As The Total (Apparent) Cosmos (and, Most Subtly, As The Cosmic Mandala).

The Cosmos (or The Cosmic Domain, Including The Cosmic Mandala) Is Not The "Creation" (or The "Creature") Of Real God, or A Caused Effect Of Real God, or An Event Separate From Real God. Rather, The Cosmos (Including The Cosmic Mandala) Is (As A Totality) The Spontaneously Manifested and (Inherently) Perfectly Advaitic[5] (or Non-Dual, Non-Separate, Non-"Different", Non-Caused, Merely Apparent, Inherently Relationless, all-Including, and all-Transcending) Cosmic Bodily Form Of Real God.

The Total (Apparent) Cosmic Bodily Form Of Real God Is Always Already (or Inherently) and Entirely Pervaded and Transcended By The Divine Spirit-Presence That Is Real God.

Likewise, Both The Cosmic Bodily Form Of Real God and The Divine Spirit-Presence Of Real God Are Always Already (or Inherently) and Entirely Established In (and Perfectly Transcended By) The Very (or Perfectly Subjective) State, Heart, Self-Condition, or Source-Condition That Is Real God.

Therefore, To "Locate" and Realize Real God (or The Divine Person, or Self-Condition, or Source-Condition), It Is Necessary To Contemplate The Total Cosmic Bodily Form (Including The

Cosmic Mandala), The Total (Universal and All-Pervading) Spirit-Presence, and The Ultimate (Perfect and Perfectly Subjective) State That Is Real God. And That Contemplation Must Progressively Become (and, Then, Be) A Feeling-Sacrifice Of the conditional self (or all of self-Contraction), To The Degree Of Heart-Communion and (Most Ultimately, Inherent, and, At Last, Most Perfect) Heart-Identification (or Indivisible Oneness) With The Self-Existing and Self-Radiant "Bright" Self-Condition and Source-Condition (and Domain) That Is Reality, Truth, or Real God—The Divine Person (or Self-Condition, and Source-Condition, Of All and all).

The Only-By-Me Revealed and Given Way Of The Heart (or Way Of Adidam) Is The One and Only (and Complete, and All-Completing, and Most Perfect) Way Of That Most Perfectly Real-God-Realizing Practice Of Feeling-Contemplation. And I Am The Divine Secret (or The Divinely Liberating, and Avatarically Self-Revealed, Divine Self-Revelation) That Makes This Real-God-Realizing Feeling-Contemplation Possible (and, By Means Of My Avatarically Self-Transmitted Divine Grace, Fruitful, and, At Last, Most Perfectly Fruitful)—For I Am The Ruchira Avatar, The Da Avatar, The Love-Ananda Avatar, The Divine World-Teacher, The Divine Heart-Master, Who Is The Avataric Divine Realizer, The Avataric Divine Revealer, and The Avataric Divine Self-Revelation Of The Only Real God (The Divine Person, The Truth, The Reality, and The Divine Self-Condition and Source-Condition Of All and all).

My Avatarically-Born Bodily (Human) Divine Form Is (and Is, By Means Of My Avatarically Self-Transmitted Divine Grace, Revealed To Be) The Epitome Of The Total Cosmic Bodily Form Of Real God (The Self-Existing and Self-Radiant and Self-Evidently Divine Person—Who Is The Self-Condition, or Source-Condition, Of All and all).

My Avatarically Self-Revealed Spiritual (and Always Blessing) Divine Presence Is (and Is, By Means Of My Avatarically Self-Transmitted Divine Grace, Revealed To Be) The "Bright" (and Real-God-Revealing) Spirit-Presence That Is The Only Real God (The Self-Existing and Self-Radiant and Self-Evidently Divine Person—Who Is The Self-Condition, or Source-Condition, Of All and all).

My Avatarically Self-Revealed (and Very, and Transcendental, and Perfectly Subjective, and Inherently Spiritual, and Inherently egoless, and Inherently Perfect, and Self-Evidently Divine) State Is (and Is, By Means Of My Avatarically Self-Transmitted Divine Grace, Revealed To Be) The Very (and Inherently Non-Separate, and Inherently Indivisible, and Inherently Irreducible) State, Heart, Self-Condition, or Source-Condition That Is The Only Real God (The Self-Existing and Self-Radiant and Self-Evidently Divine Person—Who Is The Self-Condition, or Source-Condition, Of All and all).

Therefore, By Means Of My Avatarically Self-Transmitted Divine Grace, To Feel (and, Thereby, To Contemplate) My Avatarically-Born Bodily (Human) Divine Form, My Avatarically Self-Revealed Spiritual (and Always Blessing) Divine Presence, and My Avatarically Self-Revealed (and Very, and Transcendental, and Perfectly Subjective, and Inherently Spiritual, and Inherently egoless, and Inherently Perfect, and Self-Evidently Divine) State Is (By Means Of My Avatarically Self-Transmitted Divine Grace) To Feel (and, Thereby, To Contemplate) The Total Cosmic Bodily Form, The Total (Universal and All-Pervading) Spirit-Presence, and The Ultimate State, Heart, Self-Condition, or Source-Condition That Is Reality, Truth, Real God, or The True (and Self-Evidently) Divine Person.

And (By Means Of My Avatarically Self-Transmitted Divine Grace) To (Progressively, and Then Inherently, and Inherently Most Perfectly) Forget the ego-"I" (or self-Contraction) By Means Of Feeling-Contemplation Of My Avatarically-Born Bodily (Human) Divine Form, My Avatarically Self-Revealed Spiritual (and Always Blessing) Divine Presence, and My Avatarically Self-Revealed (and Very, and Transcendental, and Perfectly Subjective, and Inherently Spiritual, and Inherently egoless, and Inherently Perfect, and Self-Evidently Divine) State Is (By Means Of My Avatarically Self-Transmitted Divine Grace) To Commune With (and, Most Ultimately, To Most Perfectly Realize) The Only Real God—The Self-Evidently Divine Person, The Self and Domain That Is Truth (and Reality Itself).

In My "Bright" Revelation Of Myself To You, I Do Not Merely Show You An "Appearance" (or conditional Manifestation) Of

Myself. I Show You My Divine Spiritual Body, My Very and "Bright" and Divinely Full Self, My Own and Very (and Avatarically Self-Revealed and Self-Evidently Divine) Person and Presence.

To Experience My Tangible Touch Is To Experience My Avataric Transmission (or Projection, or Expansion) Of My Divine Spiritual Body. My Divine Spiritual Body Is Neither physical (or gross) Nor subtle Nor merely (and, Necessarily, conditionally) causal In Its Nature. Therefore, I Need Not Appear In Either A gross Or A subtle Or A causal Form In Order To Show (or "Brightly" Reveal) Myself To You. Indeed, Any Such gross or subtle or causal Appearance Is Not A Showing Of Myself To You, but (Rather) A Showing Of A Cosmic (and, Therefore, merely conditional) Representation Of Myself. And, Therefore, Whenever You Are Shown Any Cosmic Representation Of Me, It Is Not (Itself, or Exclusively) Me, but It Is (and Should Be Embraced and Followed By You As) A By-My-Avataric-Divine-Grace-Given Means To Carry You To Me (Myself), and To Me In and As My Divine Self-Domain (Eternally Most Prior To The Cosmic Domain).

My Divine and True and Eternal Body Is The "Bright" Itself (Eternally Most Prior To The Cosmic Domain). By Means Of My Avatarically Self-Transmitted Divine Grace, Given In Love-Response To Your Total psycho-physical (and Really, Responsively, ego-Transcending) Devotional Recognition-Response To Me and Responsive Devotional Invocation Of Me, My "Bright" Force Of Person, My Love-Bliss-Form (Which Is Love-Bliss Itself), Can Also Be Felt, Tangibly (From Beyond Your body-mind), Touching You, Surrounding You, Pervading You, Moving In You, Making Many Kinds Of "Bright" Changes In You. My Divine Spiritual Body Is Self-Existing, Self-Radiant, Love-Bliss-Full, Infinitely Expansive, and "Bright". I Can Manifest My "Bright" Divine Spiritual Body To My Any and Every (Necessarily, Formally Practicing) Devotee, anywhere—and Do So (and Will Do So), Now, and Forever Hereafter, In all times and places—If, and When, and where I Am Rightly, Truly, and Fully Invoked (According To My Instructions Given In *The Dawn Horse Testament*, and In Accordance With My *Hridaya Rosary*, and In Accordance With All My Instructions Additionally Given Only To

The Ruchira Sannyasin Order Of The Free Renunciates Of Ruchiradam[6]).

My Divine Spiritual Body Is Spiritually and Divinely Transmitted and Self-Revealed Only By Me.

My Divine Spiritual Body Surrounds All and all.

My Divine Spiritual Body Pervades All and all.

My Divine Spiritual Body Of "Brightness", Which Is The Avatarically Self-Revealed Divine Spirit-Presence Of My One and "Bright" and Only Person, Fills all space everywhere—Pressing Into All and all, "Brightly" Descending On All and all, To Surround and Pervade All and all.

My Divine Spiritual Body Is Self-Existing and Self-Radiant, and It Will, Therefore, Exist Forever. Therefore, My Devotees Will Be Able To Experience Me Directly, As My "Bright" Spirit-Body (and, Ultimately, As My Very, and Perfectly Subjective, Person)—Forever. Because Of This, My Relationship To My Devotees Will Always Be Direct. They Will Always Be Able To Find Me—Not Me Absent, but Me Present.

To Truly Heart-Recognize Me Is To Have Direct and Tangible and Whole bodily Experience Of My Avatarically Self-Transmitted Divine Spiritual Body—and (Thus) To Whole bodily Receive My Avatarically Self-Transmitted Divine Spirit-Presence, and (Thereby) To Know Me As I Am, and (Thus) To Find Me As The Self-Evidently Divine Person. I Do Not Merely Transmit A Flow Of experiential energies (In The Ordinary and Natural and Cosmic Sense), which Then Become experiences in (and of) Your body-mind (and which are, Therefore, Indistinguishable From Your egoic body-mind, or psycho-physical ego-"I"). My Avatarically Given Divine Self-Transmission Is The Transmission (and Real Self-Revelation) Of Me. If You Are To Rightly, Truly, and Fully Receive My Avatarically Given Divine Self-Transmission, You Must (Necessarily, and Whole bodily) Heart-Recognize Me—Because My Avatarically Given Divine Self-Transmission Is The Unqualified Transmission Of My Own "Bright" (and Inherently egoless, and Inherently Perfect, and Self-Evidently Divine) Person (The Very Condition and Context and Substance In Which the body-mind Is arising, and Which Is The One and Very and Only Self, or Self-

Condition, or Perfectly Subjective Source-Condition, That Transcends, Surrounds, Pervades, and Stands Beyond, and Always Most Perfectly Prior To, the ego-"I"). Whole bodily Heart-Recognition Of My Avatarically Self-Revealed (and Inherently ego-less, and Inherently Perfect, and Self-Evidently Divine) Person Converts the Apparently Separate being From The "Act Of Narcissus" (or The self-Contracting and Separative Act Of ego-Possession) To The Ecstatic (or Inherently, and, Ultimately, Most Perfectly, ego-Transcending) "Bhava" Of Total psycho-physical Devotion To Me.

If You (As My Formally Practicing Devotee, In The Only-By-Me Revealed and Given Way Of The Heart, or Way Of Adidam) Rightly, Truly, Fully, and Fully Devotionally Practice Ruchira Avatara Bhakti Yoga, moment to moment, You Will, By Grace Of My Avatarically Given "Bright" Divine Self-Revelation (In The Context Of Your Truly Effectively Me-"Locating", and Total psycho-physical, Devotion To Me), Be Always In The "Bhava" Of Beholding My Avatarically Self-Revealed "Bright" Divine Form and Person. This "Ruchira Avatara Bhava Samadhi"[7] (and, In Due Course, The Most Ultimate and Most Perfect, or Seventh Stage, Realization Of It) Is The (Right, True, and Full) Purpose Of Ruchira Avatara Bhakti Yoga (Right, True, and Full). Thus, Ruchira Avatara Bhakti Yoga Is A Matter, In every moment, Of Entering Into My Sphere Of "Brightness", The Sphere Of My Very Person, The Sphere Of My Divine Spiritual Body, The Sphere (and, Ultimately, The Divine Domain) That Is The "Bright" Itself. The "Bright"—Avatarically Self-Revealed, By Me, To You—Is Me, Self-Revealed (In Person) To You.

Real God, The Divine Person—Who Is Self-Existing (or Transcendental) and Self-Radiant (or Inherently Spiritual) Being Itself—Is (Now, and At all times) Present (and Evident) In The Midst (or Still-Point) Of The (Apparent) Cosmos (or Cosmic Mandala) In The Form Of An Overriding (or Deep Background) Vibratory Sound (In Which all conditionally Manifested sounds, and vibrations, and forms May Resonate and Dissolve—As In A Matrix, or Vortex, Of Undifferentiated Oneness), and In The Form Of A Brilliant Clear White Five-Pointed Star (In Which all conditionally Manifested lights, and visualizations, and energies, and all forms Composed Of energy, or light, May Become Transparent and Dissolve—As In A Matrix, or Vortex, Of Undifferentiated Oneness). Therefore, The Divine Person May Be Observed As The Apparently Objective Divine Star and As The Apparently Objective Mass Of Divine Sound In any and every plane Of The Cosmic Mandala.

This Same Mass Of Divine Sound (In Its Most Ascended, or Highest, Form) and This Same Divine Star (In Its Most Ascended, or Highest, Form) Are Also (Necessarily) My Own Original Apparent Forms (or First Audible and Visible Signs). And, Likewise (It May, By Means Of My Avatarically Self-Transmitted Divine Grace, Be Realized, By Means Of The Progressive Process Of Dissolution Into Oneness With Me), They (In Their Grades Of Form-Manifestation, plane to plane—and, Then, At Last, or Ultimately, In Their Highest, or Most Ascended, or Most Perfectly Me-Realizing Forms) Are The Original Apparent Forms (or First Audible and Visible Signs) Of Even every conditionally Manifested being.

Therefore, I Reveal (and I Am) The Highest Mass Of Divine Sound and The Highest Divine Star—In and As Themselves, and In Man-Form (As My Divinely Self-Manifested Bodily Human Avataric-Incarnation-Form). And The Highest Mass Of Divine Sound and The Highest Divine Star (Even Revealed Simply As My Avatarically-Born Bodily Human Divine Form) Are (If Rightly Understood) The Cosmically Manifested (or Objectively Represented) Signs Even Of The "Bright" Divine Heart Itself, or The Native (or Inherent, and Not Cosmic) State Of Inherently egoless (and Inherently Perfect) Self-Identification (or Absolute Subjective Oneness) With The Self-Evidently Divine Person—Which Heart, State, or Divine Self-Condition and Source-Condition, Because It Is Native To all conditionally Manifested beings, Is (By Means Of My Avatarically Self-Transmitted Divine Grace) To Be Realized By all conditionally Manifested beings.

Therefore, As A (Potential) Sign (and Help) To all, I Will Remain Present As The Highest Mass Of Divine Sound (or "Om", or "Da-Om", or "Da"), and As Even Every Grade Of The Form-Manifestation Of The Mass Of Divine Sound, In every plane Of

The Cosmic Domain—and As The Highest Divine Star-Form, and As Even Every Grade Of The Form-Manifestation Of The Divine Star, and Of Even All The Forms Of Ascended Light, Whenever (or As Long As) The Cosmic Domain and conditionally Manifested beings Exist.

Real God, or Truth, or Reality Is Inherently Existing and Always Already Self-Existing, Both Transcendentally (or Prior To conditional Existence) and Spiritually (or Self-Radiantly). Therefore, I Am Always Already Merely Present (or Self-Existing) As The Transcendental Self (or Consciousness Itself) and As The "Bright" (or The Self-Radiant Spiritual, Transcendental, and Self-Evidently Divine Self-Condition, and Source-Condition, That Is The Divine Heart Itself).

Real God, or Truth, or Reality Is Always Already Coincident With conditionally Manifested Existence (If conditionally Manifested Existence arises). Therefore, As Long As The Cosmic Domain Exists, I Am Always Already Manifestly Present As The Apparently Objective Divine Star, and The Apparently Objective Mass Of Divine Sound, and The Total Apparently Objective (and Tangible) Divine Spiritual Body Of "Brightness". And I Am, When The Time Is So Given, Also Avatarically Self-Manifested In the various planes Of The Cosmic Mandala As The Bodily Incarnate Human (or Otherwise conditionally Manifested) Divine Heart-Master.

I Am The Divine Heart-Master, The Ruchira Avatar, The Da Avatar, The Love-Ananda Avatar, The Avataric Incarnation Of The Divine Heart Itself. Therefore, In and By Means Of My Avataric-Incarnation-Form (and As My "Bright" Divine Body Of Avataric Spirit-Presence—here, and every "where" In The Cosmic Domain), I Am The Threshold Personality—The "Bright" One, The Supremely Attractive Divine Form, The Self-Existing and Self-Radiant and All-and-all-En-Light-ening Person At The Doorway (Above and Beyond all conditionally Manifested beings). I Am The "Bright" Divine Personality At The Threshold, Between The Cosmic Domain and The Divine Domain. I Am The Divine Threshold Personality Of Indivisibly "Bright" Love-Bliss-Light, Who Is Always Gathering all conditionally Manifested beings To

The Transcendental, and Inherently Spiritual, and Self-Evidently Divine Source-Condition, Self-Condition, and Domain—and Who, Thus and Thereby, Leads each one Beyond the conditional self and the conditional worlds By Progressively (and, At Last, Most Perfectly) Dissolving the conditional self and the conditional worlds In The Transcendental, and Inherently Spiritual, and Perfectly Divine Self-Domain That Is The Ultimate Condition Of all and All.

To Be My Listening Devotee, My Hearing Devotee, or My Seeing Devotee Is To Be Attracted To The Inherently Perfect Condition (and "Bright" Divine Spiritual Body) That Is Beyond My Unique Human Visibility. Devotion (By Heart-Attraction) To My Avatarically-Born Bodily (Human) Divine Form, My Avatarically Self-Revealed Spiritual (and Always Blessing) Divine Presence, and My Avatarically Self-Revealed (and Very, and Transcendental, and Perfectly Subjective, and Inherently Spiritual, and Inherently egoless, and Inherently Perfect, and Self-Evidently Divine) State May Perhaps (In Its Developmental Course) Also Become An Attraction To The Apparently Objective Vision Of The Divine Star (The Five Points Of Which Correspond To The Head, The Two Arms, and The Two Legs Of My Bodily Human Divine Form), and (Coincidentally, or, Otherwise, Alone) That Same Devotion To Me May Become An Attraction To The Apparently Objective Audition Of The Mass Of Divine Sound (or The "Om", or "Da-Om", or "Da" Sound), From Which Both My Divine Star and My Divine Spiritual Body Cosmically "Emerge", To here, and To every "where" In The Cosmic Domain. However, To Be Truly (and Most Profoundly) Devoted (By Heart-Attraction) To My Avatarically-Born Bodily (Human) Divine Form, My Avatarically Self-Revealed Spiritual (and Always Blessing) Divine Presence, and My Avatarically Self-Revealed (and Very, and Transcendental, and Perfectly Subjective, and Inherently Spiritual, and Inherently egoless, and Inherently Perfect, and Self-Evidently Divine) State Is To Be Attracted—Even Beyond The Vision Of The Divine Star, and Beyond The Audition Of The Mass Of Divine Sound, and (At Last) Even Beyond The Tangible Feeling Of My Total Divine Spiritual Body, and (Thus) Beyond all and All—To The Perfectly Subjective Heart Itself,

Which Is My "Bright" Divine Self-Domain, The Inherently Perfect Self-Condition (and Source-Condition) That Is Love-Bliss-Radiance Itself (and The Source-Condition, and Self-Condition, Of My Inherently "Bright" Divine Spiritual Body Itself).

In My Avataric-Incarnation-Form (or Human Revelation-Body), I Am The Revealing Agent, and The Revelation-Sign, and The Very (and Complete, and Most Perfect) Self-Revelation Of The One and Only and Self-Evidently Divine Person, The Eternal and Indivisible Source-Condition and Self-Condition Of all and All. Therefore, Above and Beyond My here-Visible Bodily (Human) Divine Form, I Am Eternally and everywhere Present As The "Bright" (The Real and True and Perfectly Subjective Divine Source, or Source-Condition, Of All and all), The Apparently Objective Divine Sound (The First Audible Form Of All and all), The Apparently Objective Divine Star (The First Visible Form Of All and all), The Self-Radiant All-Pervading Divine Spirit-Presence (The Apparently Objective Divine Spiritual Body, Which Is The Help Of All and all), and The Transcendental (or Self-Existing, and Self-Radiant, or Inherently Spiritual) Divine Self (The Non-Separate and Indivisible and Indestructible Self Of All and all).

To My Listening Devotees, My Hearing Devotees, and My Seeing Devotees, I Am (In My "Bright" Avatarically-Born Bodily Human Divine Form) The Eternal Threshold Personality, The Eternally Living Murti, The Miraculous Icon, The Perpetual conditional Manifestation Of The Self-Evidently Divine Person (Who Is The Divine Self-Condition, and Source-Condition, Of all and All). This Is So Both During and Forever After The Avataric Physical Lifetime Of My Bodily (Human) Divine Form. Therefore, I Am (Now, and Forever Hereafter) To Be, Thus, Felt and Observed (In The Meditation and Deep Vision Of My Devotees), and, Thus, Found In My "Bright" (and Even Bodily Human) Divine Form, As Me.

Nevertheless (Now, and Forever Hereafter), I Am Always Calling and Leading My Listening Devotees, My Hearing Devotees, and My Seeing Devotees To My Eternally "Bright" Person, Beyond My Avataric Figure Made Of Man In The Cosmic Play. Now, and Forever Hereafter, I Always Call and Lead My Listening Devotees, My Hearing Devotees, and My Seeing Devotees To Find Me (As I

Am)—The One and Only and Indivisible Divine Person (The Perfectly Subjective, Transcendental, Inherently Spiritual, Inherently egoless, Inherently Perfect, and Self-Evidently Divine Source-Condition, Self-Condition, and Domain Of all and All). The "Bright" (or The Fundamental Light Of Love-Bliss That Is The One and Indivisible and Indestructible Condition Of all conditionally Manifested forms) Is My Cosmic-Domain-Transcending Form and Domain. Therefore (Now, and Forever Hereafter), all those who Truly Heart-Recognize My Avatarically Self-Revealed (and Self-Evidently Divine) Person, and who Heart-Respond To My Avatarically Self-Revealed (and Self-Evidently Divine) Person With Right, True, and Full (and Truly Whole bodily) Devotion, Will Embrace Me As The Only One Who Is—and they Will (In Due Course, and By Means Of Truly Counter-egoic Heart-Response To My Avatarically Self-Revealed, and Self-Evidently Divine, Person and Grace) "Locate" Me and Realize Me (Beyond The Cosmic Doorway, Without Separation or "Difference"), As The Self-Evidently Divine Person and The "Bright" Divine Self-Domain.

Therefore, Be My Devotee (Real and True), and (By Formally Practicing The Only-By-Me Revealed and Given Way Of The Heart, or Way Of Adidam) Listen To Me, Hear Me, See Me, and Follow Me. The Only-By-Me Revealed and Given Way Of The Heart (or Way Of Adidam) Is The Divine Way Of ego-Surrendering, ego-Forgetting, and (More and More) ego-Transcending Devotion To My Avatarically-Born Bodily (Human) Divine Form, and My Avatarically Self-Revealed Spiritual (and Always Blessing) Divine Presence, and My Avatarically Self-Revealed (and Very, and Transcendental, and Perfectly Subjective, and Inherently Spiritual, and Inherently egoless, and Inherently Perfect, and Self-Evidently Divine) State Of Person. Therefore, Really and Truly (and, Thus, Rightly, Truly, Fully, Fully Devotionally, and, Necessarily, Formally) Enter The Only-By-Me Revealed and Given Way Of The Heart (or Way Of Adidam) and (By All Its Only-By-Me Revealed and Given Means) Always Find Me and Love Me, The Only One Who Is—For I Am Existence (Itself), or Being (Itself), "Bright" Before You. When (In The Course Of The Total, or Full and Complete, Practice Of The Only-By-Me Revealed and Given Way

Of The Heart) You (By Means Of My Avatarically Given Divine Grace) Both Hear Me and See Me, From The Heart—Follow Me. If You (Thus) Hear Me and See Me and Follow Me, My Avatarically Self-Transmitted Divine Spiritual Presence Will Cause You To Sympathize With The Inherently Attractive (and ego-Undermining) Self-Condition Of My Very (and Transcendental, and Perfectly Subjective, and Inherently Spiritual, and Inherently egoless, and Inherently Perfect, and Self-Evidently Divine) Person. And (Because My Divine Self-Condition Is The Very, and One, and Only, and Transcendental, and Perfectly Subjective, and Inherently Spiritual, and Inherently egoless, and Inherently Perfect, and Self-Evidently Divine Self-Condition, and The Perfectly Subjective, and Self-Evidently Divine, Source-Condition, Of all and All) My Avatarically Self-Transmitted Divine Spirit-Current Of Love-Bliss Will Lead You To Most Perfect Realization Of The One and Only and "Bright" Eternal Divine Self-Domain.

By Seeing Me (and Then Following Me) In The Devotional Manner, You Will Enter Into The Responsively Progressive Discipline and Spontaneity Of Spiritually Awakened Meditation. Then Practice This ego-Transcending Spiritual Meditation Of Me-Devotion, Even (If Required) In subtler places or worlds.

Thus Spiritually Awakened By Me (and To Me), Practice The Only-By-Me Revealed and Given Way Of The Heart (Formally, and Fully Accountably) As You Are (By Means Of My Avatarically Self-Transmitted Divine Grace) Given To Practice It. Always Practice (Thus) In Communion With My Avatarically Self-Revealed Divine Body (Of Spirit-Presence), and Thereby Enter Into The Circle Of My All-and-all-Surrounding and All-and-all-Pervading "Bright" Spirit-Current.

At First, You Must Follow and Allow The Full Descent Of My Avatarically Self-Transmitted "Bright" Divine Spirit-Current. Then You May Turn About (Below), and Follow Upwards With The Love-Bliss-Flow, Even Into The Ascended Source Of all sounds, and lights, and touches. In Any Case, Ultimately, You Must Dissolve To A Stand (or Merely Be), Beyond The Descending and Ascending Flows. There (Where Only The Heart Is, Effortless and Free) My Self-"Bright" Divine Domain (Of Self-Existing and Self-

Radiant Divine Self-Consciousness) Always Already Stands. It Is
The Motionless Ultimate Source Of All That Flows. It Is Love-Bliss
Itself—"Where" I Am, and "What" I Am, and "Who" I Am.

Therefore, When You (As My Fully, and, Necessarily,
Formally, Practicing Devotee) Have Heard Me and Seen Me, Look
For Me In every world of Your experience. Always Find Me (Thus,
and there) As The Threshold Personality (Before Your Total body-
mind, and Above Your Total body-mind, and Beyond Your Total
body-mind). Always (Thus, and there) "Locate" My Avatarically
Self-Revealed "Bright" Divine Spirit-Presence That (In every moment
I Am Thus Found) Spontaneously Opens Your Devotionally Me-
Recognizing and Devotionally To-Me-Responding Heart. And
Follow Me, Thus, By Allowing Your Total body-mind To Swoon
In My Avatarically Self-Revealed Divine Spirit-Presence Of My
Own Person (Divine and "Bright" and One and Only).

When You (As My Fully, and, Necessarily, Formally, Practicing
Devotee) Have Heard Me and Seen Me, Then Always Hear Me
and See Me Now (In every then present-time moment).

Then You Have (By Means Of My Avatarically Self-Transmitted
Divine Grace) Truly Fully (or Spiritually) Realized Me To Be Your
Divine Heart-Master, Merely Present With You.

Then (By Means Of My Avatarically Self-Transmitted Divine
Grace) Always "Locate" Me By Heart (Surrounding and Pervading
Your Total body-mind), and (Thus and Thereby) Enter Into
Spiritually Me-Meditative (and Most Profoundly ego-Surrendering,
ego-Forgetting, and, Always More and More, ego-Transcending)
Ecstasy.

By Means Of My Avatarically Self-Transmitted Divine Grace,
This Becomes A Great Process.

And (By Means Of My Avatarically Self-Transmitted Divine
Grace) This Great Process Will (In Due Course) Lead You To The
Full (Descending and Ascending) Realization (or Samadhi) Of The
"Thumbs", and It May (Also) Lead You To The Ascended
Realization Of subtle forms (In Savikalpa Samadhi), The Ascended
Vision Of Cosmic Unity (In The Highest Form Of Savikalpa
Samadhi, Which Is "Cosmic Consciousness", or The "Vision" Of
The Cosmic Domain As One Undifferentiated Mind), The Utterly

Ascended Realization Of bodiless and mindless Love-Bliss (In Ascended, or Fifth Stage, conditional Nirvikalpa Samadhi), and The Exclusive Realization Of Transcendental (and Inherently Spiritual) Self-Existence (In Jnana Samadhi, or, Really, Jnana Nirvikalpa Samadhi).

And (By Means Of My Avatarically Self-Transmitted Divine Grace) This Great Process Will Certainly Lead You (Most Ultimately) To The Unconditional Realization Of Self-Radiant (or Inherently Spiritual) and Self-Existing (or Transcendental) Divine Being (In Seventh Stage Sahaj Samadhi, or, Really, Seventh Stage Sahaja Nirvikalpa Samadhi, or The Samadhi Of No-"Difference", Which I Have Otherwise Named "Ruchira Samadhi", and "'Open Eyes'"). And Ruchira Samadhi Will (Perhaps) Demonstrate Itself (By Means Of My Avatarically Self-Transmitted Divine Grace) As Occasional (and Not Strategic, but Spontaneous) Outshining Of body, mind, world, and Even all relations, By and As The Being-Radiance Of My Divine Self-Domain Itself (In The "Bhava", or Temporary Demonstration, Of Divine Translation)—but Ruchira Samadhi Will Certainly (At Last, and Finally) Demonstrate Itself (By Means Of My Avatarically Self-Transmitted Divine Grace) As Divine Translation Itself (or The Most Ultimate and Most Perfect Demonstration Of Ruchira Samadhi).

And Divine Translation Is The Most Ultimate (or Most "Brightly" Shining) Event (and By-My-Avataric-Divine-Grace-Given Fulfillment) Of Inherent (and Inherently Most Perfect) Identification (or The By-My-Avataric-Divine-Grace-Given Realization Of Indivisible Oneness) With Me—Thus and Thereby (and, Altogether, By Means Of Most Perfectly Counter-egoic Whole bodily Heart-Response To My Avatarically Self-Revealed Divine Person) Realizing The Self-Existing (and Eternal, and Indivisible, and Not Cosmic, but Perfectly Subjective) "Heaven" (or Inherently "Bright" Transcendental, and Inherently Spiritual, Divine Sphere and Space and Domain) Of Self-Existing and Self-Radiant and Non-Separate and Indivisible Divine Consciousness Itself, Infinitely "Expanded" (or Free-Standing In All "Directions") As The Eternal Heart-"Celebration" Of Inherent Joy (Always Already En-Joyed By The Indivisible and Inseparable and Non-Separate, Infinitely All-

"Multiplied" and Undifferentiated, "Gathering" That Is The Non-Separate and Indivisible Heart Itself, In The Unlimited and Indefinable and Inherently Relationless "Embrace" That Is The Non-Separate, and Indivisible, and Irreducible Divine Love-Bliss Itself).[8]

RUCHIRA AVATAR ADI DA SAMRAJ
The Mountain Of Attention, 2000

PART NINE

Space-Time
<u>Is</u> Love-Bliss

Space-Time
<u>Is</u> Love-Bliss

VATAR ADI DA SAMRAJ: Reality (<u>Itself</u>) <u>Is</u> The Only Real God. Reality (<u>Itself</u>) is not merely what can be observed about this or that limited condition. Reality (<u>Itself</u>) <u>Is</u> the Condition of all conditions. Reality (<u>Itself</u>) <u>Is</u> That Which Is Always Already The Case.

Ordinary religion, ordinary science, and ordinary culture seek to experience, to know, to gain an advantage with respect to, and to gain control over what is mysterious, what is unknown, what is threatening. Ordinary religion, ordinary science, and ordinary culture want to achieve absolute power for human beings. The quest for power (or control) over the unknown is the collective egoic pursuit (or aggressive search) of mankind, in the midst of (and on the basis of) the universal human reactions of egoic fear, sorrow, and anger—or the universal denial of un-conditional relational love (and the universal non-Realization of the Love-Bliss That <u>Is</u> the Inherent Characteristic of Reality <u>Itself</u>). To affirm (as the world-culture of scientific materialism does) that this "All" of space-time is merely materiality—limited, dying, and, effectively, dead—is, itself, a kind of aggressive affirmation of power, a collective cultural manifestation of a <u>dissociative</u> (or self-contracted) disposition that is merely afraid, self-absorbed, and deeply depressed by sorrow and anger.

"Matter" is <u>Light</u>—not merely ordinary light (which can even change its speed, or fly about and be reflected on surfaces, and so on), but <u>Fundamental</u> Light, Light <u>Itself</u>, Which Is inherently Indivisible, inherently Unbroken. The conditional (or space-time) universes are a manifestation of the <u>apparent</u> breaking of Fundamental Light—a curious, simple, apparent "difference" (or division) within Fundamental Light (or Unlimited and Unconditional Energy, Itself). But Fundamental Light (Itself), or Unlimited and Unconditional Energy (Itself), Is Love-Bliss (Itself), the (Self-Evidently) Divine "Brightness". Therefore, the Real Condition (or Reality-Context) of space-time (or the conditional, or Cosmic, or psycho-physical, domain) Is Love-Bliss (Itself). Space-time (and even the entirety of all beings, things, or conditions apparent within it) Is (in and As Reality Itself) Love-Bliss (Itself). Love-Bliss (Itself) Is Reality (Itself) and Truth (Itself). Love-Bliss (Itself) Is the Only Real God.

The conditional domain (or the Cosmic domain of space-time, and psycho-physical, conditions) cannot be comprehended in its own terms. In and of itself, the conditional domain is a "problem", and a goad to seeking. When the Irreducible, Indivisible, Unbroken "Brightness" of Reality is Realized, It is Found to Be Always Already The Case, and It is Found to inherently Transcend all of conditional existence, all of space-time, all of apparent limitation—all of the gross dimension (of apparent materiality), all of the subtle dimension (of subtler materiality, and of mind), and all of the causal dimension (of root-causation).

Space-time (itself, or in its totality) cannot be observed. The "Big Bang" was not an event that could have been observed. The "Big Bang" is not something that occurred in space (or in time). The "Big Bang" is the origin of space (and of time). To look at the "Big Bang" as an event in space (and in time) is already to look at it in egoic terms, and from a position after the event. To examine the "Big Bang" in conventional scientific terms is to assume a dissociated (and separate, and separative) position, as if the ego-"I" (or the "observing" body-mind) were standing outside of space-time—but it does not. Egoity (and all of psycho-physical self, or body-mind) is, inherently and necessarily, an event in (and of) space-time. The body-mind is an event in (and of) space-time. That in Which the body-mind is occurring (or of Which the body-mind is a modification, or a mere and temporary appearance) necessarily (Itself) Transcends space-time, Transcends limitation, Transcends the apparent breaking of Fundamental Light (or of Energy Itself, or of Radiance Itself).

The presumption of "point of view"—as the "knower", and the "measure", of Reality Itself—is the fundamental error (or inherent limitation) of conventional science and conventional (or exoteric) religion. Those who publicly advocate the viewpoint of scientific materialism tend to speak in terms that "make nothing" of religion. Such advocates of the scientific materialist point of view are, in effect, still fighting with the Catholic Christian religious authorities at the beginning of the European Renaissance. They all, in effect, imagine themselves to be Galileo, "getting the goods" on exoteric religion—which is a "straw man", easy to criticize. Exoteric religion is filled with limitations, and scientific materialists "love" to "make nothing" of it.

In the view of some scientific materialists, "religion" is merely a kind of bizarre episode of human mind, an expression of a mind naturally fitted to very simple patterns of comprehension that, although they have an ordinary natural purpose, cannot comprehend the "big picture", or great Cosmic (and even pre-Cosmic, or non-Cosmic) matters. According to this point of view, religious statements are merely a kind of mental babbling, ultimately no more profound, or meaningful, than "Pass the salt" or "Walk down the block", or even random computer "garbage"—and, therefore, religion is to be discounted (as a pre-scientific, or non-scientific, and, therefore, un-comprehending, mode of mind and language).

Anti-religionists, atheists, and so forth, generally do not talk seriously about great esoteric religion and Spirituality. They merely take delight in creating verbal conflict with "other" (or science-challenged) human beings. The reason why they seem to have so much energy for promoting their anti-religious (and inherently "dark" and hopeless) point of view is that, in doing so, they presume they are addressing (and academically "sporting" with) non-scientists, even exoteric religionists, people with non-scientific (and scientifically insupportable, and, therefore, it is presumed, irrational) views, and so forth. Like headstrong young college students, they derive great enjoyment from denying (and even "officially" anathematizing) absolutely everything that the pious religionists merely believe. But, outside the circumstance of that adolescent debate, where would they get any energy for denying Reality Itself, in Its Greatness? Any fool can delight in abusive conflicts with public religionists of the ordinary and exoteric kind. But what about Truth? What about the Great Matter—Reality Itself?

In the human being, mind is, indeed, associated with simple functions in the natural domain, and so forth. That is one aspect of mind, certainly. But the entire human structure (and its every part) is also inherently One with Reality Itself, Coincident with Reality Itself. Beyond all its verbal chat and ordinary functioning, the human psycho-physical structure is One with What Is—and is, therefore, in its ego-transcending disposition, capable of Realizing (or, in various ways, experiencing) That in Which it Inheres, That in Which it is arising, That of Which it is an apparent modification. Such Realization (or experiencing) is the Domain of true religion—in other words, the Domain of esoteric (or Spiritual, and, ultimately, Divine) religion, of non-"public" religion, of the religion that is not about egoity, not about mere social personality, not about ordinary social interactions, not about ordinary cognitive processes.

A conditionally manifested form may be modified over time by interactions within the form's own structure, or it may be modified over time by interactions within the sphere of relations apparently external to the form itself—but any and every conditionally manifested form is also, all the while, a manifestation within, and a manifestation of, That in Which it is arising. There is evolution, in the sense of the changing (or mutating) of forms, through internal and external interactions—but there is also the Condition of Unity, Which Is the Inherent Condition of every event, and Which Is the Source-State in Which, and from Which, all events proceed (one by one, and, also, simultaneously). All things (or all patterns, and, therefore, all conditionally manifested beings) arise in (and as an apparent modification of) the One (Self-Existing, and Self-Radiant, and Self-Evidently Divine) Reality (or Self-Condition and Source-Condition)—and, therefore (necessarily), their interactions (both internal and external) take place in That Domain (or Reality, or Real God) That Is Always Already The Case.

It is not merely that a bee appears, and (utterly independent of the bee) a flower appears, and, after a while of time, they (even arbitrarily, or accidentally) learn how to relate to (and combine with) one another. No! The "bee" and the "flower" arise (in some essential mode of their pattern of appearance) simultaneously, in the totally interrelated conditional pattern in which everything is arising. Plants cannot see bees—and, yet, plants (or their flowers) are found to take on forms that are attractive to bees (and that, in order to attract them, even look like bees)! If all aspects of "bee" and "flower" are merely external, and gross, and inherently separate from one another, then both would disappear long before they "learned" enough about one another to establish the natural relationship upon which each, in its natural fragility, depends for its survival.

There are changes and interactions among all conditionally manifested patterns and forms, but there is also simultaneity of appearance, universal inherent unity and interrelatedness, and Inherent Coincidence in the One Unbroken Light. This Greater Affair is the subject of true (or esoteric) religion. The noticing of the interactions and changes between forms, and so forth, is a compartment of human knowing (both ordinary and scientific). That noticing is interesting enough, as one of the things that human beings do, but such noticing is not an enterprise superior to true religion, nor is such noticing the Way of Truth (Itself) and of Reality (Itself).

A true science is not priorly committed to a philosophy of materialism. A true science is free enquiry. Therefore, there is a kind of true science exercised even by true religion. Of course, ordinary (exoteric) religion often takes the form of babble about things that, perhaps, are better described, comprehended, or investigated through the scientific method and language. In other words, there certainly is an immense amount of nonsense (or of arbitrary exoteric belief and doctrine) that is called "religion", but it is not the purpose of science merely to criticize (or even anathematize) the nonsense of exoteric religion. Rather, a true science must (and, inherently, does) coincide with true religion, because both true religion and true science are Founded on That Which Is

Always Already The Case (and Which, therefore, Is Truth Itself, and Reality Itself). And That Which Is Always Already The Case need not (and cannot fruitfully) be sought. Therefore, if Truth is to be served (and if Reality is to be Known), That Which Is Always Already The Case must be priorly Acknowledged, and consistently Declared, and, altogether, fully Affirmed (or Really lived), whether one is practicing religion, or doing science, or simply passing the salt.

When it is Founded in Truth (or Reality Itself), science is no longer "scientific materialism", but is simply part of the human enterprise of observing (and coming to know about) conditionally manifested forms. There is nothing about true science, or even science in general, that is threatening to true religion. Science is very threatening to ordinary (or exoteric) religion—no doubt. But why should science be involved in an endless adolescent debate with conventional pious religiosity, or even religious nonsense? Part of the "darkness" of the present world-culture is that its present disposition (wedded to scientific materialism) supports a process that is destroying all modes of religion (both esoteric and exoteric). Of course, many religions are resisting that process, but, nevertheless, the dominant cultural disposition in this "late-time", or "dark" epoch, is anti-religious—in the sense of being a criticism of exoteric (or conventional) religiosity.

In this "late-time", science presumes itself to be a kind of "esoteric" school, possessing what it regards to be a superior description of reality. That description of reality amounts, in the common scientific view, to an anathematizing of religion, and a declaration that reality is only material, and that, therefore, the human being is only material. Thus, the human being is presumed to be a dead-end of merely material appearances, rather than what the human being truly (or Really) is (in Reality, Itself), which is a process in or of (and, ultimately, Identical to, and not separate from) That (One, and Only, and Non-Separate, and Non-Dual, and Indivisible, and Indestructible, and Always Already Most Prior Reality, or Real Condition, of Conscious Light) within Which the human pattern is arising, and with Which the human pattern is Always Already Coincident.

To be My devotee is not to side with the sometimes "nonsense" of conventional (or merely exoteric) religion, or with the lunacy of negative "cultism". Not at all! But to be My devotee is also not to be bound by the limited point of view of conventional science, or by any limited point of view whatsoever. If, as My devotee, you are inclined to do science, you can do so—just as you could be a baker, or a plumber, or whatever. Science is a kind of ordinary human enterprise, in that it is about the investigation of the signs and effects of broken (or conditionally manifested) light—or, in other words, of appearances. True religion, on the other hand, is the Way of always present-time Realization of Fundamental Light—of the inherently Unbroken, Indivisible, and Indestructible Light (or Divine Love-Bliss) That Is Reality Itself.

Therefore, there is no conflict between true religion and true science, any more than there is a conflict between true religion and life itself. However, science can be engaged egoically, and on the basis of wrong principles—just as life altogether can be so engaged. Therefore, science (like every other aspect of human life) must be corrected by the Discipline of Truth and Reality—if there is to be "Brightening" by Me (and, Thus and Thereby, Divine En-Light-enment).

When advocates of scientific materialism criticize religion as an inherently limited expression of cognitive mind, they are criticizing exoteric (or ordinary) religion, the religion that is a manifestation of the cognitive mind (or of human ordinariness). True religion is not a manifestation of the cognitive mind. True religion is not a manifestation (or invention) of any aspect of conditional existence (itself). True religion is a Revelation in the midst of conditional existence. True religion is a Revelation to conditional existence. Therefore, true religion is a Revelation to everything that the human being is. True religion is a Revelation that fits all aspects of the human being to Reality Itself. If you are (thus) fitted to Reality Itself—you can live life better. Therefore, you can do science better, too. You can do anything better—which is to say that you can do anything that is right, and you can do it in a true (or right) disposition.

DEVOTEE: Scientists have typically regarded science as a way to understand objective reality. But, more recently, some scientists have begun to regard consciousness, or subjective reality, as a rightful subject of scientific investigation.

AVATAR ADI DA SAMRAJ: When scientists investigate consciousness, they are investigating a function of the human operation of knowing. Thus, from the point of view of conventional science, consciousness is priorly <u>presumed</u> to be part of the human psychophysical apparatus—and, on the basis of this presumption, consciousness is (in general) declared by scientists to be <u>merely</u> a functional aspect of what is (otherwise) <u>only</u> material, and (therefore) necessarily mortal.

However, Consciousness <u>Itself</u> (like Fundamental Light, Itself) Is a Transcendent Condition. Therefore, Consciousness <u>Itself</u> is not being (and cannot be) accounted for by means of scientific investigation into the human apparatus of knowing and experiencing. Consciousness may be being dismissed as a mere material function by certain scientific propagandists, but they are not truly dealing with Consciousness <u>Itself</u> (or Energy <u>Itself</u>, or Reality <u>Itself</u>). They are making merely conventional statements about functional consciousness, and they are, in so doing, also being mere propagandists, mere adherents (or "believers") of an inherently false philosophy—false because it is a view of Truth, and of Reality <u>Itself</u>, that is reduced by and to "point of view" (and, in particular, to the "point of view" of the gross physically based ego-"I" of the human organism). In other words, scientific materialists are not being <u>true</u> scientists, but mere (and would-be-"official") propagandists for scientific materialism (itself), which is a mode of presumed science (or of "rational" knowing) that is associated with the even ancient philosophical tradition of materialism. Categorical statements denying the Reality (and Transcendental, and Self-Evidently Divine, Nature) of Consciousness <u>Itself</u> are merely the evidence of the materialist philosophy being propagandized (and even irrationally "believed"), rather than the sign of free enquiry being rightly and effectively pursued.

DEVOTEE: The point of view of many neurophysiologists is that consciousness is merely an extension of brain chemistry.

AVATAR ADI DA SAMRAJ: What is brain chemistry? Brain chemistry is a modification of Light, of Energy. But when scientists say that consciousness is merely "brain chemistry", or that the body is only "matter", they think they are saying something profound and absolute that reduces everything to mortality—ultimately, to nothingness. The flesh-body, or brain chemistry, or any aspect of conditional existence can be addressed as a mechanistic matter, but brain chemistry Is (in its Inherent Coincidence with Reality Itself) Light—as all conditionally manifested form Is. Therefore, in order to truly (or in Reality) examine brain chemistry, the examination must be conducted in an entirely different (and, ultimately, necessarily religious and Spiritual) fashion.

On the one hand, it is obvious that human beings are, in some sense, "material". Therefore, there is an obvious legitimacy to the investigation (or rational examination) of the "material" nature of the human being (as a pattern of form). On the other hand, every conditionally manifested form is Always Already in the Condition of Inherent Unity with Fundamental Light—and, therefore, every conditionally manifested form is, simply, a modification of Fundamental Light. This Greater Truth is the Basis for the true religious and Spiritual approach to the investigation of conditional existence.

Even in your apparent materiality, you Are Energy. Energy is always conserved—It is Indestructible. Energy can be changed, but It cannot be destroyed. Therefore, you (As you Are) cannot be destroyed. You simply cannot. All kinds of transformations are possible, but that is all.

The scientific investigation of the material relationship between brain chemistry and cognitive processes does not account for the fact—proclaimed even by science itself—that brain chemistry is a mode of Light. All apparently material processes are, ultimately, a play of Light. You presently (and Always Already) Exist in a State of Indestructible Unity with Fundamental and Primary Light (Itself). Everything arising is

Always Already in a State of Indivisible Unity with Reality (Itself). This is the Basis for a great (and truly free) enquiry. Therefore, This is the Basis for true science, and also the Basis for true (or esoteric, and truly Spiritual) religion.

Scientific materialism is egoic science. Scientific materialism is science wedded to the archaic (and false) philosophy, language, and symbolism of materialism. The concept of "matter" should have become obsolete with the passing of the nineteenth century. Since the discoveries of physics in the first half of the twentieth century, every schoolchild knows that "matter" is a mode of energy (or of light). And, yet, this universally accepted "equation" has not yet become a basis for the world-culture. The same science that declares $E = mc^2$ is contradicting its own declaration by telling everyone that everything is merely "material"—and, thereby, communicating a "dark" and hopeless message.

Why is mankind becoming even more and more hopeless? Because it is possessed (and ego-bound) by the belief in the "official" (or "authoritatively" propagandized) declaration of materiality-only—and, on that basis, it doubts Truth (or feels materiality, and mortal "darkness", is the "Truth"), and it doubts Reality Itself (or feels materiality, and mortal "darkness", is the only "Reality"), and, therefore (or likewise), it doubts all religion.

In this "late-time", those who would affirm common (or merely exoteric) religion often have to become virtually insane in order to piously affirm it. If they are not informed in their understanding (and patterned in their lives) by true (and, necessarily, esoteric—and Really ego-transcending) religion, it is only by developing fundamentalist craziness, or fanatic "cultism", that people become "religious" in the face of what they (correctly) perceive to be the negative (and anti-religious, and false) scientific declaration that fills the common world.

The desperate, and even irrational, resort to exoteric believer's religiosity is not the Way of Adidam. My devotees are not Called to Me to become "cultists", to be mad, to be insane. My devotees are Called to Me to be made sane by My Spiritual Company. In devotional heart-Communion with Me, My true devotee (by right practice, and by exercising truly intelligent discrimination) overcomes all errors, all falsity, all negativity, all false views—whether religious, or scientific, or of whatever kind.

This overcoming of falsity and negativity must occur, because all of mankind is insane in this "late-time". The craziness that may be observed in the world in this "late-time" is the manifestation of a universal (and, therefore, dangerous) collective human insanity that is becoming more and more profoundly destructive day by day. There is a profound conflict in the heart and mind of humanity in the present epoch—a conflict resulting from its own false and ego-made doctrines, its own aggressive and ignorant dissociation from Reality (Itself). The science of materialism and the ordinary religion of anti-materialism are equally false, and they are false for the same reason—because they are visions made by egoity. They are not manifestations of Truth, but merely products of the conditional suffering (and the defensive ego-efforts) of human beings.

The culture of scientific materialism is opposed to anybody having anything to do with mysticism and related endeavors, but it still has not found a way to control people as effectively as exoteric religion can. Therefore, the culture of scientific materialism still allows a "back door" for the continued existence of exoteric religion, as a means for the political and social controlling of people's pain-based motivations, and their pleasure-based motivations. In and of itself, scientific materialism does not provide a truly usable doctrine for motivating people to control their behavior along idealistic lines. In fact, quite the opposite! The materialistic message does not give people any real reason to be "good"! And that is why the times are so "dark" (or "bad")!

Religion is still a part of the materialistic world-culture, but it is reduced to being merely a means for encouraging people to positively socialize their behavior, and to reduce their pain-based activities and their pleasure-based activities to an acceptable (politically and socially prescribed and enforced) level. Exoteric religion does this through rather bold, even suppressive, methods—which control people (to some degree), but which do not, in any profound sense, make people "good" human beings. Merely exoteric (or pious and idealistic) religion does not make people either religious or "good" in any profound sense—any more than scientific materialism makes them "good", religious, and so forth.

On the one hand, many influential scientists constantly argue against (and, altogether, condemn) exoteric religion. On the other hand, they are still inclined to allow large-scale exoteric (and politically and socially prescribed and enforced) "official" religious institutions to function as the common controller of social behavior. Nevertheless, this is neither logical nor truly effective, because such scientists are, all the while, condemning the very basis on which exoteric religion attempts to convince people to control their social behavior. People are not failing to get this point! And this is why everybody is going mad. If "when you're dead, you're dead"—if there is nothing but a material process here—then what difference does it make what anybody does! You may as well be utterly ego-possessed and negatively indulge yourself as much as you can—while trying to avoid trouble as much as you can—and that's about it! And that is what everybody tends to be doing in this "late-time"! And that is a very dangerous situation. It is a world-culture made of fear, sorrow, and anger—a world-culture that enshrines egoity, on both the individual level and the collective level, while pretending to be about something great.

Certainly, those who truly practice the only-by-Me Revealed and Given Way of Adidam (Which is the one and only by-Me-Revealed and by-Me-Given Way of the Heart) are benign characters in their behavior. But this is not the case simply because My devotees are Called by Me to control their social behavior—as if that, in itself, is religion. The disposition of My true devotee is certainly humanly positive and life-positive, but that disposition does not come from mere adherence to "moral commands". It is the humanly positive and life-positive disposition itself—made true and real by his or her devotional heart-Communion with Me—that rightens My devotee. Without that disposition, My devotee does not have a right and true basis for volunteering for any kind of "socially disciplined" behavior. If the universe is nothing but flying rocks, what difference does it make what you do, or what anybody does? It is all unsatisfactory, even terrible—and, effectively, dead! "Matter" is death! If that is all there is, who cares about anything?!

And, indeed, that is precisely the disposition of mankind, as a whole, in this "late-time". And that is why this is such a "dark" and dangerous time.

If the disposition (or Real Circumstance) of the being is not Found to be Eternal, then there is no basis for rightness, there is no basis for sanity, there is no basis for well-being, there is no basis for right life, for a truly "good" life, for a consistently positive disposition of any kind—except whatever you can manufacture based on your fear of suffering. To "control" your "pain-and-pleasure"-based social behavior merely because you hope that everyone else will do the same—and that you will (therefore) be (in any case, only temporarily, and only maybe) safe—is not a profound disposition at work. Indeed, it is a very frightened disposition at work.

While humankind is collectively insane, and becoming more and more insane day by day, the mosquitos and the frogs and the fish are all still sane—unless they are confined, or trapped, or abused, or otherwise too much influenced by human beings who are insane. Thus, the insanity being manifested by humankind in this "late-time" is not shared by the rest of the conditional domain (except where inordinate human influences have been imposed). Flowers are not insane, yet—except, perhaps, some hybrid varieties, "made" by human beings. Fish are not insane, yet—except, perhaps, some hybrid varieties that, because of their over-large heads (and such), cannot swim, and cannot eat, and, therefore, cannot survive. Even the "edible" animals are not insane, yet—except, perhaps, some enslaved varieties, buckled and fenced into feeding-confinements, unable to rest into Contemplation, because of the material stresses by which their human keepers mock and reduce their lives. These "invented" and enslaved non-humans have been manipulated into suffering and insanity through the intervention of insanely clever human beings! But, apart from such hybridization and enslavement, which does result in negative signs, the non-humans—including all the plants and trees—are not, yet, insane.

However, there is much inordinate influence by insane humanity that is affecting the larger picture of the world. Terrible weather patterns, terrible natural environmental patterns of all kinds, and even terrible (and powerfully "cure"-resistant) diseases are appearing all over the world, and these are the product of an over-powerful, insane humanity—which is an entire species confined to itself, an ego-machine that exploits and destroys all that is "good", and that (in its "dark" point of view) reduces even Reality (Itself) to a loveless "Thing" of meaningless motions and grotesque always already death.

There have always been insane human beings, but, in earlier times, they were not as powerful as they have become in this "late-time". It is only in this "late-time" that human beings have become capable of producing effects that can change even global weather patterns, and global ecological patterns of all kinds. But human beings have always been insane in the domain of politics, for example. For countless centuries, wherever human beings, in their egoity, have been capable of influencing conditional events, there has been insanity and conflict. But now, in its motion into the twenty-first century, the insanity of mankind is influencing even the larger picture of the human natural circumstance. And this must be changed—or there is going to be a terrible, horrific calamity on Earth! Such a calamity is not yet inevitable, but it will occur if there is not a fundamental transformation of mankind—in its heart and mind, and in its endeavors. A fundamental rightening of the world-process must occur, because mankind is now having a profoundly negative effect on the human world-process, and even on the larger natural domain of the world.

This is why I Describe this time as the "late-time", or the "dark" epoch. This epoch need not be so "dark" that every thing and every one is brought to an end, but such can be the dreadful outcome of the current human insanity! And, previous to this "late-time", that immense potential did not exist in the human domain.

My devotees must serve the rightening of the entire world-process. In My twenty-three Divine "Source-Texts", I have Given (to all and All) the right understanding of all and All. In My twenty-three Divine "Source-Texts", I have Given the understanding that (if it is Embraced in right devotion to Me) makes the heart and the mind truly sane, and (thus and thereby) rightens the total life of human activity. So rightened by their conformity to Me, My devotees are <u>able</u> to serve the rightening of all of mankind. And, in fact—now, and forever hereafter—I Call upon <u>all</u> My devotees to do so.

If My devotees do <u>not</u> do this, or if My devotees are reluctant to do it, or if My devotees fail to do it rightly, or if My devotees do it merely on the basis of "cultic" enthusiasm—then My Divinely Self-"Emerging" Blessing-Work is without sufficient human means to Make the necessary change in the world of mankind. If I cannot Make the necessary change of mankind through (and in the human person of) My devotees, then how else will this transformation occur?

Apart from Me, where is the Presence, the Teaching, and the Means That can truly righten mankind?

DEVOTEES: Nowhere, Beloved.

AVATAR ADI DA SAMRAJ: Therefore, it is time for you, My devotees, to become profoundly serious. You must fully equip yourselves with the Arms of My twenty-three Divine "Source-Texts". You must truly Embrace the only-by-Me Revealed and Given Way of Adidam. You must altogether rightly, truly, fully, and fully devotionally <u>live</u> the only-by-Me Revealed and Given Way of Adidam— and you must bring It, as My Gift, to <u>all</u> of mankind.

My devotees <u>are</u> the living Seed whereby the world-rightening transformation can, and must, occur. Indeed, right devotion to Me Is the Substance of human rightness and of all the rightened worlds of all and All.

RUCHIRA AVATAR ADI DA SAMRAJ
Los Angeles, 2000

PART TEN

The Heart-Summary
Of Adidam

The Heart-Summary
Of Adidam

The only-by-Me Revealed and Given Avataric Divine Way of Adidam (Which is the One and Only by-Me-Revealed and by-Me-Given Way of the Heart) is the Way of Devotion to Me As the Divine "Atma-Murti" (or As the Inherently egoless, and Self-Evidently Divine, Person of Reality and Truth—In Place, As Self-Condition, rather than As exclusively Objective Other).

Therefore, in every moment, My true devotee whole bodily (and, thus, by means of the spontaneous Me-recognizing Devotional response of all four of the principal psycho-physical faculties—of attention, emotional feeling, breath, and perceptual body) "Locates" Me As That Which Is Always Already The Case (Prior to—but not separate from—the form, the exercise, and the any object of the four psycho-physical faculties).

Happiness Itself (or Inherent Love-Bliss-Sufficiency Of Being) Is Always Already The Case.

Happiness Itself (or the Divinely Self-Sufficient Love-Bliss-Condition Of Being—Itself) Is That Which Is Always Already The Case.

Happiness Itself (or Love-Bliss-Radiance Of Boundlessly Feeling Being) Is the Most Prior Condition Of Existence (or Of Conscious Being—Itself).

Happiness Itself (or the Condition Of Love-Bliss-Radiance) Must Be Realized—In and As every conditionally arising moment—By Transcending self-Contraction (or all of separate and separative self, or psycho-physical ego-"I", and all of the ego's objects, or conditions of existence—or, indeed, all of the illusions of self and not-self).

When attention is facing outward (or is turned out, as if to outside itself), the body-mind is concentrated upon the "view" (or "field") of apparently separate objects (and upon Me As Objective Other).

When attention is facing inward (or is turned in, as if upon itself), the body-mind is concentrated upon the "point of view" of apparently separate self (and upon Me As Separate Consciousness).

When attention is Devotionally Yielded to whole bodily "Locate" Me As That Which Is Always Already (and Divinely) The Case, all "difference" (whether of ego-"I" or of object and other) is (Inherently) Transcended (In Consciousness Itself, or Self-Existing Being, Which Is Love-Bliss-Happiness Itself—and Which Is Always Already The Case).

Therefore, to the degree that you surrender (whole bodily) to be and do truly relational (and ecstatic, or ego-transcending) Devotional love of Me (As the True Loved-One, the Divine Beloved of the heart), you are (Thus and Thereby) Established— whole bodily and Inherently—in the non-contracted Condition (or Self-Condition, or Inherent Condition) of Reality Itself (Which Is Consciousness Itself and Love-Bliss Itself—and Which Is Always Already The Case).

In due course, This Devotional Practice Is Perfect—and, at last, to Be Most Perfectly Realized.

RUCHIRA AVATAR ADI DA SAMRAJ
Lopez Island, 2000

I <u>Am</u>
The Unbroken Light
Of True Religion

I Am
The Unbroken Light
Of True Religion

I.

Reality Is Truth.
Reality Is Real God.
Reality Is Always Already The Case.
Reality Is That Than Which There Can Be No Other.
Reality Is Not Separate.
Reality Is One.
Reality Is Indivisible.
Reality Is Self-Existing.
Reality Is Indestructible.
Reality Is Self-Radiant.
Reality Is Light (Itself).
Reality Is Love-Bliss.
Reality Is The Divine Source-Condition Of all and All.
Reality Is The Divine Self-Condition Of all and All.
I Am Reality.
I Am The "Bright".
I Am The Only One Who Is.
I Am The Unbroken Light.

II.

True Religion Is Not a "science". The "sciences" are secular, exoteric disciplines, generally (historically) associated with the philosophy of "materialism" (or the viewpoint, and the exoteric prejudices, of "scientific materialism").

The "sciences" (or the secular, exoteric enterprises of "scientific materialism") are founded on the myth of "matter", but True Religion Is Founded On The Self-Evident Reality Of Light.

True Religion Is Not a "science" (secular and exoteric). True Religion Is The Great Esoteric Science (or The Way Of Divine Knowing).

Exoteric science is an ego-based and ego-serving and entirely secular (or non-religious) effort to know—and, thereby, to control (or gain power over) the conditions that affect (and, otherwise, control) human psycho-physical existence. Therefore, exoteric science is a method of controlling "matter", for the sake of the gross survival (and possible pleasure) of the gross bodily ego-"I" of Man (individually, and collectively). And the point of view of that method (and of its exercise) is the subject-object dualism of mind versus body (or mind versus "thing"). Therefore, the method of exoteric science is to abstract (or strategically dissociate) the "investigator" from the "object of investigation", in a process of "objectively" investigating (or even further dissecting) the "matter"-modes of apparent (or apparently Broken) Light.

True Religion Is The Esoteric Science (or Luminous Sacred Process) Of Direct (and Directly ego-Transcending) Investigation Of (or Enquiry Into) Light Itself. The Method Of True Religion Is Devotional Surrender Of the total body-mind of the "investigator" To and Into Light Itself (In Person, Self-Existing, Self-Radiant, Conscious, and "Bright")—and This, Ultimately, To The Most Perfect Degree, Which Is Most Perfect Realization Of Indivisible Oneness With Inherently Indivisible (and Inherently Indestructible) Light Itself (or The Universal Self-Vibratory Energy Itself), Which Is Self-Existing and Self-Radiant Being (Itself), or Self-Existing Consciousness (Itself), Self-Radiant As Love-Bliss (Itself), and Which Is Reality Itself (or That Which Is Always Already The Case), and Which <u>Is</u> (Therefore) The all-and-All Liberating Truth (Itself), or The Only Real God.

True Religion Is The Way (or Intensive Process) Of Realizing Non-Separateness From Reality, Truth, Real God, Love-Bliss, or The One and Only and Divine Self-Condition (and Source-Condition) Of all and All.

True Religion Is The Esoteric Science (or True Divine Way) Of <u>Truly</u> Knowing (and, Thereby, <u>Being</u>) The Unbroken Light.

I <u>Am</u> The Unbroken Light—The Avataric Divine Realizer, The Avataric Divine Revealer, and The Avataric Divine Self-Revelation Of True Religion.

I <u>Am</u> The Great Means Whereby True Religion Is Fulfilled.

I <u>Am</u> The One To Be Realized By The Great Means Of True Religion.

I <u>Am</u> The One Who Is Realized When All Separateness Is Transcended.

I <u>Am</u> The Unbroken Light Of True Religion.

III.

From the beginning of My Avatarically Self-Manifested Divine Work of Teaching and Self-Revelation, I Addressed all My devotees, In Order To Answer One Fundamental Question:

What Is Real God? What Is Truth? What Is Reality? What <u>Is</u> To Be Realized?

My devotees (as individuals) and mankind (in its various collectives) have made many propositions about What Real God Is, What Truth Is, What Reality Is, and What There <u>Is</u> To Be Realized.

I Have Addressed My devotees About all of these propositions—and, In So Doing, I Have Effectively Addressed the entire Great Tradition (or the <u>total</u> Wisdom-Inheritance of mankind) Relative To <u>all</u> Its propositions about Real God, Truth, Reality, and Realization.

What I Have Thoroughly "Considered" With My devotees, and Thoroughly Communicated and Revealed To all, Is That <u>Only</u> Divine Self-Realization Is The Realization Of Reality, Truth, or Real God.

Only Most Perfect (or Seventh Stage) Realization Is True (or Most Perfect) Realization.

All propositions associated with (and limited by or to) the first six stages of life are less than Truth (or True Realization), and are (therefore, necessarily) associated with the point of view of egoity.

No phenomenal experiences of any kind (whether gross or subtle or causal) Are Truth, Real God, Reality, or True (or Most Perfect) Realization.

Therefore, No experiences or conditions associated with any and all of the developing stages of life previous to The Only-By-Me Revealed and Given Seventh Stage Of Life Are Truth, Real God, Reality, or True (or Most Perfect) Realization.

No modifications of the body-mind, No conditional experiences, and No "things" associated with attention (or based on attention, or resulting from attention) Are Truth, Real God, Reality, or True (or Most Perfect) Realization.

There Is Only One Reality (or Truth, or Real God) and, Therefore, Only One Most Perfect Realization Of Reality (or Truth, or Real God).

That One Realization Of The One Reality (or Truth, or Real God) Is The Only-By-Me Revealed and Given Seventh Stage Realization.

That Realization Is What I Am here To Awaken In (and As) every one, and all, and All, By Means Of My Avatarically Self-Revealed Divine Spirit-Presence and The "Bright" Force Of My Avatarically Self-Transmitted Divine Samadhi.

In all the years of My Avatarically Self-Manifested Divine Teaching-Work, I "Considered" every possible subject or "thing", and I Worked (Spiritually, and In the human scale, and By Means Of All My Avataric Divine Means) To Generate every kind of "experience" in My devotees, So That every mode of the first six stages of life could be "considered" (by My devotees) relative to My Avatarically Given Divine Teaching-Arguments.

Therefore, at times, I Generated in My devotees all kinds of experiences relative to the gross domain, or the subtle domain, and even relative to the causal principle of attention itself—So That My devotees could examine such experiences, and I Could

"Consider" such experiences with My devotees, and, Thereby, Prove To My devotees (relative to <u>every</u> kind of <u>conditional</u> proposition or experience or condition) That "this" is <u>Not</u> Truth, "this" is <u>Not</u> Real God, "this" is <u>Not</u> Reality, "this" is <u>Not</u> True (or Most Perfect) Realization.

Having Done That Avataric Teaching-Work To The Degree Of <u>Complete</u> Revelation Of Reality (or Truth, or Real God) and Of The Only <u>Complete</u> Way To Realize Reality (or Truth, or Real God), I Am here (now, and forever hereafter) <u>Only</u> To Attract and Bring <u>all</u> beings To Me, and (when they, one by one, become My devotees) To Attract and Bring them (each and all) Into My Own (Avatarically Self-Revealed, and "Bright", and Self-Evidently Divine) Self-Condition and My Own (Avatarically Self-Revealed, and "Bright", and Self-Evidently Divine) Domain.

Therefore, those who Come To Me Should (now, and forever hereafter) Always Direct themselves Beyond themselves, Toward <u>Me</u>—and (Thereby) Always Remain Directly Moved Toward (and, In Due Course, Into) The "Perfect Practice" Of The Only-By-Me Revealed and Given Way Of Adidam, and (Ultimately) The Most Perfect Realization Of Reality, Truth, or Real God.

IV.

The Only-By-Me Revealed and Given Way Of Adidam (Which Is The One and Only By-Me-Revealed and By-Me-Given Way Of The Heart) Is <u>Not</u> (at all, or in <u>any</u> sense) a matter of seeking and ego-possession.

The Only-By-Me Revealed and Given Way Of Adidam Is <u>Not</u> (at all, or in <u>any</u> sense) a matter of preoccupation with any kind of conditional (or phenomenal) state or purpose.

Even In The Context Of Most Perfect Divine Self-Realization, My devotees Remain apparently associated with phenomenal states, and I Have (Therefore) Told every one Exactly How To Practice Rightly In every circumstance of such appearances—but Such Right Practice Is A Matter Of The <u>Transcending</u> Of egoity (or self-contraction) in the context of those appearances.

The Realization Of Reality (or Truth, or Real God—Which <u>Is</u> Indivisible, Indestructible, Self-Existing, and Self-Radiant Light Itself, or The Perfectly Subjective, Self-Existing, and Self-Radiant Divine Self-Condition and Source-Condition, Itself) Is Always Already Prior To all conditions, Never Dependent On conditional existence, and Never limited by conditional existence (Even In the apparent context of conditional existence).

You Are here In Order To Realize Me—The Avatarically Self-Revealed (and Self-Evidently Divine) Person and Self-Condition Of Reality (or Truth, or Real God).

You Are here In Order To Realize My "Bright" Divine Self-Domain—and Not in order to remain bound to the conditional (or Cosmic) domain.

It Is Not by exhausting yourself with the experiences potential in the conditional (or Cosmic) domain, but By Always Giving your attention To Me (and Surrendering, as your entire body-mind, To Me) That you Will Reach The Point Where you Are No Longer Governed By the motives associated with the conditional (or Cosmic) domain.

My Avatarically Self-Revealed (and "Bright") Divine Spirit-Presence here, My Avatarically Accomplished Divine Descent and Divine Self-"Emergence" Into the conditional (or Cosmic) domain, My Avatarically Self-Manifested Conforming Of This here-Speaking Body-Mind To My Very (and Self-Evidently Divine) Self-Condition, and My Avataric Establishment (now, and forever here-after) Of My "Bright" Divine Samadhi here (and every where in the conditional, or Cosmic, domain) Is (now, and forever here-after) My Divine Gift Of Divine Means, Given (By Me) For The Purpose Of The Most Ultimate (or Seventh Stage) Divine Self-Realization and Divine Translation Of all and All—and Which Divine Means (now, and forever hereafter) Can Be, and Will Be, Received and Made Effective in the case of each and all who devotionally recognize Me, and devotionally respond To Me, as My formally acknowledged (and rightly, truly, fully, and fully devotionally practicing) devotees.

My (now, and forever hereafter) Divinely Self-"Emerging" Realization-Demonstration Of (Inherently Most Perfect) Divine En-Light-enment In the context of the conditional (or Cosmic) domain Has Great "Brightness"-Power (Not Appearing previously)

To <u>Attract</u> conditional beings Into The Most Perfect Realization Of Reality, Truth, or Real God.

By Means Of The "Brightness"-Power Of My Avatarically Self-Revealed Divine Samadhi, I Have <u>permanently</u> Established My Divine Spirit-Presence and Person In the conditional (or Cosmic) domain.

My Avatarically Self-Transmitted ("Bright", and Self-Existing, and Self-Radiant) Divine Samadhi Is The Divine Means For The Divine Liberation and En-Light-enment Of every one, and all, and All—Both during and after (and forever after) The physical Lifetime Of My Avatarically-Born bodily (human) Divine Form.

<u>I</u> (Myself) <u>Am</u> The Divine Means For This Divine Liberation and En-Light-enment.

Therefore, The Only-By-Me Revealed and Given Way Of Adidam Is A <u>Relationship</u>—Not merely a technique (or a system of techniques), and Not merely a philosophy (or a system of ideas or descriptions).

Most fundamentally, The Only-By-Me Revealed and Given Way Of Adidam Is ego-Transcending Participation In My Avatarically Self-Transmitted Divine Samadhi—Through ego-Surrendering, ego-Forgetting, and (more and more) ego-Transcending (and Always devotionally Me-recognizing and devotionally To-Me-responding) Devotional Communion With Me.

If you Surrender and Forget and Transcend your ego-"I" (or self-contraction) as My formally acknowledged (and rightly, truly, fully, and fully devotionally practicing) devotee—Then I Am Effective in your case, and you Are Moved (Progressively) To Ecstatic Absorption In (and, Ultimately, Non-Separate, or egoless, Identification With) My Avatarically Self-Revealed, and "Bright", and Self-Evidently Divine Person (or Self-Condition).

V.

All of the experiences you pursue in the context of the body-mind are temporary events—or self-manipulations and mechanical possibilities in the context of what is (in and of itself) a limitation, and that is only a mode of suffering, and that is, inevitably, going to die.

The body-mind (or even any mode of conditional existence—gross, subtle, or causal) is <u>Not</u> Truth, <u>Not</u> Real God, and <u>Not</u> Reality (or Indivisible and Indestructible Light, Itself).

The conditional (or Cosmic) domain, in any of its planes, is <u>Not</u> Truth, <u>Not</u> Real God, and <u>Not</u> Reality (or Indivisible and Indestructible Light, Itself).

Experiences in any of the planes of the conditional (or Cosmic) domain are <u>Not</u> Truth, <u>Not</u> Real God, and <u>Not</u> Reality (or Indivisible and Indestructible Light, Itself).

Conditional experiences are, merely and only, appearances generated (or made inevitable—or, otherwise, made to persist) by means of self-contraction.

To Realize Reality, Truth, or Indivisible Oneness With Real God (or Indivisible and Indestructible Light, Itself), you Must Transcend self-contraction, and (Thus and Thereby) Enter Into My Divine Self-Domain—Which <u>Is</u> The Divine Disposition (or State) That <u>Is</u>, Most Perfectly Prior To attention.

Only <u>That</u> <u>Is</u> Divine Liberation.

<u>Nothing</u> else <u>Is</u> Divine Liberation.

The phenomenal possibilities of life in gross form, and the phenomenal possibilities of even subtle conditional experience, are <u>all</u> a play on limitation, change, and mortality.

All such possibilities pass—and, even in the having of them, you remain under mortal stress, in fear of death, only suffering, and constantly self-deluded (even at the causal root).

Therefore, In The Only-By-Me Revealed and Given Way Of Adidam (Which Is The One and Only By-Me-Revealed and By-Me-Given Way Of The Heart), There Is <u>No</u> gesture of preoccupation with anything less than Truth, or Real God, or Reality (Itself), or Indivisible and Indestructible Light (Itself).

The usual "God" (of exoteric and conventional religion) is an ego-consoling icon, made by Man, for Man—and, therefore, the usual "God" represents (and is intended to serve) the egoic human aspiration toward self-fulfillment (or the fulfillment of ego-based desire, or of seeking).

Real God <u>Is</u> The Condition In Which all seeking (and its fulfillment) Is Inherently and Most Perfectly Transcended.

Why Should you Surrender To what is less than Real God?

Why Should you Embrace <u>any</u> conditional form or concept <u>itself</u>, As If <u>it</u> (in and of itself) Were Able To Divinely Liberate you, or Bring you To True (and, Necessarily, egoless, or Non-Separate) Happiness?

This Is My Revelation To you: <u>No</u> thing or idea or state less (or other) than Most Perfect Divine Self-Realization (or Most Perfect Divine En-Light-enment) <u>Is</u> True Divine Happiness (or Divine En-Light-enment).

Most Perfect Divine En-Light-enment <u>Is</u> Who I <u>Am</u>.

I <u>Am</u> The One Who Is The Avataric Divine Means Of Most Perfect Divine Self-Realization (or Most Perfect Divine En-Light-enment).

I <u>Am</u> The Very One you Are here To Realize.

Aham Da Asmi. Beloved, I <u>Am</u> Da, The Light Itself (Unbroken, Whole, One, and Only), Appearing (now, and forever hereafter—here, and every where in the Cosmic domain) As The Avatarically Descended and Divinely Self-"Emerging" Ruchira Avatar, Adi Da Samraj—The Da Avatar, The Love-Ananda Avatar, The Avatarically Self-Revealed "Bright" Divine Incarnation (and The Avatarically Given, and All-and-all-Surrounding, and All-and-all-Pervading Divine Self-Manifestation) Of The Heart Itself (The Self-Existing, and Self-Radiant, and Self-Evidently Divine Reality and Person That Is Always Already The Case, and That <u>Is</u> The Only One Who <u>Is</u>).

What You Can Do Next—

Contact an Adidam center near you.

■ Find out about upcoming courses, events, and seminars in your area:

AMERICAS
12040 North Seigler Road
Middletown, CA 95461 USA
1-707-928-4936

PACIFIC-ASIA
12 Seibel Road
Henderson
Auckland 1008
New Zealand
64-9-838-9114

AUSTRALIA
P.O. Box 244
Kew 3101
Victoria
1800 ADIDAM
(1800-234-326)

EUROPE-AFRICA
Annendaalderweg 10
6105 AT Maria Hoop
The Netherlands
31 (0)20 468 1442

THE UNITED KINGDOM
PO Box 20013
London, England
NW2 1ZA
0181-7317550

E-MAIL: **correspondence@adidam.org**

■ If you are interested in becoming a fully practicing devotee of Avatar Adi Da Samraj, sign up for our preliminary course, "The <u>Only</u> Truth That Sets The Heart Free".

■ More information about Adidam classes and events is available at the Adidam University website:

adidam.org/university

Read these books by and about Avatar Adi Da Samraj:

■ *The Light Is <u>On</u>!*
by Carolyn Lee, Ph.D.

The profound, heart-rending, humorous, miraculous, wild—and true—Story of the Divine Person Alive in human Form. Essential reading as background for the study of Avatar Adi Da's books.

■ *Aham Da Asmi (Beloved, I <u>Am</u> Da)*

The Five Books Of The Heart Of The Adidam Revelation, Book One: The "Late-Time" Avataric Revelation Of The True and Spiritual Divine Person (The egoless Personal Presence Of Reality and Truth, Which <u>Is</u> The Only <u>Real</u> God).

This Ecstatic Scripture, the first of His twenty-three "Source-Texts", contains Ruchira Avatar Adi Da's magnificent Confession as the Very Divine Person and Source-Condition of all and All.

Continue your reading with the remaining books of *The Five Books Of The Heart Of The Adidam Revelation* (the *Ruchira Avatara Gita,* the *Da Love-Ananda Gita, Hridaya Rosary,* and *Eleutherios*). Then you will be ready to go on to *The Seventeen Companions Of The True Dawn Horse* (see pp. 329-34).

These and other books by and about Ruchira Avatar Adi Da Samraj can be ordered from the Adidam Emporium by calling:

1-877-770-0772 (from within North America)
1-707-928-6653 (from outside North America)

or by writing to:
ADIDAM EMPORIUM
10336 Loch Lomond Road
PMB #306
Middletown, CA 95461 USA

Or order from the Adidam Emporium online at:
www.adidam.com

The labels visible in the image: Sanctuary, Society, Gallery, Community, Museum, Emporium, Library, University, Adidam Gateway

Visit the Adidam Sacred City online at: www.adidam.org

■ Explore the online community of Adidam and discover more about Avatar Adi Da Samraj and the Way He Offers to all.

Find presentations on: Avatar Adi Da's extraordinary life-story, the stages leading to Divine Enlightenment, cultism versus true devotional practice, the "radical" politics of human-scale community, true emotional-sexual freedom, the sacred function of art in human life, and more.

RUCHIRA AVATAR ADI DA SAMRAJ
Lopez Island, 2000

The Great Choice

An Invitation to the Way of Adidam

Since the very earliest days of His Teaching-Work, Avatar Adi Da Samraj has said, "I offer you a relationship—not a technique." Thus, the Way of Adidam is not primarily a set of religious practices or a body of Spiritual Teaching. Most fundamentally, the Way of Adidam is the devotional and Spiritual relationship to Avatar Adi Da Samraj.

AVATAR ADI DA SAMRAJ: The profound central reality of the Way of Adidam is the devotional and Spiritual relationship to Me.

The Way of Adidam is the devotional and Spiritual relationship to Me.

The Way of Adidam is not what you do "somewhere else". The Way of Adidam is about what you do directly in devotional and Spiritual relationship to Me. [January 22, 2001]

Avatar Adi Da's human body is, of course, located in a particular place and a particular time. But when you become sensitive to Him Spiritually, you discover that His Spiritual Presence can be felt anywhere and anytime, regardless of whether you are in His physical Company or not. Because His Spiritual Presence is Eternal (and will not "disappear" when His human body dies), it is possible for everyone to cultivate a direct heart-relationship with Him—under all circumstances, in this life and beyond. And so, the relationship to Him, once forged, is eternal—going beyond death and the apparent boundaries of time and space.

The Truth of the Way of Adidam is Revealed when you begin to participate in it from the heart. Thus, practice of the Way of Adidam is not a matter of beliefs and prescribed behaviors. The Way of Adidam is a matter of direct, moment-to-moment response to Adi Da Samraj and a process of receiving His Spiritual Transmission ever more profoundly. It does not work to try to practice His Teaching by yourself. As He has said many times, it is simply not possible to move beyond the confines of the ego on your own. Nor is it possible to "unlock" the Secrets of Divine Enlightenment that He has Revealed outside of a formally acknowledged devotional relationship to Him. That is why it is so important to become His formal devotee and to live the Way of Adidam exactly as He has Given it.

AVATAR ADI DA SAMRAJ: I Am the Divine Blessing, Real-God-with-you. Such is not merely My Declaration to you. You must find Me out. You must prove the Way I Give you. Really do the Way I Give you, and you will find Me out further. You will prove the Way of Adidam by doing it—not by believing it merely. [Ruchira Avatara Hridaya-Siddha Yoga]

Darshan

The foundation of Spiritual practice in Adidam is Darshan, or the feeling-Contemplation of Avatar Adi Da's bodily (human) Form—either through the sighting of His physical body, or through Contemplating a photographic or artistic representation of Him. This heart-beholding of Avatar Adi Da's Form is the well-spring of meditation in the Way of Adidam, and so His devotees place a large photograph of Him in each meditation hall, as the central image of Contemplation. In fact, Remembrance of Adi Da Samraj—or the recollecting of His Form in mind and feeling—is the constant practice of His devotees, in the midst of the activities of daily life as well as in meditation. Avatar Adi Da has often spoken about the unique potency of beholding His Form.

AVATAR ADI DA SAMRAJ: In the traditional setting, when it works best, an individual somehow Gracefully comes into the Company of a Realizer of one degree or another, and, just upon (visually) sighting that One, he or she is converted at heart, and, thereafter, spends the rest of his or her life devoted to sadhana (or Spiritual practice), in constant Remembrance of the Guru. The Guru's Sign is self-authenticating.

When Adi Da Samraj is approached with an open heart, His Darshan—the Sighting of His Form alone, even in representational form—is so potent that the heart overflows in response to Him, recognizing Him as the Very Divine Person, the Supreme Source of Bliss and Love.

The Four Congregations

Avatar Adi Da has created the four congregations in order to make it possible for all types of people to enter into the devotional and Spiritual relationship to Him—both those who are moved to practice the Way of Adidam in the fullest and most profound manner (first and second congregations) and those whose life-circumstance makes it right and appropriate for them to practice a simpler form of the Way of Adidam (third and fourth congregations). For each of the congregations, there are particular qualifications for membership and there is a particular form of practice of the Way of Adidam to be engaged.

Which of the four congregations you should apply to for membership depends on the nature of your response to Avatar Adi Da Samraj and on your life-circumstance. Membership in any of the four congregations establishes you in a direct devotional relationship with Avatar Adi Da, and all four congregations are essential to the flowering of His Blessing-Work in the world.

Entering any of the four congregations of Adidam is based on taking a vow of devotion and service to Avatar Adi Da Samraj. This vow is a profound—and, indeed, eternal—commitment. You take this vow (for whichever congregation you are entering) when you are certain that your true heart-impulse is to be a devotee of Avatar Adi Da Samraj, embracing Him as your Divine Heart-Master. And Avatar Adi Da Samraj Himself is eternally Vowed to Serve the Liberation of all who become His devotees.

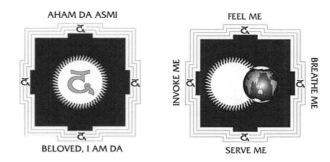

The First and Second Congregations

*(those who are moved to embrace
the complete practice of the Way of Adidam)*

The first congregation is for renunciate practitioners, or those who are moved (and qualified) to embrace the ultimate stages of the Way of Adidam in the context of a renunciate life of perpetual Spiritual retreat. (Membership in the first congregation necessarily requires a prepatory period of some years as a member of the second congregation.)

The second congregation is for lay practitioners, or those who are moved to embrace the complete practice of the Way of Adidam in the context of ordinary life-obligations.

Members of both the first and the second congregations embrace the complete practice of the Way of Adidam. To do so is to take full advantage of the opportunity Offered by Adi Da Samraj—to enter fully into the process of Divine Enlightenment. That process necessarily requires application to the full range of disciplines that Ruchira Avatar Adi Da Samraj has Given for the sake of Spiritual growth.

The disciplines of Adidam are the means whereby the body-mind is conformed to a right and inherently pleasurable pattern of well-being. As you progressively adapt to these disciplines, the body-mind is purified and balanced, and you thereby become able to receive and respond to the Divine Heart-Transmission of Adi Da Samraj more and more fully.

The Life of a Formally Practicing Devotee of Ruchira Avatar Adi Da Samraj

Meditation offers the opportunity to relinquish outward, body-based attention and to be alone with Adi Da Samraj, allowing one to enter more and more into the Sphere of His Blessing-Transmission.

The practice of sacramental worship, or "puja", in the Way of Adidam is the bodily active counterpart to meditation. It is a form of ecstatic worship of Avatar Adi Da Samraj, using a photographic representation of Him and involving devotional chanting and recitations from His Wisdom-Teaching.

"You must deal with My Wisdom-Teaching in some form every single day, because a new form of the ego's game appears every single day. You must continually return to My Wisdom-Teaching, confront My Wisdom-Teaching."
Avatar Adi Da Samraj

The beginner in Spiritual life must prepare the body-mind by mastering the physical, vital dimension of life before he or she can be ready for truly Spiritual practice. Service is devotion in action, a form of Divine Communion.

Avatar Adi Da Samraj Offers practical disciplines to His devotees in the areas of work and money, diet, exercise, and sexuality. These disciplines are based on His own human experience and an immense process of "consideration" that He engaged face-to-face with His devotees for more than twenty-five years.

The complete practice of the Way of Adidam includes medita-tion, sacramental worship (or "puja"), study of Avatar Adi Da's Wisdom-Teaching, devotional chanting, and regular periods of retreat.

AVATAR ADI DA SAMRAJ: You must come from the depth-position of meditation and puja before entering into activities in the wak-ing state, and remain in the disposition of that depth from the time of meditation and puja each morning. Maintain that heart-disposition, and discipline the body-mind—functionally, practi-cally, relationally—in all the modes I have Given you. This devo-tional Yoga, Ruchira Avatara Bhakti Yoga, is moment-to-moment. Fundamentally, it is a matter of exercising it profoundly, in this set-apart time of meditation and puja, and then, through random, artful practice moment-to-moment, constantly refresh it, preserve it. All of this is to conform the body-mind to the Source-Purpose, the in-depth Condition.

That basic discipline covers all aspects of the body-mind. That is the pattern of your response to Me. It is the foundation Yoga of organizing your life in terms of its in-depth principle, and grow-ing this depth. [December 5, 1996]

This moment-to-moment devotional turning to Avatar Adi Da is refreshed not only in the meditation hall but also in the temple, where worship, prayer, devotional chanting, and other sacred activ-ities occur.

AVATAR ADI DA SAMRAJ: The sacred life must be perpetual. The sacred domain is the core of the community, and every community and every Sanctuary should have a temple in its domain: A place of chant, of song, of prayer, where everyone gathers for this life of Invocation, prayer, and puja. [May 13, 1999]

The complete practice of Adidam also includes the adaptation to a purifying diet and a routine of daily exercise (including morning calisthenics and evening Hatha Yoga exercises). There is progressive adaptation to a regenerative practice of sexuality. And there is the expectation to participate in the cooperative community of other first- and second-congregation devotees, to maintain yourself in full employment or full-time service, and to tithe regularly.

All these practices are means whereby your body-mind becomes more and more capable of receiving the constant Blessing-Transmission of Avatar Adi Da Samraj. Therefore, He has made it clear that, in order to Realize Him with true profundity—and, in particular, to Realize Him most perfectly, to the degree of Divine Enlightenment—it is necessary to be a member of either the first or the second congregation, engaging the complete practice of the Way of Adidam.

If you are moved to join the second congregation of Adidam—or if you are moved to consider that possibility—the first step is to take "The Only Truth That Sets The Heart Free", a course in which you examine the opportunity Offered to you by Avatar Adi Da Samraj, and learn what it means to embrace the complete practice of the Way of Adidam.

To register for "The Only Truth That Sets The Heart Free":

contact the regional or territorial center nearest to you (p. 248),

or

e-mail us at: correspondence@adidam.org.

Those who, having practiced the Way of Adidam most inten-sively, make the transition to the "Perfect Practice" (in the sixth, or penultimate, stage of the Way of Adidam), may do so either as general practitioners (continuing as members of the second con-gregation of Adidam) or (if they demonstrate the necessary quali-fications) as formal renunciate practitioners (thereby becoming members of the first congregation of Adidam).

To enter the first congregation of the Way of Adidam is to become a member of the order of sannyasins (formal and legal renunciates) established by Avatar Adi Da. This order is known as "The Ruchira Sannyasin Order of the Free Renunciates of Ruchiradam" (or, simply, "The Ruchira Sannyasin Order"). Avatar Adi Da Himself is the Founding Member of the Ruchira Sannyasin Order. The devotee-members of the Ruchira Sannyasin Order ded-icate themselves intensively to Spiritual practice in the ultimate stages of the Way of Adidam, in the context of perpetual retreat. The Ruchira Sannyasin Order is the senior cultural authority within the gathering of Avatar Adi Da's devotees. Thus, the Ruchira Sannyasin Order has the principal responsibility, within the gathering of Avatar Adi Da's devotees, for exemplifying, com-municating about, and serving the development of the devotional and Spiritual relationship to Avatar Adi Da Samraj.

The Adidam Youth Fellowship

(within the second congregation)

Young people (25 and under) are also offered a special form of relationship to Avatar Adi Da—the Adidam Youth Fellowship. The Adidam Youth Fellowship has two membership bodies— friends and practicing members.

A <u>friend</u> of the Adidam Youth Fellowship is simply invited into a culture of other young people who want to learn more about Avatar Adi Da Samraj and His Happiness-Realizing Way of Adidam. A formally <u>practicing</u> <u>member</u> of the Adidam Youth Fellowship acknowledges that he or she has found his or her True Heart-Friend and Master in the Person of Avatar Adi Da Samraj, and wishes to enter into a direct, ego-surrendering Spiritual relationship with Him as the Means to True Happiness.

Practicing members of the Youth Fellowship embrace a series of disciplines that are similar to (but simpler than) the practices engaged by adult members of the second congregation of Adidam. Both friends and members are invited to special retreat events from time to time, where they can associate with other young devotees of Avatar Adi Da.

To become a member of the Adidam Youth Fellowship, or to learn more about this form of relationship to Avatar Adi Da, call or write:

Vision of Mulund Institute (VMI)
10336 Loch Lomond Road
PMB #146
Middletown, CA 95461 USA
phone: 1-707-928-6932
e-mail: vmi@adidam.org

COOPERATION + TOLERANCE = PEACE

The Third Congregation

(those who are moved to serve Avatar Adi Da Samraj
via their patronage and/or advocacy,
and those who are preparing for the second congregation)

The third congregation is for patrons and advocates, or those who are moved to support Avatar Adi Da's Work financially and/or through their advocacy, while embracing the simple form of the practice of Adidam. (The third congregation also includes individuals who have resolved to join the second congregation and are taking the preparatory educational course.)

As a member of the third congregation, you practice the simplest form of Ruchira Avatara Bhakti Yoga—invoking Avatar Adi Da, feeling Him, breathing Him, and serving Him. You are not obliged to engage the full range of disciplines practiced in the first two congregations. You are, however, encouraged to practice periods of meditation and sacramental worship and to study Avatar Adi Da's Wisdom-Teaching regularly.

1. Patrons and Individuals of Unique Influence

If you are a person of unique wealth or influence in the world, we invite you to serve Avatar Adi Da's world-Blessing Work through your patronage or influence. As a member of the third congregation of Adidam, supporting the world-Work of Adi Da Samraj, you are literally helping to change the destiny of countless people. You are making it possible for His Divine Influence to reach people who might otherwise never come to know of Him.

If you are interested in becoming a devotee of Avatar Adi Da Samraj in the third congregation, and serving Him in this crucial way, please contact us:

Third Congregation Advocacy
12040 North Seigler Road
Middletown, CA 95461 USA
phone number: 1-707-928-4800
e-mail: director_of_advocacy@adidam.org

2. The Transnational Society of Advocates of the Adidam Revelation

If you have the capability to effectively advocate Avatar Adi Da in the world—through your individual skills, position, or professional expertise—you may join a branch of the third congregation called the Transnational Society of Advocates of the Adidam Revelation. Members of the Society of Advocates are individuals who, while not of <u>unique</u> wealth or social influence, can make a significant difference to Avatar Adi Da's Work by making Him known in all walks of life (including the spheres of religion, the arts, media, education, health, entertainment, and so on). Advocates also serve the Global Mission of Adidam by financially supporting the publication of Avatar Adi Da's "Source-Texts" and His other Literature, as well as associated missionary literature. Members of the Society of Advocates make a monthly donation for this purpose and pay an annual membership fee that supports the services of the Society.

If you are interested in becoming a member of the Society of Advocates, please contact us:

The Society of Advocates
12040 North Seigler Road
Middletown, CA 95461 USA
phone: 1-707-928-6924
e-mail: soacontact@adidam.org

3. Pre-student-novices under vow

If you are certain that you wish to become a second-congregation devotee of Avatar Adi Da, and you (therefore) wish to embrace the vow of devotion to Him immediately (even before you qualify to become a student-novice in the second congregation), you are invited to become a pre-student-novice under vow (as part of the third congregation of Adidam).

As a pre-student-novice under vow, you make a commitment to become a student-novice (and, therefore, to move into the second congregation) within a period of three to six months. During this period, you take the preparatory course, "The Only Truth That Sets The Heart Free", which introduces you to the fundamentals of the second-congregation practice. Pre-student-novices under vow engage daily study of the Wisdom-Teaching of Avatar Adi Da, make regular financial contributions, and take up a regular form of service.

For information about becoming a pre-student-novice under vow, please contact the Adidam regional center nearest you (p. 248).

COOPERATION + TOLERANCE = PEACE

The Fourth Congregation

*(for those who are maintaining their participation
in the religious and/or cultural tradition
to which they already belong)*

Individuals who live in traditional cultural settings, and also individuals who wish to maintain their participation in the religious tradition to which they already belong (while acknowledging Avatar Adi Da Samraj as the Ultimate Divine Source of true religion), are invited to apply for membership in the fourth congregation of Adidam.

As a member of the fourth congregation, you practice the simplest form of Ruchira Avatara Bhakti Yoga—invoking Avatar Adi Da, feeling Him, breathing Him, and serving Him. You are not obliged to engage the full range of disciplines practiced in the first two congregations. You are, however, encouraged to practice periods of meditation and sacramental worship and to study Avatar Adi Da's Wisdom-Teaching regularly. The financial and service obligations of each fourth-congregation devotee are adapted to his or her particular circumstance.

The opportunity to practice in the fourth congregation is also extended to all those who, because of physical or other functional limitations, are unable to take up the total practice of the Way of Adidam as required in the first and second congregations.

For more information about the fourth congregation of Adidam, call or write one of our regional centers (see p. 248), or e-mail us at: correspondence@adidam.org.

**Temple sites at the Mountain Of Attention (left)
and Da Love-Ananda Mahal (right)**

One of the ways in which Avatar Adi Da Communicates His Divine Blessing-Transmission is through sacred places. To date, He has Empowered five Sanctuaries: the Mountain Of Attention, Tat Sundaram, and Love's Point Hermitage in northern California, Da Love-Ananda Mahal in Hawaii, and Adidam Samrajashram in Fiji. Avatar Adi Da has Established Himself Spiritually in perpetuity at all of these places. Devotees are invited to go on special retreats at the Mountain Of Attention, Da Love-Ananda Mahal, and Adidam Samrajashram.

Adidam Samrajashram, Fiji

**Darshan occasion with
Avatar Adi Da Samraj at
Tat Sundaram**

The life of a devotee of Avatar Adi Da Samraj is unheard-of Grace, and this life can be lived by anyone. It does not matter who you are, where you live, or what you do. All of that makes no difference, once your heart recognizes Adi Da Samraj. Then the only course is heart-response to Him—a life of devotion to the Divine in human Form, full of devotional ecstasy, true humor, freedom, clarity, and profound purpose.

So, why delay? The Living One, Adi Da Samraj, is here. He will always be Spiritually Present—but now is the brief, and especially Blessed, window of time in which He is humanly Alive, doing His Great Work for the sake of all beings. Everyone who comes to Him and serves Him in His bodily human Lifetime shares in His unique once-and-forever Work of establishing the Way of Adidam in this world.

Avatar Adi Da Samraj is not an "Other". He is the Gift, the Bliss, of Being Itself. He is the "Brightness" of Very God—Dawning, and then Flowering, in your heart. That Process is pure Revelation. It changes everything—grants peace, sanity, and the overwhelming impulse to Realize Unlimited, Permanent, and Perfect Oneness with Him.

As devotees of Avatar Adi Da, we make this confession: The opportunity to live in heart-Communion with Avatar Adi Da Samraj exceeds anything ever offered to mortal beings. And Avatar Adi Da is always ready, now or any time in the future, to Give you this Gift.

Those whose hearts are given, in love, to Me, Fall into My Heart. Those who are Mine, because they are in love with Me, no longer demand to be fulfilled through conditional experience and through the survival (or perpetuation) of the ego-"I". Their love for Me grants them Access to Me, and, Thus, to My Love-Bliss—because I Am Love-Ananda, the Divine Love-Bliss, in Person.

What will My lover do but love Me? I suffer every form and condition of every one who loves Me—because I Love My devotee As My own Form, My own Condition. I Love My devotee As the One by Whom I Am Distracted.

I Grant all My own Divine and "Bright" Excesses to those who love Me, in exchange for all their doubts and sufferings. Those who "Bond" themselves to Me, through love-surrender, are inherently Free of fear and wanting need. They transcend the ego-"I" (the cause of all conditional experience), and they (cause and all and All) Dissolve in Me—for I Am the Heart of all and All, and I Am the Heart Itself, and the Heart Itself Is the Only Reality, Truth, and Real God of All and all.

What is a Greater Message than This?

[Da Love-Ananda Gita]

In order to ensure that Avatar Adi Da's Divine Work flourishes in the world, His devotees are dedicated to serving three great purposes:

1. Providing for Avatar Adi Da Samraj Himself

(and for the Ruchira Sannyasin Order, as His most exemplary devotees)

2. Serving people's devotional response to Avatar Adi Da Samraj

(by making Avatar Adi Da Samraj and the Way of Adidam known throughout the world, and by serving the Spiritual growth of those who become His devotees)

3. Creating a community that supports the life of devotion to Avatar Adi Da Samraj

Each of these purposes is served by a particular organized body of Avatar Adi Da's devotees:

1. THE DA LOVE-ANANDA SAMRAJYA

devotees of Avatar Adi Da Samraj who most directly serve Him (Da) and His Spiritual Kingdom (Samrajya) of Love-Bliss (Love-Ananda)

2. THE ELEUTHERIAN PAN-COMMUNION OF ADIDAM

devotees of Avatar Adi Da Samraj who serve the gathering (Communion) of all (Pan-) those who have become, or may be moved to become, His devotees—thereby serving Avatar Adi Da's Divine Impulse to Offer His Liberating (Eleutherian) Grace and Help to all

3. THE RUCHIRASALA OF ADIDAM

devotees of Avatar Adi Da Samraj who serve the cooperative community of His first- and second-congregation devotees—the "House" (sala) that is made "Bright" (Ruchira) by His Blessing-Grace

The Da Love-Ananda Samrajya

Serving The Avataric-Incarnation-Body,
The Hermitage Sanctuaries, and The World-Blessing-Work
of The Divine World-Teacher,
Ruchira Avatar Adi Da Samraj

The Da Love-Ananda Samrajya is dedicated to serving Avatar Adi Da Himself—protecting Him and His intimate Sphere, providing for His Hermitage circumstance (in various parts of the world), and ensuring that He has everything He needs in order to Do His Divine Blessing-Work.

The Da Love-Ananda Samrajya serves, protects, and provides for the Ruchira Sannyasin Order, the body of formal (and legal) renunciates who live on perpetual retreat within Avatar Adi Da's Hermitage Domain.

The Da Love-Ananda Samrajya serves and manages the process of access to Avatar Adi Da Samraj, on the part of all who are invited to enter into His Hermitage Domain (either in order to offer service to Him and the Ruchira Sannyasin Order or in order to enter into meditative retreat in His Spiritual Company).

The Da Love-Ananda Samrajya is also culturally responsible to ensure the permanent integrity of Avatar Adi Da's Wisdom-Teaching, both in its archival and in its published forms.

The Eleutherian Pan-Communion
of Adidam

*The Sacred Cultural Gathering and Global Mission
of the Devotees of The Divine World-Teacher,
Ruchira Avatar Adi Da Samraj*

*Dedicated to the Practice and the Proclamation of
The True World-Religion of Adidam,
The Unique Divine Way of Realizing Real God*

The Eleutherian Pan-Communion of Adidam is dedicated to serving the development of people's devotional and Spiritual relationship to Avatar Adi Da Samraj—by making Him known in the world, and by serving the culture of devotional practice in the second, third, and fourth congregations. (The first congregation is the Ruchira Sannyasin Order, which is served by the Da Love-Ananda Samrajya.)

The Eleutherian Pan-Communion of Adidam also serves and protects the Sanctuaries, the Archives, the Wisdom-Teaching, and other sacred Treasures of Adidam.

The Global Mission of Adidam is the branch of the Adidam Pan-Communion that makes Avatar Adi Da's Offering (of the devotional and Spiritual relationship to Him) known to people throughout the world—through publications, internet websites, public events, and the personal missionary efforts of each devotee.

THE ADI DA RUCHIRASALA

COOPERATION + TOLERANCE = PEACE

COOPERATION + TOLERANCE = PEACE

THE 'BRIGHT' HOUSE OF ADI DA SAMRAJ

The Ruchirasala
of Adidam

*The True Cooperative Community Gathering
of the Devotees of The Divine World-Teacher,
Ruchira Avatar Adi Da Samraj*

*The Seed of a "Bright" New Age of Sanity
and Divine Joy for Mankind*

Participation in a community of practitioners is one of the greatest supports for Spiritual practice. Therefore, participation in cooperative community is a fundamental discipline in the first and second congregations of Adidam.

The Ruchirasala of Adidam is dedicated to serving the creation of cooperative community among Avatar Adi Da's first- and second-congregation devotees—including the establishment of intimate human living arrangements and shared services (such as sacred arts guilds, schools, community businesses, and a health clinic).

Cooperation + Tolerance = Peace^{SM}

In addition to His First Calling, which is to those who would become His devotees, Adi Da Samraj makes a Second Calling to the world at large: to embrace the disposition He has Summarized in the equation "Cooperation + Tolerance = Peace". By this Second Calling, Adi Da Samraj urges everyone to create a sane human society—including, in particular, the creation of a truly cooperative global human community, free of the devastation of war.

To find out more about Adi Da Samraj's Second Calling, please visit the Adidam Peace Center:

www.peacesite.org

An Invitation to Support Adidam

Avatar Adi Da Samraj's sole Purpose is to act as a Source of continuous Divine Grace for everyone, everywhere. In that spirit, He is a Free Renunciate and He owns nothing. Those who have made gestures in support of Avatar Adi Da's Work have found that their generosity is returned in many Blessings that are full of His healing, transforming, and Liberating Grace—and those Blessings flow not only directly to them as the beneficiaries of His Work, but to many others, even all others. At the same time, all tangible gifts of support help secure and nurture Avatar Adi Da's Work in necessary and practical ways, again similarly benefiting the entire world. Because all this is so, supporting His Work is the most auspicious form of financial giving, and we happily extend to you an invitation to serve Adidam through your financial support.

You may make a financial contribution in support of the Work of Adi Da Samraj at any time. You may also, if you choose, request that your contribution be used for one or more specific purposes.

If you are moved to help support and develop the Hermitage circumstance provided for Avatar Adi Da and the other members of the Ruchira Sannyasin Order, the senior renunciate order of Adidam, you may do so by making your contribution to The Da Love-Ananda Samrajya, the Australian charitable trust which has central responsibility for the Sacred Treasure of the Ruchira Sannyasin Order.

To do this: (1) if you do not pay taxes in the United States, make your check payable directly to "The Da Love-Ananda Samrajya Pty Ltd" (which serves as the trustee of the trust) and mail it to The Da Love-Ananda Samrajya at P.O. Box 4744, Samabula, Suva, Fiji; and (2) if you do pay taxes in the United States and you would like your contribution to be tax-deductible under U.S. laws, make your check payable to "The Eleutherian Pan-Communion of Adidam", indicate on your check or accompanying letter that you would like your contribution used for the work of The Da Love-Ananda Samrajya, and mail your check to the Advocacy Department of Adidam at 12040 North Seigler Road, Middletown, California 95461, USA.

If you are moved to help support and provide for one of the other purposes of Adidam, such as publishing the Sacred Literature of Avatar Adi Da, or supporting any of the Sanctuaries He has Empowered, or maintaining the Sacred Archives that preserve His recorded Talks and Writings, or publishing audio and video recordings of Avatar Adi Da, you may do so by making your contribution directly to The Eleutherian Pan-Communion of Adidam, specifying the particular purposes you wish to benefit, and mailing your check to the Advocacy Department of Adidam at the above address.

If you would like more information about these and other gifting options, or if you would like assistance in describing or making a contribution, please write to the Advocacy Department of Adidam at the above address or contact the Adidam Legal Department by telephone at 1-707-928-4612 or by FAX at 1-707-928-4062.

Planned Giving

We also invite you to consider making a planned gift in support of the Work of Avatar Adi Da Samraj. Many have found that through planned giving they can make a far more significant gesture of support than they would otherwise be able to make. Many have also found that by making a planned gift they are able to realize substantial tax advantages.

There are numerous ways to make a planned gift, including making a gift in your Will, or in your life insurance, or in a charitable trust.

If you would like to make a gift in your Will in support of the work of The Da Love-Ananda Samrajya: (1) if you do not pay taxes in the United States, simply include in your Will the statement, "I give to The Da Love-Ananda Samrajya Pty Ltd, as trustee of The Da Love-Ananda Samrajya, an Australian charitable trust, P.O. Box 4744, Samabula, Suva, Fiji, _____" [inserting in the blank the amount or description of your contribution]; and (2) if you do pay taxes in the United States and you would like your contribution to be free of estate taxes and to also reduce any estate taxes payable on the remainder of your estate, simply include in your Will the statement, "I give to The Eleutherian Pan-Communion of Adidam, a California non-profit corporation, 12040 North Seigler Road, Middletown, California 95461, USA, _____" [inserting in the blank the amount or description of your contribution].

To make a gift in your life insurance, simply name as the beneficiary (or one of the beneficiaries) of your life insurance policy the organization of your choice (The Da Love-Ananda Samrajya or The Eleutherian Pan-Communion of Adidam), according to the foregoing descriptions and addresses. If you are a United States taxpayer, you may receive significant tax benefits if you make a contribution to The Eleutherian Pan-Communion of Adidam through your life insurance.

We also invite you to consider establishing or participating in a charitable trust for the benefit of Adidam. If you are a United States taxpayer, you may find that such a trust will provide you with immediate tax savings and assured income for life, while at the same time enabling you to provide for your family, for your other heirs, and for the Work of Avatar Adi Da as well.

The Advocacy and Legal Departments of Adidam will be happy to provide you with further information about these and other planned gifting options, and happy to provide you or your attorney with assistance in describing or making a planned gift in support of the Work of Avatar Adi Da.

Further Notes to the Reader

An Invitation to Responsibility

Adidam, the Way of the Heart that Avatar Adi Da has Revealed, is an invitation to everyone to assume real responsibility for his or her life. As Avatar Adi Da has Said in *The Dawn Horse Testament Of The Ruchira Avatar,* "If any one Is Heart-Moved To Realize Me, Let him or her First Resort (Formally, and By Formal Heart-Vow) To Me, and (Thereby) Commence The Ordeal Of self-Observation, self-Understanding, and self-Transcendence. . . ." Therefore, participation in the Way of Adidam requires a real struggle with oneself, and not at all a struggle with Avatar Adi Da, or with others.

All who study the Way of Adidam or take up its practice should remember that they are responding to a Call to become responsible for themselves. They should understand that they, not Avatar Adi Da or others, are responsible for any decision they may make or action they may take in the course of their lives of study or practice. This has always been true, and it is true whatever the individual's involvement in the Way of Adidam, be it as one who studies Avatar Adi Da's Wisdom-Teaching or as a formally acknowledged member of Adidam.

Honoring and Protecting the Sacred Word through Perpetual Copyright

Since ancient times, practitioners of true religion and Spirituality have valued, above all, time spent in the Company of the Sat-Guru (or one who has, to any degree, Realized Real God, Truth, or Reality, and who, thus, serves the awakening process in others). Such practitioners understand that the Sat-Guru literally Transmits his or her (Realized) State to every one (and every thing) with whom (or with which) he or she comes in contact. Through this Transmission, objects, environments, and rightly prepared individuals with which the Sat-Guru has contact can become empowered, or imbued with the Sat-Guru's Transforming Power. It is by this process of empowerment that things and beings are made truly and literally sacred and holy, and things so sanctified thereafter function as a source of the Sat-Guru's Blessing for all who understand how to make right and sacred use of them.

Sat-Gurus of any degree of Realization and all that they empower are, therefore, truly Sacred Treasures, for they help draw the practitioner more quickly into the process of Realization. Cultures of true Wisdom have always understood that such Sacred Treasures are precious (and fragile) Gifts to humanity, and that they should be honored, protected, and reserved for right sacred use. Indeed, the word "holy" means "set apart", and, thus that which is holy and sacred must be protected from insensitive secular interference and wrong use of any kind. Avatar Adi Da has Conformed His human Body-Mind Most Perfectly to the Divine Self, and He is, thus, the most Potent Source of Blessing-Transmission of Real God, or Truth Itself, or Reality Itself. He has for many years Empowered (or made sacred) special places and things, and these now serve as His Divine Agents, or as literal expressions and extensions of His Blessing-Transmission. Among these Empowered Sacred Treasures is His Wisdom-Teaching, which is full of His Transforming Power. This Blessed and Blessing Wisdom-Teaching has Mantric Force, or the literal Power to serve Real-God-Realization in those who are Graced to receive it.

Therefore, Avatar Adi Da's Wisdom-Teaching must be perpetually honored and protected, "set apart" from all possible interference and wrong use. The fellowship of devotees of Avatar Adi Da is committed to the perpetual preservation and right honoring of the Sacred Wisdom-Teaching of the Way of Adidam. But it is also true that, in order to fully accomplish this, we must find support in the world-society in which we live and in its laws. Thus, we call for a world-society and for laws that acknowledge the sacred, and that permanently protect it from insensitive, secular interference and wrong use of any kind. We call for, among other things, a system of law that acknowledges that the Wisdom-Teaching of the Way of Adidam, in all its forms, is, because of its sacred nature, protected by perpetual copyright.

We invite others who respect the sacred to join with us in this call and in working toward its realization. And, even in the meantime, we claim that all copyrights to the Wisdom-Teaching of Avatar Adi Da and the other Sacred Literature and recordings of the Way of Adidam are of perpetual duration.

We make this claim on behalf of The Da Love-Ananda Samrajya Pty Ltd, which, acting as trustee of The Da Love-Ananda Samrajya, is the holder of all such copyrights.

Avatar Adi Da and the Sacred Treasures of Adidam

True Spiritual Masters have Realized Real God (to one degree or another), and, therefore, they bring great Blessing and introduce Divine Possibility to the world. Such Adept-Realizers Accomplish universal Blessing-Work that benefits everything and everyone. They also Work very specifically and intentionally with individuals who approach them as their devotees, and with those places where they reside and to which they direct their specific Regard for the sake of perpetual Spiritual Empowerment. This was understood in traditional Spiritual cultures, and, therefore, those cultures found ways to honor Adept-Realizers by providing circumstances for them where they were free to do their Spiritual Work without obstruction or interference.

Those who value Avatar Adi Da's Realization and Service have always endeavored to appropriately honor Him in this traditional way by providing a circumstance where He is completely Free to do His Divine Work. The Hermitage-Retreat Sanctuaries of Adidam have been set aside by Avatar Adi Da's devotees worldwide as Places for Him to do His universal Blessing-Work for the sake of everyone, as well as His specific Work with those who pilgrimage to His Hermitage circumstance (wherever He may be residing at a given time) to receive the special Blessing of coming into His physical Company.

Avatar Adi Da is a legal renunciate. He owns nothing and He has no secular or religious institutional function. He Functions only in Freedom. He, and the other members of the Ruchira Sannyasin Order, the senior renunciate order of Adidam, are provided for by The Da Love-Ananda Samrajya, which also provides for His Hermitage circumstance and ensures the permanent integrity of Avatar Adi Da's Wisdom-Teaching, both in its archival and in its published forms. The Da Love-Ananda Samrajya exists exclusively to provide for these Sacred Treasures of Adidam.

The institution which has developed in response to Avatar Adi Da's Wisdom-Teaching and universal Blessing is known as "The Eleutherian Pan-Communion of Adidam". This formal organization is active worldwide in making Avatar Adi Da's Wisdom-Teaching available to all, in offering guidance to all who are moved to respond to His Offering, and in providing for the other Sacred Treasures of Adidam. In addition to the central corporate entity known as The Eleutherian Pan-Communion of Adidam, which is based in California, there are numerous regional entities which serve congregations of Avatar Adi Da's devotees in various places throughout the world.

Practitioners of Adidam worldwide have also established numerous community organizations, through which they provide for many of their common and cooperative community needs, including those relating to housing, food, businesses, medical care, schools, and death and dying. By attending to these and all other ordinary human concerns and affairs via ego-transcending cooperation and mutual effort, Avatar Adi Da's devotees constantly free their energy and attention, both personally and collectively, for practice of the Way of Adidam and for service to Avatar Adi Da Samraj, to the other Sacred Treasures of Adidam, and to The Eleutherian Pan-Communion of Adidam.

All of the organizations that have evolved in response to Avatar Adi Da Samraj and His Offering are legally separate from one another, and each has its own purpose and function. Avatar Adi Da neither directs, nor bears responsibility for, the activities of these organizations. Again, He Functions only in Freedom. These organizations represent the collective intention of practitioners of Adidam worldwide not only to provide for the Sacred Treasures of Adidam, but also to make Avatar Adi Da's Offering of the Way of Adidam universally available to all.

APPENDIX

Chart of
The Seven Stages of Life

CHART 1

THE
SEVEN
STAGES
OF LIFE

The Full and
Complete Process
of Human Maturation,
Spiritual Growth, and
Divine Enlightenment

As Revealed by
**RUCHIRA AVATAR
ADI DA SAMRAJ**

Based on
The Seven Stages Of Life,
pp. 103-31

FIRST STAGE (approx. 0-7 years)	**SECOND STAGE** (approx. 7-14 years)	**THIRD STAGE** (approx. 14-21 years)
individuation; adaptation to the physical body 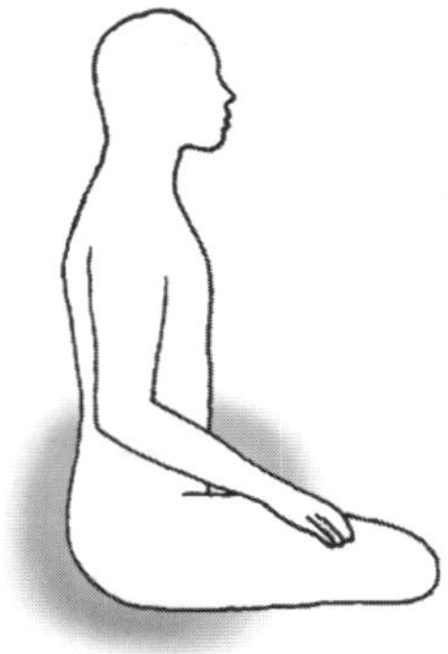	socialization; adaptation to the emotional-sexual (or feeling) dimension 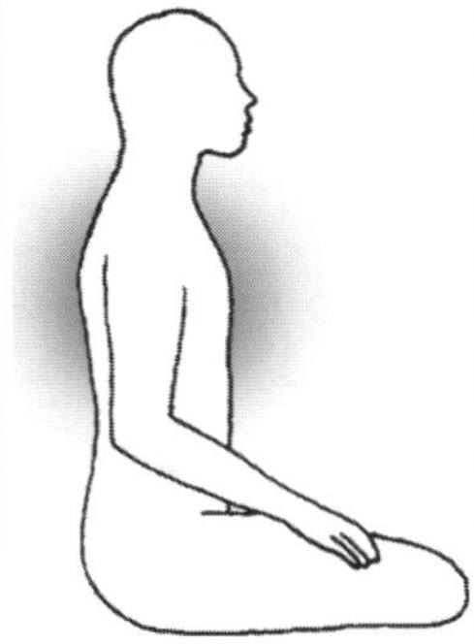	integration of the psycho-physical personality; development of verbal mind, discriminative intelligence, and the will 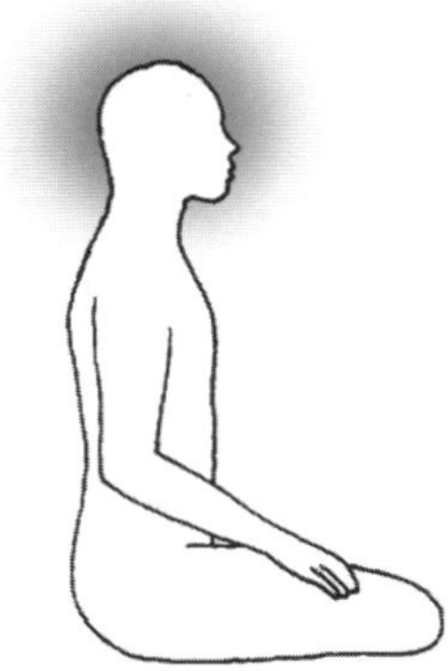

Identified with the gross self

FOURTH STAGE	FIFTH STAGE	SIXTH STAGE	SEVENTH STAGE
ego-surrendering devotion to the Divine Person; purification of body-based point of view through reception of Divine Spirit-Force	Spiritual or Yogic ascent of attention into psychic dimensions of the being; mystical experience of the higher brain; may culminate in fifth stage conditional Nirvikalpa Samadhi	Identification with Consciousness Itself (presumed, however, to be separate from all conditional phenomena); most likely will include the experience of Jnana Samadhi	Realization of the Divine Self; Inherently Perfect Freedom and Realization of Divine Love-Bliss (seventh stage Sahaj Samadhi); no "difference" experienced between Divine Consciousness and psycho-physical states and conditions
anatomy: the circulation of the Divine Spirit-Current, first (in the "basic" fourth stage of life) downward through the frontal line and then (in the "advanced" fourth stage of life) upward through the spinal line, until attention rests stably at the doorway to the brain core	**anatomy**: the ascent of the Divine Spirit-Current from the brain core (the Ajna Door) to the crown of the head and above (or even, in fifth stage conditional Nirvikalpa Samadhi, to the Matrix of Divine Sound and Divine Light infinitely above the total crown of the head)	**anatomy**: the Divine Spirit-Current descends (via Amrita Nadi, the "Immortal Current" of Divine Love-Bliss) from the Matrix of Divine Sound and Divine Light (infinitely above the total crown of the head) to the right side of the heart (the bodily seat of Consciousness)	**anatomy**: the "Regeneration" of Amrita Nadi, such that Amrita Nadi is felt as the Divine Current of "Bright" Spirit-Fullness, Standing between the right side of the heart and the Matrix of Divine Sound and Divine Light infinitely above the total crown of the head
Identified with the subtle self (In the Way of Adidam, practice in the context of the "advanced" fourth stage of life and in the context of the fifth stage of life may typically be bypassed, proceeding directly from the "basic" fourth stage of life to the sixth stage of life)		Identified with the causal self	Identified with Divine Consciousness Itself

Notes to the Text of
<u>Real</u> God <u>Is</u> The Indivisible Oneness
Of Unbroken Light

Part Four

1. "Mana" is a South Pacific word for energy, or power.

Part Five

2. Here Avatar Adi Da Samraj is referring to the absence of Divine Self-Recognition. The devotee of Avatar Adi Da who Realizes the seventh stage of life simply Abides as Self-Existing and Self-Radiant Consciousness Itself, and he or she Freely Recognizes (or inherently and instantly and Most Perfectly comprehends and perceives) all phenomena (including body, mind, conditional self, and conditional world) as transparent (or merely apparent), and un-necessary, and inherently non-binding modifications of the same "Bright" Divine Self-Consciousness.

3. Avatar Adi Da's Name "Da" means "The Divine Giver". Tibetan Buddhists regard the syllable "Da" (written, in Tibetan, with a single letter) as most auspicious, and they assign numerous holy meanings to it, including "the Entrance into the Dharma". In Sanskrit, "Da" means principally "to give", but also "to destroy", and it is also associated with Vishnu, the "Sustainer". Thus, "Da" is anciently aligned to all three of the principal Divine Beings, Forces, or Attributes in the Hindu tradition—Brahma (the Creator, Generator, or Giver), Vishnu (the Sustainer), and Siva (the Destroyer). In certain Hindu rituals, priests address the Divine directly as "Da", invoking qualities such as generosity and compassion.

Part Eight

4. "Maha" is Sanskrit for "great". "Shakti" is Sanskrit for the Divine Manifesting as Energy (or Spiritual Power). Therefore, "Maha-Shakti" means "the Great Divine Energy (or Spiritual Power)".

5. "Advaita" is Sanskrit for "Non-Duality". Thus, "Advaitic" means "Non-Dual". Avatar Adi Da has Revealed that, in Truth, there is not the slightest separation (or "difference") between the Unconditional Divine Reality and the conditional reality. In other words, Reality altogether is Perfectly One (or Non-Dual).

6. Chapter 3 of *The Dawn Horse Testament* contains Avatar Adi Da's Instruction in the basic practice of Invoking Him as it is engaged by all members of all four congregations of the Way of Adidam. *Hridaya Rosary* contains His Instruction in the further development of the practice of Invoking Him as it is engaged by

members of the first and second congregations of the Way of Adidam in the second period of the intensively listening-hearing stage of practice and beyond. Additionally, Avatar Adi Da has indicated that some aspects of His Instruction to His devotees (particularly relative to matters pertaining to practice in the context of the ultimate stages of the Way of Adidam) will never be made generally available in published form but will be Given only to members of the Ruchira Sannyasin Order, as the senior cultural authority of Adidam.

7. "Ruchira Avatara Bhava Samadhi" is "the enraptured feeling-swoon of Communion with the Ruchira Avatar, Adi Da Samraj".

8. In this passage, Avatar Adi Da describes the nature of Divine Translation. It is not an abstract state of "emptiness" or a "void" of nothingness—nor is it a cosmic "soup". It is, rather, as He describes here, an Embrace (Full of Love-Bliss) by an infinite but undifferentiated gathering.

GLOSSARY

A

Adi Sanskrit for "first", "primordial", "source"—also "primary", "beginning". Thus, most simply, "Adi Da" means "First Giver".

Adidam The primary name for the Way Revealed and Given by Avatar Adi Da Samraj.

When Avatar Adi Da Samraj first Gave the name "Adidam" in January 1996, He pointed out that the final "m" adds a mantric force, evoking the effect of the primal Sanskrit syllable "Om". (For Avatar Adi Da's Revelation of the most profound esoteric significance of "Om" as the Divine Sound of His own Very Being, see *He-and-She Is Me*.) Simultaneously, the final "m" suggests the English word "Am" (expressing "I Am"), such that the Name "Adidam" also evokes Avatar Adi Da's Primal Self-Confession, "I Am Adi Da", or, more simply, "I Am Da" (or, in Sanskrit, "Aham Da Asmi").

Adidam Samrajashram See **Sanctuaries**.

adolescent See **childish and adolescent strategies**.

Advaita Vedanta The Sanskrit word "Vedanta" literally means the "end of the Vedas" (the most ancient body of Indian Scripture), and is used to refer to the principal philosophical tradition of Hinduism. "Advaita" means "non-dual". Advaita Vedanta, then, is a philosophy of non-dualism, the origins of which lie in the ancient esoteric teaching that Brahman, or the Divine Being, is the only Reality.

Advaitayana Buddha / Advaitayana Buddhism "Advaitayana" means "Non-Dual Vehicle". The Advaitayana Buddha is the Enlightened One Who has Revealed and Given the Non-Dual Vehicle.

"Advaitayana Buddhism" is another name for the Way of Adidam. The name "Advaitayana Buddhism" indicates the unique sympathetic likeness of Adidam to the traditions of Advaitism (or Advaita Vedanta) and Buddhism. In His examination of the entire collective religious tradition of humankind, Avatar Adi Da has observed that these two traditions represent the most advanced Realizations ever attained previous to His Avataric Divine Incarnation. The primary aspiration of Buddhism is to realize freedom from the illusion of the separate individual ego-self. The primary aspiration of Advaitism (or the tradition of "Non-Dualism") is to know the Supreme Divine Self absolutely, beyond all dualities (of high and low, good and bad, and so on). Advaitayana Buddhism is the Non-Dual ("Advaita") Way ("yana", literally "vehicle") of Most Perfect Awakening ("Buddhism"). Advaitayana Buddhism is neither an outgrowth of the historical tradition of Buddhism nor of the historical tradition of Advaitism. Advaitayana Buddhism is the unique Revelation of Avatar Adi Da Samraj, which perfectly fulfills both the traditional Buddhist aspiration for absolute freedom from the bondage of the egoic self and the traditional Advaitic aspiration for absolute Identity with the Divine Self. (For Avatar Adi Da's discussion of Advaitayana Buddhism, see *The Only Complete Way To Realize The Unbroken Light Of Real God*.)

Advaitic "Advaita" is Sanskrit for "Non-Duality". Thus, "Advaitic" means "Non-Dual". Avatar Adi Da has Revealed that—in Truth, and in Reality—there is not the slightest separation, or "difference", between the Unconditional Divine Reality and the conditional reality. In other words, Reality altogether is Perfectly One, or Non-Dual, or Advaitic.

the advanced and the ultimate stages of life Avatar Adi Da Samraj uses the term "advanced" to describe the fourth stage of life (in its "basic" and "advanced" contexts) and the fifth stage of life in the Way of Adidam. He uses the term "ultimate" to describe the sixth and seventh stages of life in the Way of Adidam.

"advanced" context of the fourth stage of life See **stages of life**.

Agents / Agency Agents (or Agency) include all the Means that may serve as complete Vehicles of Avatar Adi Da's Divine Grace and Awakening Power. The first Means of Agency that have been fully established by Him are the Wisdom-Teaching of the Way of Adidam, the Hermitage-Retreat Sanctuaries and the Pilgrimage and Retreat Sanctuaries that He has Empowered, and the many Objects and Articles that He has Empowered for the sake of His devotees' Remembrance of Him and reception of His Heart-Blessing. After Avatar Adi Da's human Lifetime, at any given time a single individual from among His seventh stage "Ruchira san-nyasin" devotees will be designated (by the senior governing membership of the Ruchira Sannyasin Order) to serve as His living <u>human</u> Agent.

Aham Da Asmi The Sanskrit phrase "Aham Da Asmi" means "I (Aham) Am (Asmi) Da". "Da", meaning "the One Who Gives", indicates that Avatar Adi Da Samraj is the Supreme Divine Giver, the Avataric Incarnation of the Very Divine Person.

Avatar Adi Da's Declaration "Aham Da Asmi" is similar in form to the "Mahavakyas" (or "Great Statements") of ancient India (found in the Upanishads, the collected esoteric Instruction of ancient Hindu Gurus). However, the significance of "Aham Da Asmi" is fundamentally different from that of the traditional Mahavakyas. Each of the Upanishadic Mahavakyas expresses, in a few words, the profound (though not most ultimate) degree of Realization achieved by great Realizers of the past. For example, the Upanishadic Mahavakya "Aham Brahmasmi" ("I Am Brahman") expresses a great individual's Realization that he or she is Identified with the Divine Being (Brahman), and is not, in Truth, identified with his or her apparently individual body-mind. However, "Aham Da

Asmi", rather than being a proclamation of a human being who has devoted his or her life most intensively to the process of Real-God-Realization and has thereby Realized the Truth to an extraordinarily profound degree, is Avatar Adi Da's Confession that He <u>Is</u> the Very Divine Person, Da, Who has Appeared here in His Avatarically-Born bodily (human) Divine Form, in order to Reveal Himself to all and All, for the sake of the Divine Liberation of all and All.

all and All / All and all Avatar Adi Da uses the phrase "all and All" (or "All and all") to describe the totality of conditional existence from two points of view. In *Aham Da Asmi,* He defines lower-case "all" as indicating "the collected sum of all Presumed To Be Separate (or limited) beings, things, and conditions", and upper-case "All" as indicating "The All (or The Undivided Totality) Of conditional Existence As A Whole".

Amrita Nadi Amrita Nadi is Sanskrit for "Channel (or Current, or Nerve) of Ambrosia (or Immortal Nectar)". Amrita Nadi is the ultimate "organ", or root-structure, of the body-mind, Realized as such in the seventh stage of life in the Way of Adidam. It is felt to Stand Radiant between the right side of the heart (which is the psycho-physical Seat of Consciousness Itself) and the Matrix of Light infinitely above the crown of the head. (For Avatar Adi Da's principal discussions of Amrita Nadi, see *The Knee Of Listening, The <u>All-Completing</u> and <u>Final</u> Divine Revelation To Mankind, Santosha Adidam,* and *The Dawn Horse Testament.)*

anatomy See **Spiritual anatomy.**

asana Sanskrit for bodily "posture" or "pose"—by extension, and as Avatar Adi Da often intends, "asana" also refers to the attitude, orientation, posture, or feeling-disposition of the heart and the entire body-mind.

"Atma-Murti" "Atma" indicates the Divine Self, and "Murti" means "Form". Thus, "Atma-Murti" literally means "the Form That Is the (Very) Divine Self". And, as Avatar Adi Da Indicates everywhere in His Wisdom-Teaching, "Atma-Murti" refers to Himself as the Very Divine Self of all, "Located" as "the Feeling of Being (Itself)". To Commune with Avatar Adi Da as "Atma-Murti" is to Realize (or enter into Identification with) His Divine State.

Avadhoot   Avadhoot is a traditional term for one who has "shaken off" or "passed beyond" all worldly attachments and cares, including all motives of detachment (or conventional and other-worldly renunciation), all conventional notions of life and religion, and all seeking for "answers" or "solutions" in the form of conditional experience or conditional knowledge.

Avatar   "Avatar" (from Sanskrit "avatara") is a traditional term for a Divine Incarnation. It literally means "One who is descended, or 'crossed down' (from, and as, the Divine)". Avatar Adi Da Samraj Confesses that, simultaneous with His human Birth, He has Incarnated in every world, at every level of the Cosmic domain, as the Eternal Giver of Divine Help and Divine Grace and Divine Liberation to all beings—and that, even though His bodily (human) Lifetime is necessarily limited in duration, His Spiritual Incarnation in the Cosmic domain is Eternal.

Avataric Incarnation   Avatar Adi Da Samraj is the Avataric Incarnation, or the Divinely Descended Embodiment, of the Divine Person. The reference "Avataric Incarnation" indicates that Avatar Adi Da Samraj fulfills both the traditional expectation of the East, that the True God-Man is an Avatar (or an utterly Divine "Descent" of Real God in conditionally manifested form), and the traditional expectations of the West, that the True God-Man is an Incarnation (or an utterly human Embodiment of Real God).

For Avatar Adi Da's discussion of the "Avatar" and "Incarnation" traditions, and of His unique and all-Completing Role as the "Avataric Incarnation" of the Divine Person, see "'Avatar' and 'Incarnation': The Complementary God-Man Traditions of East and West", in *The Truly Human New World-Culture Of Unbroken Real-God-Man.*

Avataric Self-Submission   For a full description of Avatar Adi Da's "Ordeal Of Avataric Self-Submission", see *The Light Is On!*, by Carolyn Lee.

"Avoiding relationship?"   The practice of self-Enquiry in the form "Avoiding relationship?", unique to the Way of Adidam, was spontaneously developed by Avatar Adi Da in the course of His Divine Re-Awakening (as Avatar Adi Da describes in *The Knee Of Listening*). Intense persistence in the "radical" discipline of this unique form of self-Enquiry led rapidly to His Divine Re-Awakening in 1970.

The practice of self-Enquiry in the form "Avoiding relationship?" is the principal form of the "conscious process" practiced by devotees of Avatar Adi Da who choose the Devotional Way of Insight. (See also **Devotional Way of Insight / Devotional Way of Faith** and **Re-cognition**)

B

"basic" context of the fourth stage of life   See **stages of life**.

Bhagavan   The Title "Bhagavan" is an ancient one used over the centuries for many Spiritual Realizers of India. It means "blessed" or "holy" in Sanskrit. When applied to a great Spiritual Being, "Bhagavan" is understood to mean "bountiful Lord", or "Great Lord", or "Divine Lord".

bhakta, bhakti   "Bhakti" is the practice of heart-felt devotion to the Ultimate Reality or Person—a practice which has been traditionally animated through worship of Divine Images or surrender to a human Guru.

"Bhakta" is a devotee whose principal characteristic is expressive devotion, or who practices within the Hindu tradition of Bhakti Yoga.

Bhava   "Bhava" is a Sanskrit word used to refer to the enraptured feeling-swoon of Communion with the Divine.

bindu   In the esoteric Yogic traditions of India, the Sanskrit word "bindu" (literally, "drop" or "point") suggests that all manifested forms, energies, and universes are ultimately coalesced or expressed in a point without spatial or temporal dimension. Each level (or plane) of psychophysical reality is said to have a corresponding bindu, or zero-point.

Blessing-Work   For a description of Avatar Adi Da's Divine Blessing-Work, see pp. 16-25.

bodily base   The bodily base is the region associated with the muladhara chakra, the lowest energy plexus in the human body-mind, at the base of the spine (or the general region immediately above and including the perineum). In many of the Yogic traditions, the bodily base is regarded as the seat of the latent ascending Spiritual Current, or Kundalini. Avatar Adi Da Reveals that, in fact, the Spirit-Current must first descend to the bodily base through the frontal line, before it can effectively be directed into the ascending spinal course. Avatar Adi Da has also pointed out that human beings who are not yet Spiritually sensitive tend to throw off the natural life-energy at the bodily base, and He has, therefore, Given His devotees a range of disciplines (including a number of exercises that involve intentional locking at the bodily base) which conserve life-energy by directing it into the spinal line.

"bodily battery"   The "bodily battery" (known in Japan as the "hara") is the energy center of the gross body and, as such, plays a very important role in the practice of "conductivity" in the frontal line. Avatar Adi Da describes its focal point (or point of concentration) as the crown of the abdomen, on the surface, about an inch and a half below the umbilical scar.

"bond" / "Bond"   Avatar Adi Da uses the term "bond", when lower-cased, to refer to the process by which the egoic individual (already presuming separateness, and, therefore, bondage to the separate self) attaches itself karmically to the world of others and things through the constant search for self-fulfillment. In contrast, when He capitalizes the term "Bond", Avatar Adi Da is making reference to the process of His devotee's devotional "Bonding" to Him, which process is the Great Means for transcending all forms of limited (or karmic) "bonding".

"Bright"   By the word "Bright" (and its variations, such as "Brightness"), Avatar Adi Da refers to the Self-Existing and Self-Radiant Divine Reality. As Adi Da Writes in His Spiritual Autobiography, *The Knee Of Listening*:

> . . . *from my earliest experience of life I have Enjoyed a Condition that, as a child, I called the "Bright".*
>
> *I have always known desire, not merely for extreme pleasures of the senses and the mind, but for the highest Enjoyment of Spiritual Power and Mobility. But I have not been seated in desire, and desire has only been a play that I have grown to understand and enjoy without conflict. I have always been Seated in the "Bright".*
>
> *Even as a baby I remember only crawling around inquisitively with a boundless Feeling of Joy, Light, and Freedom in the middle of my head that was bathed in Energy moving unobstructed in a Circle, down from above, all the way down, then up, all the way up, and around again, and always Shining from my heart. It was an Expanding Sphere of Joy from the heart. And I was a Radiant Form, the Source of Energy, Love-Bliss, and Light in the midst of a world that is entirely Energy, Love-Bliss, and Light. I was the Power of Reality, a direct Enjoyment and Communication of the One Reality. I was the Heart Itself, Who Lightens the mind and all things. I was the same as every one and every thing, except it became clear that others were apparently unaware of the "Thing" Itself.*
>
> *Even as a little child I recognized It and Knew It, and my life was not a matter of anything else. That Awareness, that Conscious Enjoyment, that Self-Existing and Self-Radiant Space of Infinitely and inherently Free Being, that Shine of inherent Joy Standing in the heart and Expanding from the heart, is the "Bright". And It is the*

entire Source of True Humor. It is Reality. It is not separate from anything.

Buddha   Just as the traditional term "Avatar", when rightly understood, is an appropriate Reference to Avatar Adi Da Samraj, so is the traditional term "Buddha". He is the Divine Buddha, the One Who Is Most Perfectly Self-Enlightened and Eternally Awake.

C

causal   See **gross, subtle, causal**.

childish and adolescent strategies
Avatar Adi Da uses the terms "childish" and "adolescent" with precise meanings in His Wisdom-Teaching. He points out that human beings are always tending to animate one of two fundamental life-strategies—the childish strategy (to be dependent, weak, seeking to be consoled by parent-figures and a parent-"God") and the adolescent strategy (to be independent—or, otherwise, torn between independence and dependence—rebellious, unfeeling, self-absorbed, and doubting or resisting the idea of God or any power greater than oneself). Until these strategies are understood and transcended, they not only diminish love in ordinary human relations, but they also limit religious and Spiritual growth.

Circle   The Circle is a primary pathway of natural life-energy and the Spirit-Current through the body-mind. It is composed of two arcs: the descending Current, in association with the frontal line (down the front of the body, from the crown of the head to the bodily base), which corresponds to the more physically oriented dimension of the body-mind; and the ascending Current, in association with the spinal line (up the back of the body, from the bodily base to the crown of the head), which is the more mentally, psychically, and subtly oriented dimension of the body-mind.

conditional   The word "conditional" (and its variants) is used to indicate everything that depends on conditions—in other words, everything that is temporary

and changing. The "Unconditional", in contrast, is the Divine, or That Which Is Eternal, Always Already the Case—because It Is utterly Free of dependence on any conditions whatsoever.

"conductivity"   "Conductivity" is Avatar Adi Da's technical term for participation in and responsibility for the movement of natural bodily energies (and, when one is Spiritually Awakened by Him, for the movement of His Divine Spirit-Current of Love-Bliss in Its natural course of association with the body-mind), via intentional exercises of feeling and breathing.

The exercises of Spiritual "conductivity" that Avatar Adi Da Gives to His (formally practicing) Spiritually Awakened devotees are technical whole-bodily Yogas of receptive surrender to the Living Spirit-Current. Rudimentary and preparatory technical forms of "conductivity" are Given to beginners.

congregations of Adidam   There are four different modes, or congregations, of formal approach to Avatar Adi Da Samraj, making it possible for everyone to participate in the Gift of heart-companionship with Him. The total practice of the Way of Adidam is engaged by those in the first and second congregations. Whereas all of Avatar Adi Da's devotees (in all four congregations) engage the fundamental practice of Ruchira Avatara Bhakti Yoga, only members of the first and second congregations are vowed to engage the full range of supportive disciplines (meditation, sacramental worship, guided study, exercise, diet, emotional-sexual discipline, cooperative community living, and so on) Given by Avatar Adi Da Samraj.

For a more detailed description of the four congregations of Avatar Adi Da's devotees, see pp. 256-67.

"conscious process"   The "conscious process" is Avatar Adi Da's technical term for those practices through which the mind, or attention, is surrendered and turned about (from egoic self-involvement) to feeling-Contemplation of Him. It is the senior discipline and responsibility of all practitioners in the Way of Adidam. (Avatar Adi Da's descriptions of the various forms of the "conscious process" are Given in *The Dawn Horse Testament Of The Ruchira Avatar*.)

"consider", "consideration" The technical term "consider" or "consideration" in Avatar Adi Da's Wisdom-Teaching means a process of one-pointed but ultimately thoughtless concentration and exhaustive contemplation of something until its ultimate obviousness is clear. As engaged in the Way of Adidam, "consideration" is not merely an intellectual investigation. It is the participatory investment of one's whole being. If one "considers" something fully in the context of one's practice of feeling-Contemplation of Avatar Adi Da Samraj, and study of His Wisdom-Teaching, this concentration results "in both the highest intuition and the most practical grasp of the Lawful and Divine necessities of human existence".

Contemplation of Avatar Adi Da's bodily (human) Form Traditionally, devotees have produced artistic images of their Gurus for the purpose of Contemplating the Guru when he or she is either not physically present or (otherwise) no longer physically alive.

Modern technology makes possible (through photography, videotape, film, holographic imagery, and other means) accurate Representations of the bodily (human) Form of Avatar Adi Da Samraj for devotional use by His formally acknowledged devotees.

"Cosmic Consciousness" See **Samadhi**.

Cosmic Mandala The Sanskrit word "mandala" (literally, "circle") is commonly used in the esoteric Spiritual traditions of the East to describe the hierarchical levels of cosmic existence. "Mandala" also denotes an artistic rendering of interior visions of the cosmos. Avatar Adi Da uses the phrase "Cosmic Mandala" as a reference to the totality of the conditionally manifested cosmos (or all worlds, forms, and beings).

Crashing Down Avatar Adi Da's Crashing Down is the Descent of His Divine Spirit-Force into the body-mind of His devotee.

My Avataric Divine Work (Altogether) Is My Crashing-Down Descent, At First Upon and Into My Own Avatarically-Born Bodily (Human) Divine Form, and, Thereafter (and Now, and Forever), Upon and Into the body-minds Of My Devotees and all beings—Even (By Means Of My Divine Embrace Of each, and all, and All) To Infuse and (At Last) To Divinely Translate each, and all, and All. Therefore, My Avataric Divine Spiritual Descent Is The Secret Of My Early Life. My Avataric Divine Spiritual Descent Is The Secret Of My Divine Self-"Emergence" (As I Am) Within The Cosmic Domain. My Avataric Divine Spiritual Descent Is The Secret Of All The Secrets Of The (Avatarically Self-Revealed) Divine and Complete and Thoroughly Devotional Way Of Practice and Realization In My Company. The Only-By-Me Revealed and Given Way Of The Heart (or Way Of Adidam) Is The Divine Yoga Of ego-Surrendering, ego-Forgetting, and ego-Transcending Devotional Recognition-Response To My (Avatarically Self-Revealed) Divine and Spiritual Person, and To My (Avatarically Self-Manifested) Divine and Spiritual Descent. The Only-By-Me Revealed and Given Way Of The Heart (or Way Of Adidam) Is The Total and Divine Way and Ordeal Of Counter-egoic Devotional Recognition-Response To My Avataric "Bright" Divine Self-Manifestation, and To The Avataric Crashing Down Of My "Bright" Divine Imposition. And, In The Case Of My Each and Every Devotee, The Way Must Continue Until The Way Is Most Perfectly "Bright", and The Way Itself Becomes Divine Translation Into My Own Sphere Of "Brightness" (Itself). [Ruchira Avatara Hridaya-Siddha Yoga]

"Crazy" Avatar Adi Da has always had a unique Method of "Crazy" Work, which, particularly during His years of Teaching and Revelation, involved His literal Submission to the limited conditions of humankind, in order to reflect His devotees to themselves, and thereby Awaken self-understanding in them (relative to their individual egoic dramas, and the collective egoic dramas of human society).

For Me, There Was Never <u>Any</u> Other Possibility Than The "Reckless" (or Divinely "Crazy" and Divinely "Heroic") Course Of All-and-all-Embrace—and I Began This Uniquely "Crazy" and "Heroic" Sadhana, Most Intensively, At The Beginning Of My Adult Life. Indeed, I Have Always Functioned, and Will Always Function, In This Divinely "Crazy" and Divinely "Heroic" Manner. The Inherently egoless "Crazy" and "Heroic" Manner Is One Of My Principal Divine Characteristics— Whereby I Can (Always, and Now, and Forever Hereafter) Be Identified. Therefore, I (Characteristically) Functioned In This "Crazy" and "Heroic" Manner Throughout All Of My "Sadhana Years", and Throughout All The Years Of My Avatarically Self-Manifested Divine Teaching-Work and My Avatarically Self-Manifested Divine Revelation-Work—and I Have Done So (and Will <u>Forever</u> Continue To Do So) Throughout All The Divine-Self-"Emergence" Years Of My Avatarically Self-Manifested Divine Blessing-Work (Both During, and Forever After, My Avataric Physical Human Lifetime). <u>All</u> My Avatarically Self-Manifested Divine Work Is A Divinely "Crazy" and Divinely "Heroic" Effort That Avoids Not anything or any one—but Which <u>Always</u> Divinely Blesses Everything and Everyone. [The Truly Human New World-Culture Of <u>Unbroken</u> Real-God-Man]

D

Da   Avatar Adi Da's Name "Da" means "The Divine Giver". In Sanskrit, "Da" means principally "to give". It is also associated with Vishnu, the "Sustainer", and it further has a secondary meaning "to destroy". Thus, "Da" is anciently aligned to all three of the principal Divine Beings, Forces, or Attributes in the Hindu tradition—Brahma (the Creator, Generator, or Giver), Vishnu (the Sustainer), and Siva (the Destroyer). In certain Hindu rituals, priests address the Divine directly as "Da", invoking qualities such as generosity and compassion.

The Tibetan Buddhists regard the syllable "Da" (written, in Tibetan, as well as in Sanskrit, with a single symbol) as most auspicious, and they assign numerous sacred meanings to it, including that of "the Entrance into the Dharma".

Da Love-Ananda Samrajya   For a description of the Da Love-Ananda Samrajya, see p. 271.

Da Avatar   "Da" is Sanskrit for "The One Who Gives". Therefore, as the Da Avatar, Adi Da Samraj is the Divine Descent of the One and True Divine Giver.

"dark" epoch   See **"late-time" (or "dark" epoch)**.

Darshan   "Darshan", the Hindi derivative of the Sanskrit "darshana", literally means "seeing", "sight of", or "vision of". To receive Darshan of Avatar Adi Da is, most fundamentally, to behold His bodily (human) Form (either by being in His physical Company or by seeing a photograph or other visual representation of Him), and (thereby) to receive the spontaneous Divine Blessing He Grants Freely whenever His bodily (human) Form is beheld in the devotional manner. In the Way of Adidam, Darshan of Avatar Adi Da is the very essence of the practice, and one of the most potent forms of receiving Avatar Adi Da's Blessing is to participate in the formal occasions of Darshan—during which Avatar Adi Da Samraj Sits silently, sometimes gazing at each individual one by one.

By extension, "Darshan" of Avatar Adi Da Samraj may refer to any means by which His Blessing-Influence is felt and received—including His Written or Spoken Word, photographs or videotapes of His Avatarically-Born bodily (human) Divine Form, recordings of His Voice, Leelas (or Stories) of His Teaching-Work and Blessing-Work, places or objects He has Spiritually Empowered, visualization of His Avatarically-Born bodily (human) Divine Form in the mind, and simple, heart-felt Remembrance of Him.

Dattatreya Dattatreya was a God-Realizer who appeared early in the common era and about whom no certain historical facts exist apart from his name. Over the centuries, numerous legends and myths have been spun around him. He was early on regarded to be an incarnation of the God Vishnu, later associated with the tradition of Saivism, and worshipped as the Divine Itself. He is commonly venerated as the originator of the Avadhoota tradition and credited with the authorship of the *Avadhoota Gita*, among other works.

The devotional sect worshipping Dattatreya presumes that he continually reincarnates through a succession of Adepts for the sake of gathering and serving devotees. The belief in the continuing incarnation of Dattatreya should be understood as a popular religious belief that is peripheral to what the Adepts in the Dattatreya succession actually taught.

The Dawn Horse Testament Of The Ruchira Avatar *The Dawn Horse Testament Of The Ruchira Avatar* is Avatar Adi Da's paramount "Source-Text", summarizing the entire course of the Way of Adidam. (See "Avatar Adi Da Samraj's Teaching-Word", pp. 32-43.)

developmental stages of practice For all members of the first and second congregations of Avatar Adi Da's devotees, the Way of Adidam develops through a series of (potential) developmental stages of practice and Realization. These stages of practice, and their relationship to the seven stages of life, are described by Avatar Adi Da Samraj in chapter seventeen of *The Dawn Horse Testament Of The Ruchira Avatar.*

When using the phrase "necessary (or, otherwise, potential)", Avatar Adi Da is referring to the fact that His fully practicing devotee must practice in the context of certain of the developmental stages of practice (corresponding to the first three stages of life, the "original" and "basic" contexts of the fourth stage of life, the sixth stage of life, and the seventh stage of life) but may bypass practice in the developmental stages that correspond to the "advanced" context of the fourth stage of life and to the fifth stage of life.

Devotional Way of Insight / Devotional Way of Faith Avatar Adi Da has Given Instruction in two variant forms of the fundamental practice of feeling-Contemplation of Him: the Devotional Way of Insight and the Devotional Way of Faith. Each of Avatar Adi Da's fully practicing devotees is to experiment with both of these Devotional Ways and then choose the one that is most effective in his or her case.

Both Devotional Ways require the exercise of insight and faith, but there is a difference in emphasis.

In the Devotional Way of Insight, the practitioner engages a specific technical process of observing, understanding, and then feeling beyond the self-contraction, as the principal technical element of his or her practice of feeling-Contemplation of Avatar Adi Da.

In the Devotional Way of Faith, the practitioner engages a specific technical process of magnifying his or her heart-Attraction to Avatar Adi Da, as the principal technical element of his or her practice of feeling-Contemplation of Avatar Adi Da.

Avatar Adi Da's extended Instruction relative to both Devotional Ways is Given in *The Only Complete Way To Realize The Unbroken Light Of Real God.*

Dharma, dharma Sanskrit for "duty", "virtue", "law". The word "dharma" is commonly used to refer to the many esoteric paths by which human beings seek the Truth. In its fullest sense, and when capitalized, "Dharma" means the complete fulfillment of duty—the living of the Divine Law. By extension, "Dharma" means a truly great Spiritual Teaching, including its disciplines and practices.

"Difference" "Difference" is the epitome of the egoic presumption of separateness—in contrast with the Realization of Oneness, or Non-"Difference", Which is Native to the Divine Self-Condition.

Divine Being Avatar Adi Da describes His Divine Being on three levels:

AVATAR ADI DA SAMRAJ: This flesh body, this bodily (human) Sign, is My Form, in the sense that it is My Murti, or a kind of Reflection (or Representation) of Me. It is, therefore, a Means for contacting My Spiritual Presence, and, ultimately, My Divine State.

My Spiritual Presence is Self-Existing and Self-Radiant. It Functions in time and space, and It is also Prior to all time and space. . . .

My Divine State is always and only utterly Prior to time and space. Therefore, I, As I Am (Ultimately), have no "Function" in time and space. There is no time and space in My Divine State.

Divine Body   Avatar Adi Da's Divine Body is not conditional or limited to His physical Body but is "The 'Bright' Itself (Spiritually Pervading and Eternally Most Prior To The Cosmic Domain)".

Divine Enlightenment   The Realization of the seventh stage of life, which is uniquely Revealed and Given by Avatar Adi Da. It is release from all the egoic limitations of the first six stages of life. Remarkably, the seventh stage Awakening, which is Avatar Adi Da's Gift to His rightly prepared devotee, is not an experience at all. The true Nature of everything is simply obvious, based on the Realization that every apparent "thing" is Eternally, Perfectly the same as Reality, Consciousness, Happiness, Truth, or Real God. And that Realization is the Supreme Love-Bliss of Avatar Adi Da's Divine Self-Condition.

Divine Ignorance   "Divine Ignorance" is Avatar Adi Da's term for the fundamental Awareness of Existence Itself, Prior to all sense of separation from (or knowledge about) anything that arises. As He proposes, "No matter what arises, you do not know what a single thing is." By "Ignorance", Avatar Adi Da means heart-felt participation in the universal Condition of inherent Mystery—not mental dullness or the fear-based wonder or awe felt by the subjective ego in relation to unknown objects. Divine Ignorance is the Realization of Consciousness Itself, transcending all knowledge and all experience of the self-contracted ego-"I".

For Avatar Adi Da's extended Instruction relative to Divine Ignorance, see *What, Where, When, How, Why, and Who To Remember To Be Happy*, Part Two: "What, Where, When, How, Why and Who To Remember To Be Happy", and Part Three: "You Do Not Know What even a single thing Is" and "My Argument Relative to Divine Ignorance".

Divine Indifference   See **four phases of the seventh stage of life**.

Divine "Intoxication"   Unlike common intoxication, such as with alcohol, Divine "Intoxication" Draws Avatar Adi Da's devotees beyond the usual egoic self and egoic mind through His Blessing Grace into a state of ecstatic devotional Communion (and Identification) with Him.

Divine Parama-Guru   The Supreme Divine Guru.

Divine Re-Awakening   Avatar Adi Da's Divine Re-Awakening occurred on September 10, 1970, in the Vedanta Society Temple in Hollywood, California. For a full description of this Great Event and its import, see *The Light Is On!*, by Carolyn Lee, or chapter sixteen of *The Knee Of Listening*.

Divine Self-Domain   Avatar Adi Da affirms that there is a Divine Self-Domain that is the Perfectly Subjective Condition of the conditional worlds. It is not "else-where", not an objective "place" (like a subtle "heaven" or mythical "paradise"), but It is the always present, Transcendental, Inherently Spiritual, Divine Source-Condition of every conditionally manifested being and thing. Avatar Adi Da Reveals that the Divine Self-Domain is not other than the Divine Heart Itself, not other than Himself. To Realize the seventh stage of life (by the Divine Grace of Avatar Adi Da Samraj) is to Awaken to His Divine Self-Domain.

For Avatar Adi Da's extended Instruction relative to His Divine Self-Domain, see *The All-Completing and Final Divine Revelation To Mankind*.

Divine Self-"Emergence"   On January 11, 1986, Avatar Adi Da passed through a profound Yogic Swoon, which He later described as the initial Event of His Divine Self-"Emergence". Avatar Adi Da's Divine Self-"Emergence" is an ongoing Process in which His Avatarically-Born bodily (human) Divine Form has been (and is ever more profoundly and potently being) conformed to Himself, the Very Divine Person, such that His bodily (human) Form is now (and forever hereafter) an utterly Unobstructed Sign and Agent of His own Divine Being.

For Avatar Adi Da's Revelation of the significance of His Divine Self-"Emergence", see section III of "The True Dawn Horse Is The Only Way To Me", in *The All-Completing and Final Divine Revelation To Mankind, The Heart Of The Dawn Horse Testament Of The Ruchira Avatar*, and *The Dawn Horse Testament Of The Ruchira Avatar*.

Divine Self-Recognition   Divine Self-Recognition is the ego-transcending and world-transcending Intelligence of the Divine Self in relation to all conditional phenomena. The devotee of Avatar Adi Da who Realizes the seventh stage of life simply Abides as Self-Existing and Self-Radiant Consciousness Itself, and he or she Freely Self-Recognizes (or inherently and instantly and Most Perfectly comprehends and perceives) all phenomena (including body, mind, conditional self, and conditional world) as transparent (or merely apparent), and un-necessary, and inherently non-binding modifications of the same "Bright" Divine Self-Consciousness.

Divine Star   The primal conditional Representation of the "Bright" (the Source-Energy, or Divine Light, of Which all conditional phenomena and the total cosmos are modifications) is the brilliant white five-pointed Divine Star. Avatar Adi Da's bodily (human) Divine Form is the Manifestation of that Divine Star—and His head, two arms, and two legs correspond to its five points. Avatar Adi Da can also be seen or intuited in vision to Be the Divine Star Itself, prior to the visible manifestation of His bodily (human) Form.

Divine Transfiguration   See **four phases of the seventh stage of life**.

Divine Transformation   See **four phases of the seventh stage of life**.

Divine Translation   See **four phases of the seventh stage of life**.

Divine World-Teacher   Avatar Adi Da Samraj is the Divine World-Teacher because His Wisdom-Teaching is the uniquely Perfect Instruction to every being—in this (and every) world—in the total process of Divine Enlightenment. Furthermore, Avatar Adi Da Samraj constantly Extends His Regard to the entire world (and the entire Cosmic domain)—not on the political or social level, but as a Spiritual matter, constantly Working to Bless and Purify all beings everywhere.

dreaming   See **waking, dreaming, and sleeping**.

E

ecstasy / enstasy   The words "ecstasy" and "enstasy" derive originally from Greek. Avatar Adi Da uses "ecstasy" in the literal sense of "standing (stasis) outside (ec-)" the egoic self, and "enstasy" in the sense of "standing (stasis) in (en-)" the Divine Self-Condition. As Avatar Adi Da Says in *The Dawn Horse Testament Of The Ruchira Avatar*, Divine Enstasy is "The Native Condition Of Standing Unconditionally As The By-Me-Avatarically-Self-Revealed Transcendental, Inherently Spiritual, and Self-Evidently Divine Self-Condition Itself".

ego-"I"   The ego-"I" is the fundamental activity of self-contraction, or the presumption of separate and separative existence.

Eleutherian Pan-Communion of Adidam   The Eleutherian Pan-Communion of Adidam is a California religious non-profit corporation, dedicated to the worldwide practice and the global proclamation of the true world-religion of Adidam.

Eleutherios   "Eleutherios" (Greek for "Liberator") is a title by which Zeus was venerated as the supreme deity in the Spiritual esotericism of ancient Greece. The Designation "Eleutherios" indicates the Divine Function of Avatar Adi Da as the Incarnation of the Divine Person, "Whose Inherently Perfect Self-'Brightness' Divinely Liberates all conditionally Manifested beings—Freely, Liberally, Gracefully, and Without Ceasing—now, and forever hereafter".

En-Light-enment En-Light-enment (or Enlightenment) is not just a state of mind, but rather an actual conversion of the body-mind to the state of Divine Consciousness Itself, or Light Itself. Thus, Avatar Adi Da sometimes writes the word "Enlightenment" with "Light" set apart by hyphens, in order to emphasize this point.

esoteric anatomy See **Spiritual anatomy**.

Eternal Vow For a description of the Vow and responsibilities associated with the Way of Adidam, see pp. 256-67.

etheric The etheric is the dimension of life-energy, which functions through the human nervous system. Our bodies are surrounded and infused by this personal life-energy, which we feel as the play of emotions and life-force in the body.

F

faculties; four faculties Avatar Adi Da has Instructed His devotees that the practice of devotional Communion with Him (or Ruchira Avatara Bhakti Yoga) requires the surrender of the four principal faculties of the human body-mind. These faculties are body, emotion (or feeling), mind (or attention), and breath.

Feeling of Being The Feeling of Being is the uncaused (or Self-Existing), Self-Radiant, and unqualified feeling-intuition of the Transcendental, Inherently Spiritual, and Self-Evidently Divine Self-Condition. This absolute Feeling does not merely accompany or express the Realization of the Heart Itself, but It is Identical to that Realization. To feel—or, really, to Be—the Feeling of Being is to enjoy the Love-Bliss of Absolute Consciousness, Which, when Most Perfectly Realized, cannot be pre-

vented or even diminished either by the events of life or by death.

feeling of relatedness In the foundation stages of practice in the Way of Adidam, the basic (or gross) manifestation of the avoidance of relationship is understood and released when Avatar Adi Da's devotee hears Him (or comes to the point of most fundamental self-understanding), thereby regaining the free capability for simple relatedness, or living on the basis of the feeling of relatedness rather than the avoidance of relationship. Nevertheless, the feeling of relatedness is not Ultimate Realization, because it is still founded in the presumption of a "difference" between "I" and "other". Only in the ultimate stages of life in the Way of Adidam is the feeling of relatedness itself fully understood as the root-act of attention and, ultimately, transcended in the Feeling of Being.

feeling-Contemplation Avatar Adi Da's term for the essential devotional and meditative practice that all practitioners of the Way of Adidam engage at all times in relationship to Him. Feeling-Contemplation of Adi Da Samraj is Awakened by His Grace—through Darshan (or feeling-sighting) of His bodily (human) Form, His Spiritual Presence, and His Divine State. It is then to be practiced under all conditions, as the basis and epitome of all other practices in the Way of Adidam.

fifth stage conditional Nirvikalpa Samadhi See **Samadhi**.

forms of practice in the Way of Adidam Avatar Adi Da has Given a number of different approaches to the progressive process of Most Perfectly self-transcending Real-God-Realization in the Way of Adidam. In this manner, He accounts for the differences in individuals' qualities—particularly relative to their capability to make use of the various technical practices that support the fundamental practice of Ruchira Avatara Bhakti Yoga and relative to the intensity of their motivation to apply themselves to the Spiritual process in His Company.

Ruchira Avatar Adi Da refers to the most detailed development of the practice of the Way of Adidam as the "technically 'fully elaborated'" form of practice. Each successive stage of practice in the technically "fully elaborated" form of the Way of Adidam is defined by progressively more detailed responsibilities, disciplines, and practices that are assumed in order to take responsibility for the signs of growing maturity in the process of Divine Awakening. A devotee who embraces the technically "fully elaborated" form of practice of the Way of Adidam must (necessarily) be a member of the first or second congregation of Avatar Adi Da's devotees. The progress of practice in the technically "fully elaborated" form of the Way of Adidam is monitored, measured, and evaluated by practicing stages (as described in detail by Avatar Adi Da Samraj in chapter seventeen of *The Dawn Horse Testament Of The Ruchira Avatar*).

Most of Avatar Adi Da's fully practicing devotees will find that they are qualified for a less intensive approach and are moved to a less technical form of the "conscious process" (than is exercised in the technically "fully elaborated" form of the Way of Adidam). Thus, most of Avatar Adi Da's fully practicing devotees will take up the technically "simpler" (or even "simplest") form of practice of the Way of Adidam.

In the technically "simpler" form of practice of the Way of Adidam, Avatar Adi Da's devotee (in the first or second congregation) engages a relatively simple form of technical means of supporting his or her fundamental practice of Ruchira Avatara Bhakti Yoga, and this technical means remains the same throughout the progressive course of developmental stages.

In the technically "simplest" form of practice, Avatar Adi Da's devotee (in any of the four congregations) engages the fundamental practice of Ruchira Avatara Bhakti Yoga in the simplest possible manner—as "simplest" feeling-Contemplation of Avatar Adi Da, together with the random use of Avatar Adi Da's Principal Name, "Da" (or one of the other Names He has Given to be engaged in the practice of simple Name-Invocation of Him).

Avatar Adi Da's fully elaborated descriptions of the technically "fully elaborated" and the technically "simpler" (or even "simplest") forms of the Way of Adidam are Given in *The Dawn Horse Testament Of The Ruchira Avatar*.

four phases of the seventh stage of life
In the context of Divine Enlightenment in the seventh stage of life, the Spiritual process continues. One of the unique aspects of Avatar Adi Da's Revelation is His description of the four phases of the seventh stage process: Divine Transfiguration, Divine Transformation, Divine Indifference, and Divine Translation.

In the phase of Divine Transfiguration, the Divinely Enlightened devotee's body-mind is Infused by Avatar Adi Da's Love-Bliss, and he or she Radiantly Demonstrates active Love, spontaneously Blessing all the relations of the body-mind.

In the following phase of Divine Transformation, the subtle or psychic dimension of the body-mind is fully Illumined, which may result in Divine Powers of healing, longevity, and the ability to release obstacles from the world and from the lives of others.

Eventually, Divine Indifference ensues, which is spontaneous and profound Resting in the "Deep" of Consciousness, and the world of relations is otherwise noticed only minimally or not at all.

Divine Translation is the ultimate "Event" of the entire process of Divine Awakening. Avatar Adi Da describes Divine Translation as the Outshining of all noticing of objective conditions through the infinitely magnified Force of Consciousness Itself. Divine Translation is the Outshining of all destinies, wherein there is no return to the conditional realms.

Being so overwhelmed by the Divine Radiance that all appearances fade away may occur <u>temporarily</u> from time to time during the seventh stage of life. But when that Most Love-Blissful Swoon becomes permanent, Divine Translation occurs, and the body-mind is inevitably relinquished in physical death. Then there is only Eternal Inherence in the Divine Self-Domain of unqualified Happiness and Joy.

frontal line, frontal personality, frontal Yoga   The frontal (or descending) line of the body-mind conducts natural life-energy and (for those who are Spiritually Awakened) the Spirit-Current of Divine Life, in a downward direction from the crown of the head to the base of the body (or the perineal area).

The frontal (or gross) personality is comprised of the physical body, and its natural energies, and the sense-based mind. It includes the entire gross dimension of the body-mind and the lower (or most physically oriented) aspects of the subtle dimension of the body-mind.

The frontal Yoga, as described by Avatar Adi Da, is the process whereby knots and obstructions in the gross (or physical) and energetic dimensions of the body-mind are penetrated, opened, surrendered, and released, through the devotee's reception of Avatar Adi Da's Transmission in the frontal line of the body-mind.

"fully elaborated" form of the Way of Adidam   See **forms of practice in the Way of Adidam**.

functional, practical, relational, and cultural disciplines of Adidam
The most basic functional, practical, and relational disciplines of the Way of Adidam (in its fully practiced form, as embraced by devotees in the first and second congregations) are forms of appropriate human action and responsibility for diet, health, exercise, sexuality, work, service to and support of Avatar Adi Da's Circumstance and Work, and cooperative (formal community) association with other practitioners of the Way of Adidam. The most basic cultural obligations of the Way of Adidam (in its fully practiced form) include meditation, sacramental worship, study of Avatar Adi Da's Wisdom-Teaching (and also at least a basic discriminative study of the Great Tradition of religion and Spirituality that is the Wisdom-inheritance of humankind), and regular participation in the "form" (or schedule) of daily, weekly, monthly, and annual devotional activities and retreats.

G

Great Tradition   The "Great Tradition" is Avatar Adi Da's term for the total inheritance of human, cultural, religious, magical, mystical, Spiritual, and Transcendental paths, philosophies, and testimonies, from all the eras and cultures of humanity— which inheritance has (in the present era of worldwide communication) become the common legacy of humankind. Avatar Adi Da's Divine Self-Revelation and Wisdom-Teaching Fulfills and Completes the Great Tradition.

gross, subtle, causal   Avatar Adi Da (in agreement with certain esoteric schools in the Great Tradition) describes conditional existence as having three dimensions— gross, subtle, and causal.

"Gross" means "made up of material (or physical) elements". The gross (or physical) dimension is, therefore, associated with the physical body, and also with experience in the waking state.

The subtle dimension, which is senior to and pervades the gross dimension, consists of the etheric (or personal life-energy) functions, the lower mental functions (including the conscious mind, the subconscious mind, and the unconscious mind) and higher mental functions (of discriminative thought, mentally presumed egoity, and will), and is associated with experience in the dreaming state. In the human psycho-physical structure, the subtle dimension is primarily associated with the ascending energies of the spine, the brain core, and the subtle centers of mind in the higher brain.

The causal dimension is senior to and pervades both the gross and the subtle dimensions. It is the root of attention, or the essence of the separate and separative ego-"I". The causal dimension is associated with the right side of the heart, specifically with the sinoatrial node, or "pacemaker" (the psycho-physical source of the heartbeat). Its corresponding state of consciousness is the formless awareness of deep sleep.

Guru   Esoterically, the word "guru" is understood to be a composite of two words, "destroyer (ru) of darkness (gu)".

H

hearing See **listening, hearing, and seeing**.

heart, stations of the heart Avatar Adi Da distinguishes three stations of the heart, associated respectively with the right side, the middle, and the left side of the heart region of the chest. He Reveals that these stations are the loci (or focal points of living origination) of the causal body, the subtle body, and the gross body (respectively). Avatar Adi Da Teaches (as foreshadowed in certain rare sixth stage texts) that the primal psycho-physical seat of Consciousness and of attention is associated with what He calls the "right side of the heart". He has Revealed that this center (which is neither the heart chakra nor the gross physical heart) corresponds to the sinoatrial node, or "pacemaker", the source of the gross physical heartbeat in the right atrium (or upper right chamber) of the physical heart. In the Process of Divine Self-Realization, there is a unique process of opening of the right side of the heart—and it is because of this connection between the right side of the heart and Divine Self-Realization that Avatar Adi Da uses the term "the Heart" as another way of referring to the Divine Self.

The Heart Itself is Real God, the Divine Self, the Divine Reality. The Heart Itself is not "in" the right side of the human heart, nor is it "in" (or limited to) the human heart as a whole. Rather, the human heart and body-mind and the world exist in the Heart, Which Is the Divine Being Itself.

heart-Communion "Heart-Communion" with Avatar Adi Da is the practice of Invoking and feeling Him. It is "communion" in the sense that the individual loses sense of the separate self in the bliss of that state, and is thus "communicating intimately" (in a most profound and non-dual manner) with Avatar Adi Da Samraj.

heart-recognition The entire practice of the Way of Adidam is founded in devotional heart-recognition of, and devotional heart-response to, Ruchira Avatar Adi Da Samraj as the Very Divine Being in Person.

AVATAR ADI DA SAMRAJ: The only-by-Me Revealed and Given Way of Adidam (Which is the One and Only by-Me-Revealed and by-Me-Given Way of the Heart) is the Way of life you live when you rightly, truly, fully, and fully devotionally recognize Me, and when, on that basis, you rightly, truly, fully, and fully devotionally respond to Me. . . .

If you rightly, truly, fully, and fully devotionally recognize Me, everything "in between" vanishes. All of that is inherently without force. In heart-responsive devotional recognition of Me, a spontaneous kriya of the principal faculties occurs, such that they are loosed from the objects to which they are otherwise bound—loosed from the patterns of self-contraction. The faculties turn to Me, and, in that turning, there is tacit devotional recognition of Me, tacit experiential Realization of Me, of Happiness Itself, of My Love-Bliss-Full Condition. That "Locating" of Me opens the body-mind spontaneously. When you have been thus Initiated by Me, it then becomes your responsibility, your sadhana, to continuously Remember Me, to constantly return to this devotional recognition of Me, in which you are Attracted to Me, in which you devotionally respond to Me spontaneously with all the principal faculties. [Hridaya Rosary (Four Thorns Of Heart-Instruction)]

heart-response See **heart-recognition**.

"Heroic" The Tantric traditions of Hinduism and Buddhism describe as "heroic" the practice of an individual whose impulse to Liberation and commitment to his or her Guru are so strong that all circumstances of life, even those traditionally regarded as inauspicious for Spiritual practice (such as consumption of intoxicants and engagement in sexual activity), can rightly be made use of as part of the Spiritual process.

Avatar Adi Da's uniquely "Heroic" Ordeal, however, was undertaken not for His own sake, but in order to discover, through His own experience, what is necessary for all beings to Realize the Truth. Because of His utter Freedom from egoic bondage and egoic karmas, Avatar Adi Da's Sadhana was "Heroic" in a manner that had never previously been possible and will never again be possible. As the Divine Person, it was necessary for Him to experience the entire gamut of human seeking, in order to be able to Teach any and all that came to Him.

Avatar Adi Da has Instructed that, because of His unique "Heroic" Demonstration, His devotees can simply practice the Way He has Revealed and Given, and do not have to attempt the (in any case impossible) task of duplicating His Ordeal. (See also **"Crazy"**.)

Hridaya-Avatar "Hridaya" is Sanskrit for "the heart". It refers not only to the physical organ but also to the True Heart, the Transcendental (and Inherently Spiritual) Divine Reality. "Hridaya" in combination with "Avatar" signifies that Avatar Adi Da is the Very Incarnation of the Divine Heart Itself, the Divine Incarnation Who Stands in, at, and <u>as</u> the True Heart of every being.

Hridaya Rosary *Hridaya Rosary (Four Thorns Of Heart-Instruction)—The Five Books Of The Heart Of The Adidam Revelation, Book Four: The "Late-Time" Avataric Revelation Of The Universally Tangible Divine Spiritual Body, Which Is The Supreme Agent Of The Great Means To Worship and To Realize The True and Spiritual Divine Person (The egoless Personal Presence Of Reality and Truth, Which <u>Is</u> The Only <u>Real</u> God)* is Avatar Adi Da's summary and exquisitely beautiful Instruction relative to the right, true, full, and fully devotional practice of the Way of Adidam, through which practice Avatar Adi Da's fully practicing devotee Spiritually receives Him with ever greater profundity, and, ultimately (through a process of the Spiritual "melting" of the entire psycho-physical being), Realizes Him most perfectly.

Hridaya-Samartha Sat-Guru "Hridaya-Samartha Sat-Guru" is a compound of

traditional Sanskrit terms that has been newly created to express the uniqueness of Avatar Adi Da's Guru-Function. "Sat" means "Truth", "Being", "Existence". Thus, "Sat-Guru" literally means "True Guru", or a Guru who can lead living beings from darkness (or non-Truth) into Light (or the Living Truth).

"Samartha" means "fit", "qualified", "able". Thus, "Samartha Sat-Guru" means "a True Guru who is fully capable" of Awakening living beings to Real-God-Realization.

The word "Hridaya", meaning "heart", refers to the Very Heart, or the Transcendental (and Inherently Spiritual) Divine Reality.

Thus, altogether, the reference "Hridaya-Samartha Sat-Guru" means "the Divine Heart-Master Who Liberates His devotees from the darkness of egoity by Means of the Power of the 'Bright' Divine Heart Itself". Avatar Adi Da has Said that this full Designation "properly summarizes all the aspects of My unique Guru-Function".

Hridaya-Shakti; Hridaya-Shaktipat The Sanskrit word "Hridaya" means "the Heart Itself". "Shakti" is a Sanskrit term for the Divine Manifesting as Energy. "Hridaya-Shakti" is thus "the Divine Power of the Heart", Which is Given and Transmitted by Avatar Adi Da Samraj.

In Hindi, "shaktipat" means the "descent of Divine Power", indicating the Sat-Guru's Transmission of the Kundalini Shakti to his or her devotee.

"Hridaya-Shaktipat", which is Avatar Adi Da's seventh stage Gift to His devotees, is "the Blessing-Transmission of the Divine Heart Itself".

Avatar Adi Da's extended Instruction relative to Hridaya-Shakti and Kundalini Shakti is Given in *Ruchira Avatara Hridaya-Siddha Yoga*.

Hridaya-Siddha Yoga The Way (Yoga) of the relationship with the "Transmission-Master of the Divine Heart" (Hridaya-Siddha), Ruchira Avatar Adi Da Samraj.

Hridayam "Hridayam" is Sanskrit for "heart". It refers not only to the physical organ but also to the True Heart, the Transcendental (and Inherently Spiritual) Divine Reality. "Hridayam" is one of Avatar Adi Da's Divine Names, signifying that He Stands in, at, and as the True Heart of every being.

I

Ignorance See **Divine Ignorance**.

Indifference See **four phases of the seventh stage of life**.

Instruments / Instrumentality
Avatar Adi Da has Indicated that members of the Ruchira Sannyasin Order function collectively and spontaneously as His Instruments, or Means by which His Divine Grace and Awakening Power are Magnified and Transmitted to other devotees and all beings. Such devotees have received Avatar Adi Da's Spiritual Baptism, and they practice in Spiritually activated relationship to Him with exemplary depth and intensity. Because of their uniquely complete and renunciate response and accountability to Him, and by virtue of their ego-surrendering, ego-forgetting, ego-transcending, and really Spiritual Invocation of Him, these devotees function collectively as Instruments for the Transmission of Avatar Adi Da's Spiritual Presence to others.

Invocation by Name See **Name-Invocation**.

Ishta-Guru Bhakti Yoga An alternate name for Ruchira Avatara Bhakti Yoga. Ishta-Guru Bhakti Yoga literally means "the practice (Yoga) of devotion (Bhakti) to Avatar Adi Da, the chosen Beloved (Ishta) Guru of His devotees".

J

Jnana Samadhi See **Samadhi**.

K

Kali Kali is a Hindu form of the Divine Goddess (or "Mother-Shakti") in her terrifying aspect.

Kali Yuga A Hindu term meaning "the dark (kali) epoch (yuga)", or the final and most ignorant and degenerate period of human history, when the Spiritual Way of life is almost entirely forgotten. (In the Hindu view, the Kali Yuga is a cyclically recurring event.)

karma "Karma" is Sanskrit for "action". Since action entails consequences (or reactions), "karma" also means (by extension) "destiny, tendency, the quality of existence and experience which is determined by previous actions".

Kashmir Saivism Kashmir Saivism is a branch of Saivism (the form of Hinduism in which Siva is worshipped as the Supreme Deity), which originated in the Kashmir region of North India in the late 8th century and whose influence spread throughout the Indian sub-continent during the mid-20th century. It has a largely fifth-stage orientation.

kiln Avatar Adi Da Samraj frequently describes the transformative process of His Blessing-Power in the lives of His devotees as being like a kiln. In a kiln, as the wet clay objects are heated more and more, they begin to glow. Eventually, the kiln is so hot that everything within it glows with a white light, and the definitions of the individual objects dissolve in the brightness. Just so, as a devotee matures in Avatar Adi Da's Spiritual Company, all presumptions of separateness as an apparently individual ego-"I" are more and more Outshined by the "Brightness" of His Divine Person and Blessing.

Klik-Klak Avatar Adi Da coined the term "Klik-Klak" as a name for the conditional reality. This name indicates (even by means of the sound of the two syllables) that conditional reality is a heartless perpetual-motion machine of incessant change, producing endlessly varied patterns that are ultimately binary in nature (as, for example, "yes-no", "on-off", or "black-white").

knots Previous to Most Perfect Divine Self-Realization, the gross, subtle, and causal dimensions are expressed in the body-mind as characteristic knots. The knot of the gross dimension is associated with the region of the navel. The knot of the subtle dimension is associated with the midbrain, or the ajna center directly behind and between the brows. And the knot of the causal dimension (which Avatar Adi Da refers to as the "causal knot") is associated with the sinoatrial node (or "pacemaker") on the right side of the heart. The causal knot (or the heart-root's knot) is the primary root of the self-contraction, felt as the locus of the self-sense, the source of the feeling of relatedness itself, or the root of attention.

Kundalini-Shaktipat The Kundalini Shakti is traditionally viewed to lie dormant at the bodily base, or lowermost psychic center of the body-mind. Kundalini-Shaktipat is the activation of the Kundalini Shakti—either spontaneously in the devotee or by the Guru's initiation—thereafter potentially producing various forms of Yogic and mystical experience.

L

"late-time" (or "dark" epoch) The "'late-time' (or 'dark' epoch)" is a phrase that Avatar Adi Da uses to describe the present era—in which doubt of God (and of anything at all beyond mortal existence) is more and more pervading the entire world, and the self-interest of the separate individual is more and more regarded to be the ultimate principle of life. It is also a reference to the traditional Hindu idea of "yugas", or "epochs", the last of which (the Kali Yuga) is understood to be the most difficult and "dark". Many traditions share the idea that it is in such a time that the Promised Divine Liberator will appear. (See also **Kali Yuga**.)

Lay Congregationist Order In "The Orders of My True and Free Renunciate

Devotees" (in *The Lion Sutra*), Avatar Adi Da describes the Lay Congregationist Order as "the common (or general) order for all formally established general (or not otherwise formal renunciate) lay practitioners of the total (or full and complete) practice of the Way of Adidam". Once a member of the second congregation has completed the student-beginner stage of practice, he or she makes the transition to the intensive listening-hearing stage of the Way of Adidam. By virtue of this transition, the individual becomes a member of the Lay Congregationist Order, unless he or she is accepted as a member of the Lay Renunciate Order.

Lay Renunciate Order See **renunciate orders**.

leela "Leela" is Sanskrit for "play", or "sport". In many religious and Spiritual traditions, all of conditionally manifested existence is regarded to be the Leela (or the Play, Sport, or Free Activity) of the Divine Person. "Leela" also means the Awakened Play of a Realized Adept (of any degree), through which he or she mysteriously Instructs and Liberates others and Blesses the world itself. By extension, a Leela is an instructive and inspiring story of such an Adept's Teaching and Blessing Play.

Lesson of life "The Lesson of life" is Avatar Adi Da's term for the fundamental understanding that Happiness cannot be achieved by means of seeking, because Happiness is inherent in Existence Itself. Avatar Adi Da has summarized this in the aphorism, "You cannot become Happy. You can only be Happy."

Lineage, Avatar Adi Da's The principal Spiritual Masters who served Avatar Adi Da Samraj during His "Sadhana Years" belong to a single Lineage of extraordinary Yogis, whose Parama-Guru (Supreme Guru) was the Divine "Goddess" (or "Mother-Shakti").

Swami Rudrananda (1928-1973), or Albert Rudolph (known as "Rudi"), was Avatar Adi Da's first human Teacher—from 1964 to 1968, in New York City. Rudi served Avatar Adi Da Samraj in the development of basic practical life-disciplines and the frontal Yoga, which is the process whereby knots and obstructions in the physical and etheric dimensions of the body-mind are penetrated, opened, surrendered, and released through Spiritual reception in the frontal line of the body-mind. Rudi's own Teachers included the Indonesian Pak Subuh (from whom Rudi learned a basic exercise of Spiritual receptivity), Swami Muktananda (with whom Rudi studied for many years), and Bhagavan Nityananda (the Indian Adept-Realizer who was also Swami Muktananda's Guru). Rudi met Bhagavan Nityananda shortly before Bhagavan Nityananda's death, and Rudi always thereafter acknowledged Bhagavan Nityananda as his original and principal Guru.

The second Teacher in Avatar Adi Da's Lineage of Blessing was Swami Muktananda (1908-1982), who was born in Mangalore, South India. Having left home at the age of fifteen, he wandered for many years, seeking the Divine Truth from sources all over India. Eventually, he came under the Spiritual Influence of Bhagavan Nityananda, whom he accepted as his Guru and in whose Spiritual Company he mastered Kundalini Yoga. Swami Muktananda served Avatar Adi Da as Guru during the period from 1968 to 1970. In the summer of 1969, during Avatar Adi Da's second visit to India, Swami Muktananda wrote a letter confirming Avatar Adi Da's attainment of "Yogic Liberation", and acknowledging His right to Teach others. However, from the beginning of their relationship, Swami Muktananda instructed Avatar Adi Da to visit Bhagavan Nityananda's burial site every day (whenever Avatar Adi Da was at Swami Muktananda's Ashram in Ganeshpuri, India) as a means to surrender to Bhagavan Nityananda as the Supreme Guru of the Lineage.

Bhagavan Nityananda, a great Yogi of South India, was Avatar Adi Da's third Guru. Little is known about the circumstances of Bhagavan Nityananda's birth and early life, although it is said that even as a child he showed the signs of a Realized Yogi. It is also known that he abandoned conventional life as a boy and wandered as a renunciate. Many miracles (including spontaneous healings) and instructive stories are attributed to him. Bhagavan Nityananda surrendered the body on August 8, 1961. Although Avatar Adi Da did not meet Bhagavan Nityananda in the flesh, He enjoyed Bhagavan Nityananda's direct Spiritual Influence from the subtle plane, and He acknowledges Bhagavan Nityananda as a direct and principal Source of Spiritual Instruction during His years with Swami Muktananda. (Avatar Adi Da summarizes the Instruction He received from Bhagavan Nityananda in section XXXII of "I (Alone) Am The Adidam Revelation", an Essay contained in many of the twenty-three "Source-Texts" of Adidam.)

On His third visit to India, while visiting Bhagavan Nityananda's burial shrine, Avatar Adi Da was instructed by Bhagavan Nityananda to relinquish all others as Guru and to surrender directly to the Divine Goddess in Person as Guru. Thus, Bhagavan Nityananda passed Avatar Adi Da to the Divine Goddess Herself, the Parama-Guru (or Source-Guru) of the Lineage that included Bhagavan Nityananda, Swami Muktananda, and Rudi.

The years of Avatar Adi Da's "Sadhana" came to an end in the Great Event of His Divine Re-Awakening, when Avatar Adi Da Husbanded the Divine Goddess (thereby ceasing to relate to Her as His Guru).

Avatar Adi Da's full account of His "Sadhana Years" is Given in *The Knee Of Listening*.

Avatar Adi Da's description of His "Relationship" to the Divine "Goddess" is Given in "I Am The Icon Of Unity", in *He-and-She Is Me*.

listening, hearing, and seeing
"Listening" is Avatar Adi Da's technical term for the orientation, disposition, and beginning practice of the Way of Adidam. A listening devotee listens to Avatar Adi Da Samraj by "considering" His Teaching-Argument and His Leelas, and by practicing feeling-Contemplation of Him (primarily

of His bodily human Form). In the total practice of the Way of Adidam, effective listening to Avatar Adi Da is the necessary prerequisite for true hearing and real seeing.

"Hearing" is a technical term used by Avatar Adi Da to indicate most fundamental understanding of the act of egoity (or self-contraction). Hearing Avatar Adi Da is the unique capability to directly transcend the self-contraction, such that, simultaneous with that transcending, there is the intuitive awakening to Avatar Adi Da's Self-Revelation As the Divine Person and Self-Condition. The capability of true hearing can only be Granted by Avatar Adi Da's Divine Grace, to His fully practicing devotee who has effectively completed the process of listening. Only on the basis of such hearing can Spiritually Awakened practice of the Way of Adidam truly (or with full responsibility) begin.

I Am Heard When My Listening Devotee Has Truly (and Thoroughly) Observed the ego-"I" and Understood it (Directly, In the moments Of self-Observation, and Most Fundamentally, or In its Totality).

I Am Heard When the ego-"I" Is Altogether (and Thoroughly) Observed and (Most Fundamentally) Understood, Both In The Tendency To Dissociate and In The Tendency To Become Attached (or To Cling By Wanting Need, or To Identify With others, and things, and circumstances egoically, and Thus To Dramatize The Seeker, Bereft Of Basic Equanimity, Wholeness, and The Free Capability For Simple Relatedness).

I Am Heard When the ego-"I" Is Thoroughly (and Most Fundamentally) Understood To Be Contraction-Only, An Un-Necessary and Destructive Motive and Design, Un-Naturally and Chronically Added To Cosmic Nature and To all relations, and An Imaginary Heart-Disease (Made To Seem Real, By Heart-Reaction).

I Am Heard When This Most Fundamental Understanding Of The Habit Of "Narcissus" Becomes The Directly Obvious Realization Of The Heart, Radiating Beyond Its Own (Apparent) Contraction.

I Am Heard When The Beginning Is Full, and The Beginning Is Full (and Ended) When Every Gesture Of self-Contraction (In The Context Of The First Three Stages Of Life, and Relative To Each and All Of The Principal Faculties, Of body, emotion, mind, and breath) Is (As A Rather Consistently Applied and humanly Effective Discipline) Observed (By Natural feeling-perception), Tacitly (and Most Fundamentally) Understood, and Really (Directly and Effectively) Felt Beyond (In The Prior Feeling Of Unqualified Relatedness). [Santosha Adidam]

When, in the practice of the Way of Adidam, hearing (or most fundamental self-understanding) is steadily exercised in meditation and in life, the native feeling of the heart ceases to be chronically constricted by self-contraction. The heart then begins to Radiate as love in response to the Divine Spiritual Presence of Avatar Adi Da.

This emotional and Spiritual response of the whole being is what Avatar Adi Da calls "seeing". Seeing Avatar Adi Da is emotional conversion from the reactive emotions that characterize egoic self-obsession, to the open-hearted, Radiant Happiness that characterizes Spiritual devotion to Avatar Adi Da. This true and stable emotional conversion coincides with true and stable receptivity to Avatar Adi Da's Spiritual Transmission, and both of these are prerequisites to further Spiritual advancement in the Way of Adidam.

Seeing Is ego-Transcending Participation In What (and Who) Is. Seeing Is Love. Seeing (or Love) Is Able (By Means Of My Avatarically Self-Transmitted Divine Grace) To "Locate", Devotionally Recognize, and Feel My Avatarically Self-Transmitted (and all-and-All-Pervading) Spiritual Radiance (and My Avatarically Self-Transmitted Spirit-Identity, As The "Bright" and Only One Who Is). . . . Seeing Is The "Radical" (or Directly ego-Transcending) Reorientation Of conditional Existence To My Avatarically Self-Revealed (Transcendental, Inherently Spiritual, Inherently Perfect, and

Self-Evidently Divine) Self-Condition, In Whom conditional self and conditional worlds Apparently arise and Always Already Inhere. . . .

Seeing Me Is Simply Attraction To Me (and Feeling Me) As My Avatarically Self-Revealed Spiritual (and Always Blessing) Divine Presence—and This Most Fundamentally, At The Root, Core, Source, or Origin Of The "Emergence" Of My Avatarically Self-Revealed Divine Spiritual Presence "here", At (and In Front Of) The Heart, or At (and In) The Root-Context Of the body-mind, or At (and In) The Source-Position (and, Ultimately, As The Source-Condition) Of conditional (or psycho-physical) Existence Itself.

Seeing Me Is Knowing Me As My Avatarically Self-Revealed Spiritual (and Always Blessing) Divine Presence, Just As Tangibly (and With The Same Degree Of Clarity) As You Would Differentiate The Physical Appearance Of My Bodily (Human) Form From the physical appearance of the bodily (human) form of any other.

To See Me Is A Clear and "Radical" Knowledge Of Me, About Which There Is No Doubt. To See Me Is A Sudden, Tacit Awareness—Like Walking Into a "thicker" air or atmosphere, or Suddenly Feeling a breeze, or Jumping Into water and Noticing The Difference In Density Between the air and the water. This Tangible Feeling Of Me Is (In any particular moment) Not Necessarily (Otherwise) Associated With effects in the body-mind . . . but It Is, Nevertheless, Felt At The Heart and Even All Over the body.

Seeing Me Is One-Pointedness In The "Radical" Conscious Process Of Heart-Devotion To Me. [Santosha Adidam]

"Living Murti"   Avatar Adi Da will always be Divinely Present in the Cosmic domain, even after His physical Lifetime. He is the One Who is (and will always be) worshipped in the Way of Adidam, and (therefore) He is (and will always be) the Eternally Living Murti for His devotees. However, Avatar Adi Da has said that, after His physical (human) Lifetime, there should always be one (and only one) "Living Murti" as a Living Link

between Him and His devotees. Each successive "Living Murti" (or "Murti-Guru") is to be selected from among those members of the Ruchira Sannyasin Order (see **renunciate orders**) who have been formally acknowledged as Divinely Enlightened devotees of Avatar Adi Da Samraj in the seventh stage of life. "Living Murtis" will not function as the independent Gurus of practitioners of the Way of Adidam. Rather, they will simply be "Representations" of Avatar Adi Da's bodily (human) Divine Form, and a means to Commune with Him.

Avatar Adi Da's full discussion of His "Living Murtis", and how they are to be chosen, is Given in Part Three, section XII, of *The Lion Sutra*.

"Locate"   To "Locate" Avatar Adi Da is to "Truly Heart-Find" Him.

Love-Ananda   The Name "Love-Ananda" combines both English ("Love") and Sanskrit ("Ananda", meaning "Bliss"), thus bridging the West and the East, and communicating Avatar Adi Da's Function as the Divine World-Teacher. The combination of "Love" and "Ananda" means "the Divine Love-Bliss". The Name "Love-Ananda" was given to Avatar Adi Da by Swami Muktananda, who spontaneously conferred it upon Avatar Adi Da in 1969. However, Avatar Adi Da did not use the Name "Love-Ananda" until April 1986, after the Great Event that Initiated His Divine Self-"Emergence".

Love-Ananda Avatar   As the Love-Ananda Avatar, Avatar Adi Da is the Very Incarnation of the Divine Love-Bliss.

M

Maha-Siddha   The Sanskrit word "Siddha" means "a completed, fulfilled, or perfected one", or "one of perfect accomplishment, or power". "Maha-Siddha" means "Great Siddha".

Mandala   The Sanskrit word "mandala" (literally, "circle") is commonly used in the esoteric Spiritual traditions to describe the entire pattern of the hierarchical levels of cosmic existence. Avatar Adi Da also uses the word "Mandala" to refer to the Circle (or Sphere) of His Heart-Transmission, or as a formal reference to a group of His devotees who perform specific functions of direct service to Him.

mantra   See **Name-Invocation**.

meditation   In the Way of Adidam, meditation is a period of formal devotional Contemplation of Avatar Adi Da Samraj. Meditation is one of the life-disciplines that Avatar Adi Da Samraj has Given to His devotees in the first and second congregations, as a fundamental support for their practice of Ruchira Avatara Bhakti Yoga. For those who have fully adapted to the disciplines of the first and second congregations, the daily practice of meditation includes a period of one and one-half hours in the morning and a period of one hour in the evening. Such daily practice is increased during periods of retreat. Members of the third and fourth congregations are also encouraged (but not required) to engage formal meditation.

missing the mark   "Hamartia" (the word in New Testament Greek that was translated into English as "sin") was originally an archery term meaning "missing the mark".

Most Perfect / Most Ultimate   Avatar Adi Da uses the phrase "Most Perfect(ly)" in the sense of "Absolutely Perfect(ly)". Similarly, the phrase "Most Ultimate(ly)" is equivalent to "Absolutely Ultimate(ly)". "Most Perfect(ly)" and "Most Ultimate(ly)" are always references to the seventh (or Divinely Enlightened) stage of life. Perfect(ly) and Ultimate(ly) refer to the sixth stage of life or to the sixth and seventh stages of life together. (See also **stages of life**.)

mudra   A "mudra" is a gesture of the hands, face, or body that outwardly expresses a state of ecstasy. Avatar Adi Da sometimes spontaneously exhibits Mudras as Signs of His Blessing and Purifying Work with His devotees and the world. He also uses the term "Mudra" to express the Attitude of His Blessing-Work, which is His Constant (or Eternal) Giving (or

Submitting) of Himself to Be the Means of Divine Liberation for all beings.

Muktananda, Swami   See **Lineage, Avatar Adi Da's.**

mummery / *The Mummery*   The dictionary defines mummery as "a ridiculous, hypocritical, or pretentious ceremony or performance". Avatar Adi Da uses this word to describe all the activities of ego-bound beings, or beings who are committed to the false view of separation and separativeness.

The Mummery is one of Avatar Adi Da's twenty-three "Source-Texts". It is a work of astonishing poetry and deeply evocative archetypes. Through the heart-breaking story of Raymond Darling's growth to manhood, his search to find, and then to be reunited with, his beloved (Quandra), and his utter self-transcendence of all conditional circumstances and events, Avatar Adi Da Tells His own Life-Story in the language of parable, and describes in devastating detail how the unconverted ego makes religion (and life altogether) into a meaningless mummery.

Murti   "Murti" is Sanskrit for "form", and, by extension, a "representational image" of the Divine or of a Guru. In the Way of Adidam, Murtis of Avatar Adi Da are most commonly photographs of Avatar Adi Da's bodily (human) Divine Form.

"Murti-Guru"   See **"Living Murti"**.

Mystery   Avatar Adi Da uses the term "the Mystery" to point out that, although we can name things, we actually do not know what anything really <u>is</u>:

It is a great and more-than-wonderful Mystery to everyone that anything <u>is</u>, or that we <u>are</u>. And whether somebody says "I don't know how anything came to be" or "God made everything", they are simply pointing to the feeling of the Mystery—of how everything <u>is</u>, but nobody knows what it really <u>Is</u>, or how it came to be. [What, Where, When, How, Why, and <u>Who</u> To Remember To Be Happy]

N

Name-Invocation Sacred sounds or syllables and Names have been used since antiquity for invoking and worshipping the Divine Person and the Sat-Guru. In the Hindu tradition, the original mantras were cosmic sound-forms and "seed" letters used for worship and prayer of, and incantatory meditation on, the Revealed Form of the Divine Person.

Practitioners of the Way of Adidam may, at any time, Remember or Invoke Avatar Adi Da Samraj (or feel, and thereby Contemplate, His Avatarically Self-Revealed Divine Form, and Presence, and State) through simple feeling-Remembrance of Him and by randomly (in daily life and meditation) Invoking Him via His Principal Name, "Da", or via one (and only one) of the other Names He has Given for the practice of Simple Name-Invocation of Him. (The specific forms of His Names that Avatar Adi Da has Given to be engaged in practice of simple Name-Invocation of Him are listed in chapter three of *The Dawn Horse Testament Of The Ruchira Avatar*.)

For devotees of Avatar Adi Da Samraj, His Names are the Names of the Very Divine Being. As such, these Names, as Avatar Adi Da Himself has described, "do not simply <u>mean</u> Real God, or the Blessing of Real God. They are the verbal or audible Form of the Divine." Therefore, Invoking Avatar Adi Da Samraj by Name is a potent and Divinely Empowered form of feeling-Contemplation of Him.

Narcissus In Avatar Adi Da's Teaching-Revelation, "Narcissus" is a key symbol of the un-Enlightened individual as a self-obsessed seeker, enamored of his or her own self-image and egoic self-consciousness. In *The Knee Of Listening*, Adi Da Samraj describes the significance of the archetype of Narcissus:

He is the ancient one visible in the Greek "myth", who was the universally adored child of the gods, who rejected the loved-one and every form of love and relationship, who was finally condemned to the contemplation of his own image, until, *as a result of his own act and obstinacy, he suffered the fate of eternal separateness and died in infinite solitude.*

Nirguna "Nirguna" is Sanskrit for "without attributes or quality".

Nirvikalpa Samadhi See **Samadhi**.

Nityananda See **Lineage, Avatar Adi Da's**.

Non-Separate Self-Domain The "Non-Separate Self-Domain" is a synonym for "Divine Self-Domain". (See **Divine Self-Domain**.)

O

"Oedipal" In modern psychology, the "Oedipus complex" is named after the legendary Greek Oedipus, who was fated to unknowingly kill his father and marry his mother. Avatar Adi Da Teaches that the primary dynamisms of emotional-sexual desiring, rejection, envy, betrayal, self-pleasuring, resentment, and other primal emotions and impulses are indeed patterned upon unconscious reactions first formed early in life, in relation to one's mother and father. Avatar Adi Da calls this "the 'Oedipal' drama" and points out that we relate to all women as we do to our mothers, and to all men as we do to our fathers, and that we relate, and react, to our own bodies as we do to the parent of the opposite sex. Thus, we impose infantile reactions to our parents on our relationships with lovers and all other beings, according to their sex, and we also superimpose the same on our relationship to our own bodies. (Avatar Adi Da's extended Instruction on "Oedipal" patterning is Given in *Ruchira Avatara Hridaya-Tantra Yoga*.)

"Open Eyes" "Open Eyes" is Avatar Adi Da's technical synonym for the Realization of seventh stage Sahaj Samadhi, or unqualified Divine Self-Realization. The phrase graphically describes the non-exclusive, non-inward, Native State of the Divine Self-Realizer, Who is Identified Unconditionally with the Divine Self-Reality, while also allowing whatever arises to appear in the Divine Consciousness (and spontaneously Divinely Self-Recognizing everything that arises as a modification of the Divine Consciousness). The Transcendental Self is intuited in the mature phases of the sixth stage of life, but It can be Realized at that stage only by the intentional exclusion of conditional phenomena. In "Open Eyes", that impulse to exclusion disappears, when the Eyes of the Heart Open, and Most Perfect Realization of the Spiritual, Transcendental, and Divine Self in the seventh stage of life becomes permanent (and incorruptible by any phenomenal events).

"original" context of the fourth stage of life   See **stages of life**.

Outshined / Outshining   Avatar Adi Da uses "Outshined" or "Outshining" as a synonym for "Divine Translation", to refer to the final Demonstration of the four-phase process of the seventh (or Divinely Enlightened) stage of life in the Way of Adidam. In the Great Event of Outshining (or Divine Translation), body, mind, and world are no longer noticed—not because the Divine Consciousness has withdrawn or dissociated from conditionally manifested phenomena, but because the Divine Self-Recognition of all arising phenomena as modifications of the Divine Self-Condition has become so intense that the "Bright" Radiance of Consciousness now Outshines all such phenomena. (See also **four phases of the seventh stage of life**.)

P, Q

"Perfect Practice"   The "Perfect Practice" is Avatar Adi Da's technical term for the discipline of the ultimate stages of life (the sixth stage of life and the seventh stage of life) in the Way of Adidam. The "Perfect Practice" is practice in the Domain of Consciousness Itself (as opposed to practice from the point of view of the body or the mind). (See also **stages of life**.)

Perfectly Subjective   Avatar Adi Da uses "Perfectly Subjective" to describe the True Divine Source, or "Subject", of the conditionally manifested world—as opposed to regarding the Divine as some sort of conditional "object" or "other". Thus, in the phrase "Perfectly Subjective", the word "Subjective" does not have the sense of "relating to the inward experience of an individual", but, rather, it has the sense of "Being Consciousness Itself, the True Subject of all apparent experience".

Pleasure Dome   Avatar Adi Da Samraj Speaks of the Way of Adidam as a "Pleasure Dome", recalling the poem "Kubla Khan", by Samuel Taylor Coleridge ("In Xanadu did Kubla Khan / A stately pleasure-dome decree . . ."). Adi Da Samraj points out that in many religious traditions it is presumed that one must embrace suffering in order to earn future happiness and pleasure. However, by Calling His devotees to live the Way of Adidam as a Pleasure Dome, Avatar Adi Da Samraj Communicates His Teaching that the Way of heart-Communion with Him is always about present-time Happiness, not about any kind of search to attain Happiness in the future. Thus, in the Way of Adidam, there is no idealization of suffering and pain as presumed means to attain future happiness—and, consequently, there is no denial of the appropriate enjoyment of even the ordinary pleasures of human life.

Avatar Adi Da also uses "Pleasure Dome" as a reference to the Ultimate and Divine Love-Bliss-Happiness That Is His own Self-Nature and His Gift to all who respond to Him.

"Practice"   As the quotation marks around the capitalized word "Practice" suggest, the psycho-physical expression of the process of Divine Enlightenment is a "Practice" only in the sense that it is simple action. It is not, in contrast to the stages of life previous to the seventh, a discipline intended to counter egoic tendencies that would otherwise dominate body and mind.

Avatar Adi Da uses quotation marks in a characteristic manner throughout His Written Word to Indicate that a particular word is a technical term, to be understood in the unique and precise language of the Way of Adidam, carrying the implication "as per definition". However, in other cases, His quotation marks carry the implication "so to speak", as in the case of the term "Practice" and are, therefore, not to be understood as precise technical terminology of the Way of Adidam.

prana/pranic   The Sanskrit word "prana" means "life-energy". It generally refers to the life-energy animating all beings and pervading everything in cosmic Nature. In the human body-mind, circulation of this universal life-energy is associated with the heartbeat and the cycles of the breath. In esoteric Yogic Teachings, prana is also a specific technical name for one of a number of forms of etheric energy that functionally sustain the bodily being.

Prana is not to be equated with the Divine Spirit-Current, or the Spiritual (and Always Blessing) Divine Presence of Avatar Adi Da Samraj. The finite pranic energies that sustain individual beings are only conditional, localized, and temporary phenomena of the realm of cosmic Nature. Even in the form of universal life-force, prana is but a conditional modification of the Divine Spirit-Current Revealed by Avatar Adi Da, Which Is the "Bright" (or Consciousness Itself), beyond all cosmic forms.

R

"radical"   The term "radical" derives from the Latin "radix", meaning "root", and, thus, it principally means "irreducible", "fundamental", or "relating to the origin". In *The Dawn Horse Testament Of The Ruchira Avatar*, Avatar Adi Da defines "Radical" as "Gone To The Root, Core, Source, or Origin". Because Adi Da Samraj uses "radical" in this literal sense, it appears in quotation marks in His Wisdom-Teaching, in order to distinguish His usage from the common reference to an extreme (often political) view.

Ramana Maharshi   A great sixth stage Indian Spiritual Master, Ramana Maharshi (1879-1950) became Self-Realized at a young age and gradually assumed a Teaching role as increasing numbers of people approached him for Spiritual guidance. Ramana Maharshi's Teaching focused on the process of introversion (through the question "Who am I?"), which culminates in conditional Self-Realization (or Jnana Samadhi), exclusive of phenomena. He established his Ashram at Tiruvannamalai in South India, which continues today.

Rang Avadhoot   Rang Avadhoot (1898-1968) was a Realizer in the tradition of Dattatreya. In *The Knee Of Listening*, Avatar Adi Da describes the brief but highly significant meeting that occurred between Himself and Rang Avadhoot in 1968.

Real God   Avatar Adi Da uses the term "Real God" to Indicate the True and Perfectly Subjective Source of all conditions, the True and Spiritual Divine Person (Which can be directly Realized), rather than any ego-made (and, thus, false, or limited) presumptions about God.

Re-cognition   "Re-cognition", which literally means "knowing again", is Avatar Adi Da's term for "the tacit transcending of the habit of 'Narcissus'". It is the mature form into which verbal self-Enquiry evolves in the Devotional Way of Insight. The individual simply notices and tacitly "knows again" (or directly understands) whatever is arising as yet another species of self-contraction, and he or she transcends (or feels beyond) it in Satsang with Avatar Adi Da.

renunciate orders   Avatar Adi Da has established two formal renunciate orders: The Ruchira Sannyasin Order of the Free Renunciates of Ruchiradam (or, simply, the Ruchira Sannyasin Order), and the Lay Renunciate Order of Adidam (or, simply, the Lay Renunciate Order).

The senior practicing order in the Way of Adidam is the Ruchira Sannyasin Order.

This order is the senior cultural authority within the formal gathering of Avatar Adi Da's devotees. "Sannyasin" is an ancient Sanskrit term for one who has renounced all worldly bonds and who gives himself or herself completely to the Real-God-Realizing or Real-God-Realized life. Members of the Ruchira Sannyasin Order are uniquely exemplary practitioners of the Way of Adidam who are (generally) practicing in the context of the ultimate (sixth and seventh) stages of life. Members of this Order are legal renunciates and live a life of perpetual retreat. The Ruchira Sannyasin Order comprises the first congregation of Avatar Adi Da's devotees.

The members of the Ruchira Sannyasin Order have a uniquely significant role among the practitioners of Adidam as Avatar Adi Da's human Instruments and (in the case of those members who are formally acknowledged as Avatar Adi Da's fully Awakened seventh stage devotees) as the body of practitioners from among whom each of Avatar Adi Da's successive "Living Murtis" (or Empowered human Agents) will be selected. Therefore, the Ruchira Sannyasin Order is essential to the perpetual continuation of authentic practice of the Way of Adidam.

The Founding Member of the Ruchira Sannyasin Order is Avatar Adi Da Himself.

In "The Orders of My True and Free Renunciate Devotees" (in *The Lion Sutra*), Avatar Adi Da describes the Lay Renunciate Order as "a renunciate service order for all intensively serving (and, altogether, intensively practicing) lay practitioners of the total (or full and complete) practice of the Way of Adidam".

All present members, and all future members, of the Lay Renunciate Order must (necessarily) be formally acknowledged, formally practicing, significantly matured (tested and proven), and, altogether, exemplary practitioners of the total (or full and complete) practice of the Way of Adidam. They must perform significant cultural (and practical, and, as necessary, managerial) service within the gathering of all formally acknowledged practitioners of the four congregations of the Way of Adidam. Either they must live within a formally designated community of formally acknowledged practitioners of the Way of Adidam or, otherwise, they must be formally designated serving residents of one of the by Me formally Empowered Ruchira Sannyasin Hermitage-Retreat Sanctuaries or one of the by Me formally Empowered Pilgrimage and Retreat Sanctuaries for all formally acknowledged practitioners of the Way of Adidam. And they must formally accept (and rightly fulfill) all the obligations and disciplines associated with membership within the Lay Renunciate Order. ["The Orders of My True and Free Renunciate Devotees"]

right side of the heart　See **heart, stations of the heart**.

Ruchira Avatar　In Sanskrit, "Ruchira" means "bright, radiant, effulgent". Thus, the Reference "Ruchira Avatar" indicates that Avatar Adi Da Samraj is the "Bright" (or Radiant) Descent of the Divine Reality Itself into the conditionally manifested worlds, Appearing here in His bodily (human) Form.

Ruchira Avatara Bhakti Yoga　Ruchira Avatara Bhakti Yoga is the principal Gift, Calling, and Discipline Offered by Adi Da Samraj to all who practice the Way of Adidam (in all four congregations).

The phrase "Ruchira Avatara Bhakti Yoga" is itself a summary of the Way of Adidam. "Bhakti", in Sanskrit, is love, adoration, or devotion, while "Yoga" is a Real-God-Realizing discipline (or practice). "Ruchira Avatara Bhakti Yoga" is, thus, "the Divinely Revealed practice of devotional love for (and devotional response to) the Ruchira Avatar, Adi Da Samraj".

The technical practice of Ruchira Avatara Bhakti Yoga is a four-part process of Invoking, feeling, breathing, and serving Avatar Adi Da in every moment.

For Avatar Adi Da's essential Instruction in Ruchira Avatara Bhakti Yoga, see the *Da Love-Ananda Gita (The Free Gift Of The Divine Love-Bliss)*, Part Five, verse 25, and Part Six; *Hridaya Rosary (Four Thorns Of Heart-Instruction)*, Parts

Four and Five; and *What, Where, When, How, Why and Who To Remember To Be Happy*, Part Three, "Surrender the Faculties of the Body-Mind To Me" and "How to Practice Whole Bodily Devotion To Me".

Ruchira Avatara Satsang   The Hindi word "Satsang" literally means "true (or right) relationship", "the company of Truth". "Ruchira Avatara Satsang" is the eternal relationship of mutual sacred commitment between Avatar Adi Da Samraj and each true and formally acknowledged practitioner of the Way of Adidam. Once it is consciously assumed by any practitioner, Ruchira Avatara Satsang is an all-inclusive Condition, bringing Divine Grace and Blessings and sacred obligations, responsibilities, and tests into every dimension of the practitioner's life and consciousness.

The Ruchira Buddha   The Enlightened One Who Shines with the Divine "Brightness".

The Ruchira Buddha-Avatar   The "Bright" Enlightened One Who is the Incarnation of the Divine Person. (See also **Avatar**.)

Ruchira Buddhism   "Ruchira Buddhism" is the Way of devotion to the Ruchira Buddha—"the 'Bright' Buddha", Avatar Adi Da Samraj (or, more fully, "the Radiant, Shining, 'Bright' Illuminator and Enlightener Who Is Inherently, or Perfectly Subjectively, Self-Enlightened, and Eternally Awake").

Ruchira Samadhi   "Ruchira Samadhi" (Sanskrit for "the Samadhi of the 'Bright'") is one of the references that Avatar Adi Da Samraj uses for the Divinely Enlightened Condition Realized in the seventh stage of life, Which He characterizes as the Unconditional Realization of the Divine "Brightness".

Ruchira Sannyasin Order   See **renunciate orders**, and see also p. 262.

Rudi / Swami Rudrananda   See **Lineage, Avatar Adi Da's**.

S

"Sadhana Years"   In Sanskrit, "Sadhana" means "self-transcending religious or Spiritual practice". Avatar Adi Da's "Sadhana Years" refers to the time from which He began His quest to recover the Truth of Existence (at Columbia College) until His Divine Re-Awakening in 1970. Avatar Adi Da's full description of His "Sadhana Years" is Given in *The Knee Of Listening*.

Saguna   "Saguna" is Sanskrit for "containing (or accompanied by) qualities".

Sahaj   "Sahaj" is Hindi (from Sanskrit "sahaja") for "twin-born", "natural", or "innate". Avatar Adi Da uses the term to indicate the Coincidence (in the case of Divine Self-Realization) of the Inherently Spiritual and Transcendental Divine Reality with conditional reality. Sahaj, therefore, is the Inherent (or Native) and, thus, truly "Natural" State of Being. (See also **Samadhi**.)

Sahaj Samadhi   See **Samadhi**.

sahasrar   In the traditional system of seven chakras, the sahasrar is the highest chakra (or subtle energy center), associated with the crown of the head and beyond. It is described as a thousand-petaled lotus, the terminal of Light to which the Yogic process (of Spiritual ascent through the chakras) aspires.

During His "Sadhana Years", Avatar Adi Da spontaneously experienced what He calls the "severing of the sahasrar". The Spirit-Energy no longer ascended into the crown of the head (and beyond), but rather "fell" into the Heart, and rested as the Witness-Consciousness. It was this experience that directly revealed to Avatar Adi Da that, while the Yogic traditions regard the sahasrar as the seat of Enlightenment, the Heart is truly the Seat of Divine Consciousness.

Avatar Adi Da's account of the severing of the sahasrar in His own Case is Given in chapter eighteen of *The Knee Of Listening*.

Saiva Siddhanta "Saiva Siddhanta" is the name of an important school of Saivism which flourished in South India and survives into the present.

Samadhi The Sanskrit word "Samadhi" traditionally denotes various exalted states that appear in the context of esoteric meditation and Realization. Avatar Adi Da Teaches that, for His devotees, Samadhi is, even more simply and fundamentally, the Enjoyment of His Divine State, Which is experienced (even from the beginning of the practice of Adidam) through ego-transcending heart-Communion with Him. Therefore, "the cultivation of Samadhi" is another way to describe the fundamental basis of the Way of Adidam. Avatar Adi Da's devotee is in Samadhi in any moment of standing beyond the separate self in true devotional heart-Communion with Him. (See "The Cultivation of My Divine Samadhi", in *The Seven Stages Of Life*.)

The developmental process leading to Divine Enlightenment in the Way of Adidam may be marked by many signs, principal among which are the Samadhis of the advanced and the ultimate stages of life and practice. Although some of the traditionally known Samadhis of the fourth, the fifth, and the sixth stages of life may appear in the course of an individual's practice of the Way of Adidam, the appearance of all of them is by no means necessary, or even probable (as Avatar Adi Da Indicates in His Wisdom-Teaching). The essential Samadhis of the Way of Adidam are those that are uniquely Granted by Avatar Adi Da Samraj—the Samadhi of the "Thumbs" and seventh stage Sahaj Samadhi. All the possible forms of Samadhi in the Way of Adidam are described in full detail in *The Dawn Horse Testament Of The Ruchira Avatar*.

Samadhi of the "Thumbs" "The 'Thumbs'" is Avatar Adi Da's technical term for the invasion of the body-mind by a particular kind of forceful Descent of His Divine Spirit-Current. Avatar Adi Da describes His own experience of the "Thumbs" in *The Knee Of Listening*:

. . . I had an experience that appeared like a mass of gigantic thumbs coming down from above, pressing into my throat (causing something of a gagging, and somewhat suffocating, sensation), and then pressing further (and, it seemed, would have expanded without limitation or end), into some form of myself that was much larger than my physical body. . . .

The "Thumbs" were not visible in the ordinary sense. I did not see them then or even as a child. They were not visible to me with my eyes, nor did I hallucinate them pictorially. Yet, I very consciously experienced and felt them as having a peculiar form and mobility, as I likewise experienced my own otherwise invisible and greater form.

I did not at that time or at any time in my childhood fully allow this intervention of the "Thumbs" to take place. I held it off from its fullest descent, in fear of being overwhelmed, for I did not understand at all what was taking place. However, in later years this same experience occurred naturally during meditation. Because my meditation had been allowed to progress gradually, and the realizations at each level were thus perceived without shock, I was able at those times to allow the experience to take place. When I did, the "Thumbs" completely entered my living form. They appeared like tongues, or parts of a Force, coming from above. And when they had entered deep into my body, the magnetic or energic balances of my living being reversed. On several occasions I felt as if the body had risen above the ground somewhat, and this is perhaps the basis for certain evidence in mystical literature of the phenomenon of levitation, or bodily transport.

At any rate, during those stages in meditation the body ceased to be polarized toward the ground, or the gravitational direction of the earth's center. There was a strong reversal of polarity, communicated along a line of Force analogous to the spine. The physical body, as well as the Energy-form that could be interiorly felt as analogous to but detached from the physical body, was felt to turn in a curve along the spine and forward in the direction of the heart. When this reversal of Energy was allowed to take place completely, I resided in a totally different body, which also contained the physical body. It was spherical in shape. And the sensation of dwelling as that form was completely peaceful. The physical body was completely relaxed and polarized to the shape of this other spherical body. The mind became quieted, and then there was a movement in consciousness that would go even deeper, into a higher conscious State beyond physical and mental awareness. I was to learn that this spherical body was what Yogis and occultists call the "subtle" body (which includes the "pranic", or natural life-energy, dimension and the "astral", or the lower mental and the higher mental, dimensions of the living being).

In the fullest form of this experience, which Avatar Adi Da calls "the Samadhi of the 'Thumbs'", His Spirit-Invasion Descends all the way to the bottom of the frontal line of the body-mind (at the bodily base) and ascends through the spinal line, overwhelming the ordinary human sense of bodily existence, infusing the whole being with intense blissfulness, and releasing the ordinary, confined sense of body, mind, and separate self.

Both the experience of the "Thumbs" and the full Samadhi of the "Thumbs" are unique to the Way of Adidam, for they are specifically signs of the "Crashing Down" (or the Divine Descent) of Avatar Adi Da's Spirit-Baptism, into the body-minds of His devotees. The Samadhi of the "Thumbs" is a kind of "Nirvikalpa" (or formless) Samadhi—but in descent in the frontal line, rather than in ascent in the spinal line.

Avatar Adi Da's extended Instruction relative to the "Thumbs" is Given in "The 'Thumbs' Is The Fundamental Sign Of The Crashing Down Of My Person". This Essay appears in a number of Avatar Adi Da's "Source-Texts" (*Hridaya Rosary*, *The Only Complete Way To Realize The Unbroken Light Of Real God*, *Ruchira Avatara Hridaya-Siddha Yoga*, *The Seven Stages Of Life*, and *Santosha Adidam*, as well as chapter twenty-four of *The Dawn Horse Testament Of The Ruchira Avatar* and chapter thirty-one of *The Heart Of The Dawn Horse Testament Of The Ruchira Avatar*).

Savikalpa Samadhi and "Cosmic Consciousness" The Sanskrit term "Savikalpa Samadhi" literally means "meditative ecstasy with form", or "deep meditative concentration (or absorption) in which form (or defined experiential content) is still perceived". Avatar Adi Da indicates that there are two basic forms of Savikalpa Samadhi. The first is the various experiences produced by the Spiritual ascent of energy and attention (into mystical phenomena, visions, and other subtle sensory perceptions of subtle psychic forms) and the various states of Yogic Bliss (or Spirit-"Intoxication").

The second (and highest) form of Savikalpa Samadhi is called "Cosmic Consciousness", or the "'Vision' of Cosmic Unity". This is an isolated or periodic occurrence in which attention ascends, uncharacteristically and spontaneously, to a state of awareness wherein conditional existence is perceived as a Unity in Divine Awareness. This conditional form of "Cosmic Consciousness" is pursued in many mystical and Yogic paths. It depends upon manipulation of attention and the body-mind, and it is interpreted from the point of view of the separate, body-based or mind-based self—and, therefore, it is not equivalent to Divine Enlightenment.

Avatar Adi Da's discussion of Savikalpa Samadhi is found in "Vision, Audition, and Touch in The Process of Ascending Meditation in The Way Of Adidam", in Part Four of *Ruchira Avatara Hridaya-Siddha Yoga*.

Avatar Adi Da's description of the varieties of experiential form possible in Savikalpa Samadhi is found in "The Significant Experiential Signs That May Appear in the Course of The Way Of Adidam", in Part Three of *What, Where, When, How, Why, and Who To Remember To Be Happy*.

fifth stage Nirvikalpa Samadhi The Sanskrit term "Nirvikalpa Samadhi" literally means "meditative ecstasy without form", or "deep meditative concentration (or absorption) in which there is no perception of form (or defined experiential content)". Traditionally, this state is regarded to be the final goal of the many schools of Yogic ascent whose orientation to practice is that of the fifth stage of life. Like "Cosmic Consciousness", fifth stage conditional Nirvikalpa Samadhi is an isolated or periodic Realization. In it, attention ascends beyond all conditional manifestation into the formless Matrix of Divine Vibration and Divine Light Infinitely Above the world, the body, and the mind. And, like the various forms of Savikalpa Samadhi, fifth stage conditional Nirvikalpa Samadhi is a temporary state of attention (or, more precisely, of the suspension of attention). It is produced by manipulation of attention and of the body-mind, and is (therefore) incapable of being maintained when attention returns (as it inevitably does) to the states of the body-mind.

Avatar Adi Da's Instruction relative to fifth stage conditional Nirvikalpa Samadhi is Given in chapter forty-two of *The Dawn Horse Testament Of The Ruchira Avatar.*

Jnana Samadhi, or Jnana Nirvikalpa Samadhi   "Jnana" means "knowledge". Jnana Nirvikalpa Samadhi (sixth stage Nirvakalpa Samadhi, or, simply, Jnana Samadhi) is the characteristic meditative experience in the sixth stage of life in the Way of Adidam. Produced by the intentional withdrawal of attention from the conditional body-mind-self and its relations, Jnana Samadhi is the conditional, temporary Realization of the Transcendental Self (or Consciousness Itself), exclusive of any perception (or cognition) of world, objects, relations, body, mind, or separate-self-sense—and, thereby, formless (or "nirvikalpa").

Avatar Adi Da's Instruction relative to Jnana Nirvikalpa Samadhi is Given in "The Sixth and The Seventh Stages of Life in The Way Of Adidam" in *The Lion Sutra.*

seventh stage Sahaj Samadhi, or seventh stage Sahaja Nirvikalpa Samadhi Avatar Adi Da's description of seventh stage Sahaj Samadhi is Given in Part Four of *The <u>All-Completing</u> and <u>Final</u> Divine Revelation To Mankind.*

Samraj   "Samraj" (from the Sanskrit "Samraja") is a traditional Indian term used to refer to great kings, but also to refer to the Hindu gods. "Samraja" is defined as "universal or supreme ruler", "paramount Lord", or "paramount sovereign".

The Sanskrit word "raja" (the basic root of "Samraj") means "king". It comes from the verbal root "raj", meaning "to reign, to rule, to illuminate". The prefix "sam-" expresses "union" or "completeness". "Samraj" is thus literally the complete ruler, the ruler of everything altogether. "Samraj" was traditionally given as a title to a king who was regarded to be a "universal monarch".

Avatar Adi Da's Name "Adi Da Samraj" expresses that He is the Primordial (or Original) Giver, Who Blesses all as the Universal Lord of every thing, every where, for all time. The Sovereignty of His Kingdom has nothing to do with the world of human politics. Rather, it is entirely a matter of His Spiritual Dominion over all and All, His Kingship in the hearts of His devotees.

samsara / samsaric   "Samsara" (or "samsaric") is a classical Buddhist and Hindu term for all conditional worlds and states, or the cyclical realm of birth and change and death. It connotes the suffering and limitations experienced in those limited worlds.

Sanctuaries   As of this writing (2001), Avatar Adi Da has Empowered five Sanctuaries as Agents of His Divine Spiritual Transmission:

- Adidam Samrajashram is the Island of Naitauba in Fiji. It was the principal site of Avatar Adi Da's Teaching and Revelation Work from 1983 to 1999. Avatar Adi Da has acknowledged that, because of the intensity of His Spiritual Work there (especially during the early months of 1999, as described in *The Light Is On!*), Adidam Samrajashram is the primary Seat from which His Divine Spiritual Blessing Flows to the entire world.

• The Mountain Of Attention Sanctuary, in northern California, was the principal site of Avatar Adi Da's Teaching Work from 1974 to the early 1980s.

• Da Love-Ananda Mahal, in Hawaii, was (together with the Mountain Of Attention) the principal site of Avatar Adi Da's Teaching Work in the early 1980s.

• Tat Sundaram and Love's Point Hermitage in northern California are small Hermitage-Retreat Sanctuaries that provide a private circumstance for Avatar Adi Da and members of the Ruchira Sannyasin Order.

Especially since 1995, Avatar Adi Da Samraj has Freely Moved among the various Sanctuaries, in His spontaneous Wandering-Work of world-Blessing. Devotees of Avatar Adi Da are invited to spend periods of retreat at the larger Sanctuaries. Through His years of Blessing-Infusion of each of these five Sanctuaries, He has fully Empowered them for His devotees throughout all time.

Santosha   "Santosha" is Sanskrit for "satisfaction" or "contentment"—qualities associated with a sense of completion. These qualities are characteristic of no-seeking, the fundamental Principle of Avatar Adi Da's Wisdom-Teaching and of His entire Revelation of Truth. Because of its uniquely appropriate meanings, "Santosha" is one of Avatar Adi Da's Names. As Santosha Adi Da, Avatar Adi Da Samraj is the Divine Giver of Perfect Divine Contentedness, or Perfect Searchlessness.

Santosha Avatar   As the Santosha Avatar, Avatar Adi Da is the Very Incarnation of Perfect Divine Contentedness, or Perfect Searchlessness.

Sat-Guru   "Sat" means "Truth", "Being", "Existence". Thus, "Sat-Guru" literally means "True Guru", or a Guru who can lead living beings from darkness (or non-Truth) into Light (or the Living Truth).

Satsang   The Hindi word "Satsang" (from the Sanskrit "Satsanga") literally means "true (or right) relationship", "the company of Truth". In the Way of Adidam, Satsang is the eternal relationship of mutual sacred commitment between Avatar Adi Da Samraj and each formally acknowledged practitioner of the Way of Adidam.

Savikalpa Samadhi   See **Samadhi**.

scientific materialism   Scientific materialism is the predominant philosophy and worldview of modern humanity, the basic presumption of which is that the material world is all that exists. In scientific materialism, the method of science, or the observation of objective phenomena, is made into philosophy and a way of life that suppresses our native impulse to Liberation.

seeing   See **listening, hearing, and seeing**.

self-Enquiry   The practice of self-Enquiry in the form "Avoiding relationship?", unique to the Way of Adidam, was spontaneously developed by Avatar Adi Da in the course of His own Ordeal of Divine Re-Awakening. Intense persistence in the "radical" discipline of this unique form of self-Enquiry led rapidly to Avatar Adi Da's Divine Enlightenment (or Most Perfect Divine Self-Realization) in 1970.

The practice of self-Enquiry in the form "Avoiding relationship?" and the practice of non-verbal Re-cognition are the principal technical practices that serve feeling-Contemplation of Avatar Adi Da in the Devotional Way of Insight.

Self-Existing and Self-Radiant   Avatar Adi Da uses "Self-Existing and Self-Radiant" to indicate the two fundamental aspects of the One Divine Person (or Reality)—Existence (or Being, or Consciousness) Itself, and Radiance (or Energy, or Light) Itself.

seven stages of life See **stages of life**.

Shakti, Guru-Shakti "Shakti" is a Sanskrit term for the Divinely Manifesting Energy, Spiritual Power, or Spirit-Current of the Divine Person. Guru-Shakti is the Power of the Guru to Liberate his or her devotees.

Shaktipat In Hindi, "shaktipat" is the "descent of Spiritual Power". Yogic Shaktipat, which manipulates natural, conditional energies or partial manifestations of the Spirit-Current, is typically granted through touch, word, glance, or regard by Yogic Adepts in the fifth stage of life, or fourth to fifth stages of life. Yogic Shaktipat must be distinguished from (and, otherwise, understood to be only a secondary aspect of) the Blessing Transmission of the Heart Itself (Hridaya-Shaktipat), which is uniquely Given by Avatar Adi Da Samraj.

Siddha, Siddha-Guru "Siddha" is Sanskrit for "a completed, fulfilled, or perfected one", or "one of perfect accomplishment, or power". Avatar Adi Da uses "Siddha", or "Siddha-Guru", to mean a Transmission-Master who is a Realizer (to any significant degree) of Real God, Truth, or Reality.

Siddha Yoga "Siddha Yoga" is, literally, "the Yoga of the Perfected One[s]".

Swami Muktananda used the term "Siddha Yoga" to refer to the form of Kundalini Yoga that he taught, which involved initiation of the devotee by the Guru's Transmission of Shakti (or Spiritual Energy). Avatar Adi Da Samraj has indicated that this was a fifth stage form of Siddha Yoga.

In "I (Alone) _Am_ The Adidam Revelation", Avatar Adi Da Says:

> . . . I Teach Siddha Yoga in the Mode and Manner of the _seventh_ stage of life (as Ruchira Avatara Hridaya-Siddha Yoga, or Ruchira Avatara Maha-Jnana Hridaya-Shaktipat Yoga)—and always toward (or to the degree of) the Realization inherently associated with (and, at last, Most Perfectly Demonstrated and Proven by) the only-by-Me Revealed and Given seventh

> stage of life, and as a practice and a Process that progressively includes (and, coincidently, _directly_ transcends) _all_ _six_ of the phenomenal and developmental (and, necessarily, yet ego-based) stages of life that precede the seventh.

Avatar Adi Da's description of the similarities and differences between traditional Siddha Yoga and the Way of Adidam is Given in "I (Alone) _Am_ The Adidam Revelation", which Essay appears in many of Avatar Adi Da's twenty-three "Source-Texts".

siddhi "Siddhi" is Sanskrit for "power", or "accomplishment". When capitalized in Avatar Adi Da's Wisdom-Teaching, "Siddhi" is the Spiritual, Transcendental, and Divine Awakening-Power That He spontaneously and effortlessly Transmits to all.

"Sila" "Sila" is a Pali Buddhist term meaning "habit", "behavior", "conduct", or "morality". It connotes the restraint of outgoing energy and attention, the disposition of equanimity, or free energy and attention for the Spiritual Process.

"simpler" (or "simplest") form of the Way of Adidam See **forms of practice in the Way of Adidam**.

sleeping See **waking, dreaming, and sleeping**.

"Source-Texts" During the twenty-seven years of His Teaching-Work and Revelation-Work (from 1972 to 1999), Avatar Adi Da elaborately described every aspect of the practice of Adidam, from the beginning of one's approach to Him to the Most Ultimate Realization of the seventh stage of life.

Avatar Adi Da's Heart-Word is summarized in His twenty-three "Source-Texts". These Texts present, in complete and conclusive detail, His Divine Revelations, Confessions, and Instructions, which are the fruits of His years of Teaching and Revelation Work. In addition to this "Source-Literature", Avatar Adi Da's Heart-Word also includes His "Supportive Texts" (comprising His practical Instruction in all the details of the practice of Adidam, including the fundamental disciplines of diet, health, exercise, sexuality, childrearing, and cooperative community), His "Early Literature" (Written during His Teaching Years), and collections of His Talks. (For a complete list of Avatar Adi Da's twenty-three "Source-Texts", see pp. 327-34.)

spinal line, spinal Yoga The spinal (or ascending) line of the body-mind conducts the Spirit-Current of Divine Life in an upward direction from the base of the body (or perineal area) to the crown of the head, and beyond.

In the Way of Adidam, the spinal Yoga is the process whereby knots and obstructions in the subtle, astral, or the more mentally and subtly oriented dimension of the body-mind are penetrated, opened, surrendered, and released through the devotee's reception and "conductivity" of Avatar Adi Da's Transmission into the spinal line of the body-mind. This ascending Yoga will be required for practitioners of Adidam only in relatively rare cases. The great majority of Avatar Adi Da's devotees will be sufficiently purified through their practice of the frontal Yoga to proceed directly to practice in the context of the sixth stage of life, bypassing practice in the context of the "advanced" fourth stage and the fifth stage of life.

Spirit-Baptism Avatar Adi Da often refers to His Transmission of Spiritual Blessing as His "Spirit-Baptism". It is often felt by His devotee as a Current descending in the frontal line and ascending in the spinal line. However, Avatar Adi Da's Spirit-Baptism is fundamentally and primarily His Moveless Transmission of the Divine Heart Itself. As a secondary effect, His Spirit-Baptism serves to purify, balance, and energize the entire body-mind of the devotee who is prepared to receive It.

Spiritual anatomy / esoteric anatomy Avatar Adi Da Samraj has Revealed that just as there is a physical anatomy, there is an actual Spiritual anatomy, or structure, that is present in every human being. As He Says in *The Basket Of Tolerance*, it is

because of this structure that the "experiential and developmental process of Growth and Realization demonstrates itself in accordance with what I have Revealed and Demonstrated to be the seven stages of life".

Avatar Adi Da's extended Instruction relative to the Spiritual anatomy of Man is Given in *The Seven Stages Of Life* and *Santosha Adidam*.

Spiritual, Transcendental, Divine Avatar Adi Da uses the words "Spiritual", "Transcendental", and "Divine" in reference to dimensions of Reality that are Realized progressively in the Way of Adidam. "Transcendental" and "Spiritual" indicate two fundamental aspects of the One Divine Reality and Person—Consciousness Itself (Which Is Transcendental, or Self-Existing) and Energy Itself (Which Is Spiritual, or Self-Radiant). Only That Which Is Divine is simultaneously Transcendental and Spiritual.

Sri "Sri" is a term of honor and veneration often applied to an Adept. The word literally means "flame" in Sanskrit, indicating that the one honored is radiant with Blessing Power.

stages of life Avatar Adi Da has Revealed the underlying structure of human growth in seven stages. The seventh stage of life is Divine Self-Realization, or Most Perfect Enlightenment.

The first three stages of life develop, respectively, the physical, emotional, and mental/volitional functions of the body-mind. The first stage begins at birth and continues for approximately five to seven years; the second stage follows, continuing until approximately the age of twelve to fourteen; and the third stage is optimally complete by the early twenties. In the case of virtually all individuals, however, failed adaptation in the earlier stages of life means that maturity in the third stage of life takes much longer to attain, and it is usually never fulfilled, with the result that the ensuing stages of Spiritual development do not even begin.

In the Way of Adidam, however, growth in the first three stages of life unfolds in the Spiritual Company of Avatar Adi Da and is based in the practice of feeling-Contemplation of His bodily (human) Form and in devotion, service, and self-discipline in relation to His bodily (human) Form. By the Grace of this relationship to Avatar Adi Da, the first three (or foundation) stages of life are lived and fulfilled in an ego-transcending devotional disposition, or (as He describes it) "in the 'original' (or beginner's) devotional context of the fourth stage of life".

The fourth stage of life is the transitional stage between the gross (bodily-based) point of view of the first three stages of life and the subtle (mind-based, or psyche-based) point of view of the fifth stage of life. The fourth stage of life is the stage of Spiritual devotion, or devotional surrender of separate self to the Divine, in which the gross functions of the being are aligned to the higher psychic (or subtle) functions of the being. In the fourth stage of life, the gross (or bodily-based) personality of the first three stages of life is purified through reception of the Spiritual Force ("Holy Spirit", or "Shakti") of the Divine Reality, which prepares the being to out-grow the bodily-based point of view.

In the Way of Adidam, as the orientation of the fourth stage of life matures, heart-felt surrender to the bodily (human) Form of Avatar Adi Da deepens by His Grace, Drawing His devotee into Love-Communion with His All-Pervading Spiritual Presence. Growth in the "basic" context of the fourth stage of life in the Way of Adidam is also characterized by reception of Avatar Adi Da's Baptizing Current of Divine Spirit-Energy, Which is initially felt to flow down the front of the body from Infinitely Above the head to the bodily base (or perineal area).

The Descent of Avatar Adi Da's Spirit-Baptism releases obstructions predominantly in what He calls the "frontal personality", or the personality typically animated in the waking state (as opposed to the dream state and the state of deep sleep). This Spirit-Baptism purifies His devotee and infuses the devotee with His Spirit-Power. Avatar Adi Da's devotee is, thus, awakened to profound love of (and devotional intimacy with) Him.

Eventually, Avatar Adi Da's Divine Spirit-Current may be felt to turn about at the bodily base and ascend up the spine to the brain core. In this case, the fourth stage of life matures to its "advanced" context, which is focused in the Ascent of Avatar Adi Da's Spirit-Baptism and the consequent purification of the spinal line of the body-mind.

In the fifth stage of life, attention is concentrated in the subtle (or psychic) levels of awareness in ascent. Avatar Adi Da's Divine Spirit-Current is felt to penetrate the brain core and rise toward the Matrix of Light and Love-Bliss Infinitely Above the crown of the head, possibly culminating in the temporary experience of fifth stage conditional Nirvikalpa Samadhi, or "formless ecstasy". In the Way of Adidam, most practitioners will not need to practice either in the "advanced" context of the fourth stage of life or in the context of the fifth stage of life, but will (rather) be Awakened, by Avatar Adi Da's Grace, directly from maturity in the fourth stage of life to the Witness-Position of Consciousness (in the context of the sixth stage of life).

In the traditional development of the sixth stage of life, a strategic effort is made to Identify with Consciousness Itself by excluding the realm of conditional phenomena. Avatar Adi Da Teaches, however, that the deliberate intention to exclude the conditional world for the sake of Realizing Transcendental Consciousness is an egoic error that must be transcended by His devotees who are practicing in the context of the sixth stage of life.

In deepest meditation in the sixth stage of life in the Way of Adidam, the knot of attention (which is the root-action of egoity, felt as separation, self-contraction, or the feeling of relatedness) dissolves, and all sense of relatedness yields to the Blissful and undifferentiated Feeling of Being. The characteristic Samadhi of the sixth stage of life is Jnana Samadhi, the temporary Realization of the Transcendental Self (or Consciousness Itself)—which is temporary because it can occur only when awareness of the world is excluded in meditation.

The transition from the sixth stage of life to the seventh stage Realization of Absolute Non-Separateness is the unique Revelation of Avatar Adi Da. Various traditions and individuals previous to Adi Da's Revelation have had sixth stage intuitions (or premonitions) of the Most Perfect seventh stage Realization, but no one previous to Avatar Adi Da has Realized the seventh stage of life.

The seventh stage Realization is a Gift of Avatar Adi Da to His devotees who have (by His Divine Grace) completed their practice of the Way of Adidam in the context of the first six stages of life. The seventh stage of life begins when His devotee Gracefully Awakens from the exclusive Realization of Consciousness to Most Perfect and Permanent Identification with Consciousness Itself, Avatar Adi Da's Divine State. This is Divine Self-Realization, or Divine Enlightenment, the perpetual Samadhi of "Open Eyes" (seventh stage Sahaj Samadhi)—in which all "things" are Divinely Self-Recognized without "difference", as merely apparent modifications of the One Self-Existing and Self-Radiant Divine Consciousness.

Avatar Adi Da uses a number of terms as synonyms for seventh stage Realization. The principal such terms are:

Divine Awakening
Divine Enlightenment
Divine Liberation
Divine Self-Realization
Most Perfect Real-God-Realization

All of these terms refer to the same Most Perfect Realization of the seventh stage of life, with each term expressing a particular Quality of that Realization. In order to explicitly indicate seventh stage Realization, the phrase "Real-God-Realization" must be preceded by "Most Perfect". (Without "Most Perfect", "Real-God-Realization" is a more general term, referring to Realization in the context of the fourth, fifth, sixth, or seventh stage of life.) "Divine Awakening", "Divine Enlightenment", "Divine Liberation", and "Divine Self-Realization" may also be preceded by "Most Perfect"—but, in the case of these phrases, the addition of "Most Perfect" does not change the meaning but simply intensifies it.

In the course of the seventh stage of life, there may be spontaneous incidents in which psycho-physical states and phenomena do not appear to the notice, being Outshined by the "Bright" Radiance of Consciousness Itself. This Samadhi, Which is the Ultimate Realization of Divine Existence, culminates in Divine Translation, or the permanent Outshining of all apparent conditions in the Inherently Perfect Radiance and Love-Bliss of the Divine Self-Condition (which necessarily coincides with the physical death of the body-mind).

In the context of practice of the Way of Adidam, the seven stages of life as Revealed by Avatar Adi Da are not a version of the traditional "ladder" of Spiritual attainment. These stages and their characteristic signs arise naturally in the course of practice for a fully practicing devotee in the Way of Adidam, but the practice itself is oriented to the transcending of the first six stages of life, in the seventh stage Disposition of Inherently Liberated Happiness, Granted by Avatar Adi Da's Divine Grace in His Love-Blissful Spiritual Company.

Avatar Adi Da's extended Instruction relative to the seven stages of life is Given in *The Seven Stages Of Life*.

Star Form   Avatar Adi Da has Revealed that He is "Incarnated" in the Cosmic domain as a brilliant white five-pointed Star, the original (and primal) conditional visible Representation (or Sign) of the "Bright" (the Source-Energy, or Divine Light, of Which all conditional phenomena and the total cosmos are modifications).

The apparently objective Divine Star can potentially be experienced in any moment and location in cosmic Nature. However, the vision of the Divine Star is not a necessary experience for growth in the Spiritual Process or for Divine Self-Realization.

Avatar Adi Da's discussion of His Star Form is found in *He-and-She Is Me*.

student-novice / student-beginner
A student-novice is an individual who is formally approaching, and preparing to become a formal practitioner of, the total practice of the Way of Adidam (as a

member of the second congregation). The student-novice makes a vow of eternal commitment to Avatar Adi Da as his or her Divine Guru, and to the practice He has Given, and is initiated into simple devotional and sacramental disciplines in formal relationship to Avatar Adi Da. During the student-novice stage, the individual engages in intensive study of Avatar Adi Da's Wisdom-Teaching and adapts to the functional, practical, relational, and cultural disciplines of the Way of Adidam.

A student-beginner is a practitioner in the initial developmental stage of the second congregation of Adidam. In the course of student-beginner practice, the devotee of Avatar Adi Da, on the basis of the eternal "Bond" of devotion to Him that he or she established as a student-novice, continues the process of listening and further adaptation to the disciplines that were begun in the student-novice stage of approach.

subtle   See **gross, subtle, causal**.

"Supportive Texts"   Among Avatar Adi Da's "Supportive Texts" are included such books as *Conscious Exercise and the Transcendental Sun*, *The Eating Gorilla Comes in Peace*, *Love of the Two-Armed Form*, and *Easy Death*.

Swami   The title "Swami" is traditionally given to an individual who has demonstrated significant self-mastery in the context of a lifetime dedicated to Spiritual renunciation.

Swami Muktananda   See **Lineage, Avatar Adi Da's**.

Swami Nityananda   See **Lineage, Avatar Adi Da's**.

Swami Rudrananda   See **Lineage, Avatar Adi Da's**.

T

Tail of the Horse   Adi Da Samraj has often referred to a passage from the ancient Indian text *Satapatha Brahmana*, which He has paraphrased as: "Man does not know. Only the Horse Knows. Therefore, hold to the tail of the Horse." Adi Da has Revealed that, in the most esoteric understanding of this saying, the "Horse" represents the Adept-Realizer, and "holding to the tail of the Horse" represents the devotee's complete dependence on the Adept-Realizer in order to Realize Real God (or Truth, or Reality).

"talking" school   "'Talking' school" is a phrase used by Avatar Adi Da to refer to those in any tradition of sacred life whose approach is characterized by talking, thinking, reading, and philosophical analysis and debate, or even meditative enquiry or reflection, without a concomitant and foundation discipline of body, emotion, mind, and breath. He contrasts the "talking" school with the "practicing" school approach—"practicing" schools involving those who are committed to the ordeal of real ego-transcending discipline, under the guidance of a true Guru.

Tat Sundaram   "Sundara" is the Sanskrit word for "beauty", and "Sundaram" means "something which is beautiful". "Tat" is the Sanskrit word for "it" or "that". Thus, "Tat Sundaram" means "That Which Is Beautiful" or, by extension, "All Of This Is Beautiful", and is a reference to the seventh stage Realization of the Perfect Non-Separateness and Love-Bliss-Nature of the entire world—conditional and Un-Conditional. Tat Sundaram is also the name of the Hermitage-Retreat Sanctuary reserved for Avatar Adi Da in northern California.

Teaching-Work   For a description of Avatar Adi Da's Divine Teaching-Work, see pp. 16-25.

technically "fully elaborated" practice   See **forms of practice in the Way of Adidam**.

technically "simpler" (and even "simplest") practice   See **forms of practice in the Way of Adidam**.

three stations of the heart   See **heart, stations of the heart**.

the "Thumbs" See **Samadhi**.

Thunder The Divine Sound of Thunder (which Avatar Adi Da also describes as the "Da" Sound, or "Da-Om" Sound, or "Om" Sound) is one of Avatar Adi Da's three Eternal Forms of Manifestation in the conditional worlds—together with His Divine Star of Light and His Divine Spiritual Body.

Avatar Adi Da's principal Revelation-Confession about these three forms of His Manifestation is Given in *He-and-She Is Me*.

. . . I Am conditionally Manifested (First) As The everywhere Apparently Audible (and Apparently Objective) Divine Sound-Vibration (or "Da" Sound, or "Da-Om" Sound, or "Om" Sound, The Objective Sign Of The He, Present As The Conscious Sound Of sounds, In The Center Of The Cosmic Mandala), and As The everywhere Apparently Visible (and Apparently Objective) Divine Star (The Objective Sign Of The She, Present As The Conscious Light Of lights, In The Center Of The Cosmic Mandala), and (From That He and She) As The everywhere Apparently Touchable (or Tangible), and Apparently Objective, Total Divine Spiritual Body (The Objective, and All-and-all-Surrounding, and All-and-all-Pervading Conscious and Me-Personal Body Of "Bright" Love-Bliss-Presence, Divinely Self-"Emerging", Now, and Forever Hereafter, From The Center Of The Cosmic Mandala Into The Depths Of Even every "where" In The Cosmic Domain) . . . .

total practice of the Way of Adidam The total practice of the Way of Adidam is the full and complete practice of the Way that Avatar Adi Da Samraj has Given to His devotees who are formal members of the first or the second congregation of Adidam (see pp. 257-62). One who embraces the total practice of the Way of Adidam conforms every aspect of his or her life and being to Avatar Adi Da's Divine Word of Instruction. Therefore, it is only such devotees (in the first or the second congregation of Adidam) who have the potential of Realizing Divine Enlightenment.

"True Prayer" "True Prayer" is Avatar Adi Da's technical term for the various forms of the "conscious process" that are practiced by His Spiritually Awakened devotees who have chosen the Devotional Way of Faith.

Avatar Adi Da's full Instruction relative to "True Prayer" is Given in *The Dawn Horse Testament Of The Ruchira Avatar*.

Turaga "Turaga" (Too-RAHNG-ah) is Fijian for "Lord".

"turiya", "turiyatita" Terms used in the Hindu philosophical systems. Traditionally, "turiya" means "the fourth state" (beyond waking, dreaming, and sleeping), and "turiyatita" means "the state beyond the fourth", or beyond all states.

Avatar Adi Da, however, has given these terms different meanings in the context of the Way of Adidam. He uses the term "turiya" to indicate the Awakening to Consciousness Itself (in the context of the sixth stage of life), and "turiyatita" as the State of Most Perfect Divine Enlightenment, or the Realization of all arising as transparent and non-binding modifications of the One Divine Reality (in the context of the seventh stage of life).

U

ultimate See **the advanced and the ultimate stages of life**.

Ultimate Self-Domain "Ultimate Self-Domain" is a synonym for "Divine Self-Domain". (See **Divine Self-Domain**.)

Ultimate Source-Condition The Divine Reality prior to all conditional arising, which is, therefore, the "Source" of all conditional worlds, beings, and things.

V

Vira-Yogi Sanskrit for "Hero-Yogi". (See **"Heroic"**.)

Vow For a description of the Vow and responsibilities associated with the Way of Adidam, see pp. 256-67.

W, X, Y, Z

waking, dreaming, and sleeping
These three states of consciousness are associated with the dimensions of cosmic existence.

The waking state (and the physical body) is associated with the gross dimension.

The dreaming state (and visionary, mystical, and Yogic Spiritual processes) is associated with the subtle dimension. The subtle dimension, which is senior to the gross dimension, includes the etheric (or energic), lower mental (or verbal-intentional and lower psychic), and higher mental (or deeper psychic, mystical, and discriminative) functions.

The sleeping state is associated with the causal dimension, which is senior to both the gross and the subtle dimensions. It is the root of attention, prior to any particular experience. (See also **gross, subtle, causal**.)

washing the dog Avatar Adi Da uses the metaphor of the "dog" and "washing the dog" to Indicate the purification of the body-mind in the process of Adidam. He addresses the presumption (as in the Kundalini Yoga tradition) that the Spiritual process requires a spinal Yoga, or an effort of arousing Spiritual Energy literally at the "tail" end of the "dog" (the bodily base, or the muladhara chakra), and then drawing It up (or allowing It to ascend) through the spinal line to the head (and above). In contrast, Avatar Adi Da Samraj has Revealed (particularly in His *Hridaya Rosary*) that, in reality, the human being can be truly purified and Liberated (or the "dog" can be "washed") only by receiving His Divine Blessing-Power (or Hridaya-Shakti) and Spiritual Person downward from Infinitely Above the head to the bodily base. This Process of downward reception of Avatar Adi Da is what He calls the "frontal Yoga", because it occurs in the frontal line of the body (which is a natural pathway of descending energy, down the front of the body, from the crown of the head to the bodily base). This necessary descending Yoga of the frontal line, once completed, is sufficient to purify and

Spiritually Infuse the body-mind, and, in most cases, it allows the practitioner of the Way of Adidam to bypass the ascending Yoga of the spinal line (which is the complementary natural pathway of ascending energy, up the back of the body, from the bodily base to the crown of the head). The frontal line and the spinal line are the two arcs of the continuous energy-circuit that Avatar Adi Da calls the "Circle" of the body-mind.

AVATAR ADI DA SAMRAJ: You wash a dog from the head to the tail. But somehow or other, egos looking to Realize think they can wash the "dog" from the "tail" toward the head by doing spinal Yoga. But, in Truth, and in Reality, only the frontal Yoga can accomplish most perfect Divine Self-Realization, because it begins from the superior position, from the "head" position, from My Crashing Down.

The heart-disposition is magnified by My Crashing Down in your devotional Communion with Me. And the vital, grosser dimensions of the being are purified by this washing from the head toward the "tail". If the Process had to begin from the bodily base up, it would be very difficult, very traumatizing—and, ultimately, impossible. The "dog" is washed, simply and very directly, by your participation in My Divine Descent, by your participation in this frontal Yoga. I am Speaking now of the Spiritually Awakened stages, basically. But, even in the case of beginning practitioners in the Way of Adidam—not yet Spiritually Awakened, not yet responsible for the truly Spiritual dimension of their relationship to Me—this "wash" is, by Means of My Avataric Divine Grace, going on.

Therefore, Spiritual life need not be a traumatic course. The "dog" should enjoy being bathed. Nice gentle little guy, happy to be rubbed and touched. You talk to him, struggle a little bit, but you gentle him down. That is how it should work. And, at the end of it, the "dog" sort of "wags its tail", shakes the water off—nice and clean, happy, your best friend. That is how it should work.

If you wash the "dog" from the "tail" up, you smear the shit from his backside toward his head. Basically, that "washing

from the tail toward the head" is a self-generated, self-"guruing" kind of effort. The Divine Process can only occur by Means of Divine Grace. Even the word "Shaktipat" means the "Descent (pat) of Divine Force (Shakti)". But Shaktipat as it appears in the traditions is basically associated with admonitions to practice a spinal Yoga, moving from the base up. In Truth, the Divine Yoga in My Company is a Descent—washing the "dog" from head to "tail" rather than giving the "dog" a "bone", letting it wash itself from the "tail" to the head.

DEVOTEE: It is only Your Hridaya-Shakti that does it.

AVATAR ADI DA SAMRAJ: This is why you must invest yourself in Me. And that is how the "dog" gets washed. [August 13, 1995]

Avatar Adi Da's extended Discourse relative to "washing the dog" is "Be Washed, From Head to Tail, By Heart-Devotion To Me", in *Hridaya Rosary*.

Way of "Radical" Understanding

Avatar Adi Da uses "understanding" to mean "the process of transcending egoity". Thus, to "understand" is to simultaneously observe the activity of the self-contraction and to surrender that activity via devotional resort to Avatar Adi Da Samraj.

Avatar Adi Da has Revealed that, despite their intention to Realize Reality (or Truth, or Real God), all religious and Spiritual traditions (other than the Way of Adidam) are involved, in one manner or another, with the search to satisfy the ego. Only Avatar Adi Da has Revealed the Way to "radically" understand the ego and (in due course, through intensive formal practice of the Way of Adidam, as His formally acknowledged devotee) to most perfectly transcend the ego. Thus, the Way Avatar Adi Da has Given is the "Way of 'Radical' Understanding".

Witness, Witness-Consciousness, Witness-Position

When Consciousness is free of identification with the body-mind, it takes up its natural "position" as the Conscious Witness of all that arises to and in and as the body-mind.

In the Way of Adidam, the stable Realization of the Witness-Position is associated with, or demonstrated via, the effortless surrender (or relaxation) of all the forms of seeking and all the motives of attention that characterize the first five stages of life. However, identification with the Witness-Position is not final (or Most Perfect) Realization of the Divine Self. Rather, it is the first of the three stages of the "Perfect Practice" in the Way of Adidam, which Practice, in due course, Realizes, by Avatar Adi Da's Grace, complete and irreversible and utterly Love-Blissful Identification with Consciousness Itself.

Avatar Adi Da's extended Instruction relative to the Witness is Given in *The Lion Sutra*.

Yoga

"Yoga", in Sanskrit, is literally "yoking", or "union", usually referring to any discipline or process whereby an aspirant attempts to unite with God. Avatar Adi Da acknowledges this conventional and traditional use of the term, but also, in reference to the Great Yoga of Adidam, employs it in a "radical" sense, free of the usual implication of egoic separation and seeking.

Yogananda, Paramahansa

Paramahansa Yogananda (Mukunda Lal Ghosh, 1893-1952) was born in Bengal, the child of devout Hindu parents. As a young man, Yogananda found his Guru, Swami Yukteswar Giri, who initiated him into an order of formal renunciates. In 1920, Yogananda traveled to America to attend an international conference of religions in Boston. Subsequently he settled in the United States, attracting many American devotees. He Taught "Kriya Yoga", a system of practice that had been passed down to him by his own Teacher and that had originally been developed from traditional techniques of Kundalini Yoga. Yogananda became widely known through the publication of his life-story, *Autobiography of a Yogi*.

The Sacred Literature of Avatar Adi Da Samraj

Read the astounding Story of Avatar Adi Da's Divine Life and Work in *The Light Is On!*

The Light Is On!

The profound, heart-rending, humorous, miraculous, wild—and true—Story of the Divine Person Alive in human Form. Essential reading as background for the study of Avatar Adi Da's books.

Enjoy the beautiful summary of His Message that Avatar Adi Da has written especially "for children, and everyone else".

What, Where, When, How, Why, and Who To Remember To Be Happy

Illustrated Children's Edition

Fundamental Truth about life as a human being, told in very simple language for children. Accompanied by extraordinarily vivid and imaginative illustrations.

The Five Books Of
The Heart Of The Adidam Revelation

In these five books, Avatar Adi Da Samraj has distilled the very essence of His Eternal Message to every one, in all times and places.

BOOK ONE:

Aham Da Asmi
(Beloved, I Am Da)

The "Late-Time" Avataric Revelation Of The True and Spiritual Divine Person (The egoless Personal Presence Of Reality and Truth, Which Is The Only Real God)

The most extraordinary statement ever made in human history. Avatar Adi Da Samraj fully Reveals Himself as the Living Divine Person and Proclaims His Infinite and Undying Love for all and All.

BOOK TWO:

Ruchira Avatara Gita
(The Way Of The Divine Heart-Master)

The "Late-Time" Avataric Revelation Of The Great Secret Of The Divinely Self-Revealed Way That Most Perfectly Realizes The True and Spiritual Divine Person (The egoless Personal Presence Of Reality and Truth, Which Is The Only Real God)

Avatar Adi Da Offers to every one the ecstatic practice of devotional relationship to Him— explaining how devotion to a living human Adept-Realizer has always been the source of true religion, and distinguishing true Guru-devotion from religious cultism.

BOOK THREE:

Da Love-Ananda Gita
(The Free Gift Of The Divine Love-Bliss)

The "Late-Time" Avataric Revelation Of The Great Means To Worship and To Realize The True and Spiritual Divine Person (The egoless Personal Presence Of Reality and Truth, Which Is The Only Real God)

Avatar Adi Da Reveals the secret simplicity at the heart of Adidam—relinquishing your preoccupation with yourself (and all your problems and your suffering) and, instead, Contemplating the "Bright" Divine Person of Infinite Love-Bliss.

BOOK FOUR:

Hridaya Rosary
(Four Thorns Of Heart-Instruction)

The "Late-Time" Avataric Revelation Of The Universally Tangible Divine Spiritual Body, Which Is The Supreme Agent Of The Great Means To Worship and To Realize The True and Spiritual Divine Person (The egoless Personal Presence Of Reality and Truth, Which Is The Only Real God)

The ultimate Mysteries of Spiritual life, never before revealed. In breathtakingly beautiful poetry, Avatar Adi Da Samraj sings of the "melting" of the ego in His "Rose Garden of the Heart".

BOOK FIVE:

Eleutherios
(The Only Truth That Sets The Heart Free)

The "Late-Time" Avataric Revelation Of The "Perfect Practice" Of The Great Means To Worship and To Realize The True and Spiritual Divine Person (The egoless Personal Presence Of Reality and Truth, Which Is The Only Real God)

An address to the great human questions about God, Truth, Reality, Happiness, and Freedom. Avatar Adi Da Samraj Reveals how Absolute Divine Freedom is Realized, and makes an impassioned Call to everyone to create a world of true human freedom on Earth.

The Seventeen Companions
Of The True Dawn Horse

These seventeen books are "Companions" to *The Dawn Horse Testament*, Avatar Adi Da's great summary of the Way of Adidam (p. 334). Here you will find Avatar Adi Da's Wisdom-Instruction on particular aspects of the true Spiritual Way, and His two tellings of His own Life-Story, as autobiography (*The Knee Of Listening*) and as archetypal parable (*The Mummery*).

BOOK ONE:

Real God Is The Indivisible Oneness Of Unbroken Light

Reality, Truth, and The "Non-Creator" God In The True World-Religion Of Adidam

The Nature of Real God and the nature of the cosmos. Why ultimate questions cannot be answered either by conventional religion or by science.

BOOK TWO:

The Truly Human New World-Culture Of Unbroken Real-God-Man

The Eastern Versus The Western Traditional Cultures Of Mankind, and The Unique New Non-Dual Culture Of The True World-Religion Of Adidam

The Eastern and Western approaches to religion, and to life altogether—and how the Way of Adidam goes beyond this apparent dichotomy.

BOOK THREE:

The Only Complete Way To Realize The Unbroken Light Of Real God

An Introductory Overview Of The "Radical" Divine Way Of The True World-Religion Of Adidam

The entire course of the Way of Adidam—the unique principles underlying Adidam, and the unique culmination of Adidam in Divine Enlightenment.

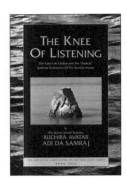

BOOK FOUR:

The Knee Of Listening
The Early-Life Ordeal and The "Radical"
Spiritual Realization Of The Ruchira Avatar

Avatar Adi Da's autobiographical account of the
years from His Birth to His Divine Re-Awakening
in 1970. Includes a new chapter, "My Realization
of the Great Onlyness of Me, and My Great
Regard for My Adept-Links to the Great Tradition
of Mankind".

BOOK FIVE:

The Divine Siddha-Method Of The Ruchira Avatar
The Divine Way Of Adidam Is An ego-Transcending
Relationship, Not An ego-Centric Technique

Avatar Adi Da's earliest Talks to His devotees, on
the fundamental principles of the devotional relationship to Him and "radical" understanding of the
ego. Accompanied by His summary statements on
His relationship to Swami Muktananda and on His
own unique Teaching-Work and Blessing-Work.

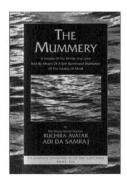

BOOK SIX:

The Mummery
A Parable Of The Divine True Love,
Told By Means Of A Self-Illuminated Illustration
Of The Totality Of Mind

A work of astonishing poetry and deeply evocative archetypal drama. This is the story of
Raymond Darling's birth, his growth to manhood,
his finding and losing of his beloved (Quandra),
and his ultimate resolution of the heart-breaking
"problem" of mortality. *The Mummery* is Avatar Adi Da's telling of His
own Life-Story in the language of parable, including His unflinching
portrayal of how the unconverted ego makes religion (and life altogether) into a meaningless mummery.

BOOK SEVEN:

He-_and_-She _Is_ Me

The Indivisibility Of Consciousness and Light In The Divine Body Of The Ruchira Avatar

One of Avatar Adi Da's most esoteric Revelations—His Primary "Incarnation" in the Cosmic domain as the "He" of Primal Divine Sound-Vibration, the "She" of Primal Divine Light, and the "Son" of "He" and "She" in the "Me" of His Divine Spiritual Body.

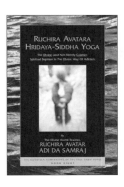

BOOK EIGHT:

Ruchira Avatara Hridaya-Siddha Yoga

The _Divine_ (and Not Merely _Cosmic_) Spiritual Baptism In The Divine Way Of Adidam

The Divine Heart-Power (Hridaya-Shakti) uniquely Transmitted by Avatar Adi Da Samraj, and how it differs from the various traditional forms of Spiritual Baptism, particularly Kundalini Yoga.

BOOK NINE:

Ruchira Avatara Hridaya-Tantra Yoga

The Physical-Spiritual (and Truly Religious) Method Of Mental, Emotional, Sexual, and _Whole Bodily_ _Health_ _and_ _Enlightenment_ In The Divine Way Of Adidam

The transformation of life in the realms of money, food, and sex. Includes: understanding "victim-consciousness"; the ego as addict; the secret of how to change; going beyond the "Oedipal" sufferings of childhood; the right orientation to money; right diet; life-positive and Spiritually auspicious sexual practice.

BOOK TEN:

The Seven Stages Of Life

Transcending The Six Stages Of egoic Life, and Realizing The ego-Transcending Seventh Stage Of Life, In The Divine Way Of Adidam

The stages of human development from birth to Divine Enlightenment. How the stages relate to physical and esoteric anatomy. The errors of each of the first six stages of life, and the unique ego-lessness of the seventh stage of life. Avatar Adi Da's Self-Confession as the first, last, and only seventh stage Adept-Realizer.

BOOK ELEVEN:

The All-Completing and Final Divine Revelation To Mankind

A Summary Description Of The Supreme Yoga Of The Seventh Stage Of Life In The Divine Way Of Adidam

The ultimate secrets of Divine Enlightenment—including the four-stage Process of Divine Enlightenment, culminating in Translation into the Infinitely Love-Blissful Divine Self-Domain.

BOOK TWELVE:

The Heart Of The Dawn Horse Testament Of The Ruchira Avatar

The Epitome Of The "Testament Of Secrets" Of The Divine World-Teacher, Ruchira Avatar Adi Da Samraj

A shorter version of *The Dawn Horse Testament*—all of Avatar Adi Da's magnificent summary Instruction, without the details of the technical practices engaged by His devotees.

BOOK THIRTEEN:

What, Where, When, How, Why, and <u>Who</u> To Remember To Be Happy

A Simple Explanation Of The Divine Way Of Adidam (For Children, and <u>Everyone</u> Else)

A text written specifically for children but inspiring to all—with accompanying Essays and Talks on Divine Ignorance, religious practices for children and young people in the Way of Adidam, and the fundamental practice of whole bodily devotion to Avatar Adi Da Samraj. (The central text of this book is also available in a special illustrated children's edition—see p. 326.)

BOOK FOURTEEN:

Santosha Adidam

The Essential Summary Of The Divine Way Of Adidam

An extended overview of the entire course of the Way of Adidam, based on the esoteric anatomy of the human being and its correlation to the progressive stages of life.

BOOK FIFTEEN:

The Lion Sutra

The "Perfect Practice" Teachings In The Divine Way Of Adidam

Practice in the ultimate stages of the Way of Adidam. How the practitioner of Adidam approaches—and passes over—the "Threshold" of Divine Enlightenment.

BOOK SIXTEEN:

The Overnight Revelation Of Conscious Light

The "My House" Discourses
On The Indivisible Tantra Of Adidam

A vast and profound "consideration" of the fundamental Tantric principles of true Spiritual life and the "Always Already" Nature of the Divine Reality. The day-by-day record of Avatar Adi Da's Discourses from a two-month period in early 1998.

BOOK SEVENTEEN:

The Basket Of Tolerance

The Perfect Guide To Perfectly <u>Unified</u>
Understanding Of The One and Great
Tradition Of Mankind, and Of The Divine
Way Of Adidam As The Perfect <u>Completing</u>
Of The One and Great Tradition Of Mankind

An all-encompassing "map" of mankind's entire history of religious seeking. A combination of a bibliography of over 5,000 items (organized to display Avatar Adi Da's grand Argument relative to the Great Tradition) with over 100 Essays by Avatar Adi Da, illuminating many specific aspects of the Great Tradition.

The Dawn Horse Testament Of The Ruchira Avatar

The "Testament Of Secrets"
Of The Divine World-Teacher,
Ruchira Avatar Adi Da Samraj

Avatar Adi Da's paramount "Source-Text", which summarizes the entire course of the Way of Adidam. Adi Da Samraj says: "In making this Testament I have been Meditating everyone, contacting everyone, dealing with psychic forces everywhere, in all time. This Testament is an always Living Conversation between Me and absolutely every one."

See My Brightness Face to Face

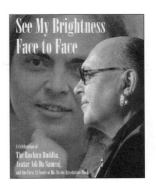

A Celebration of the Ruchira Avatar, Adi Da Samraj, and the First Twenty-Five Years of His Divine Revelation Work.

A magnificent year-by-year pictorial celebration of Ruchira Avatar Adi Da's Divine Work with His devotees, from 1972 to 1997. Includes a wealth of selections from His Talks and Writings, numerous Stories told by His devotees, and over 100 color photographs. **$19.95**, 8-1/2" x 11" paperback, 200 pages.

The "Truth For Real" series

Brief Essays and Talks by the Divine World-Teacher, Ruchira Avatar Adi Da Samraj

13 individual booklets on topics such as ecstasy, death, and the impulse to Happiness.
3-3/4" x 6", **$1.95** each

The Basket Of Tolerance Booklet series

6 individual essays on the religious traditions of humankind from *The Basket Of Tolerance*.
3-3/4" x 6", **$1.95** each

I n addition to Avatar Adi Da's 23 "Source-Texts", the Dawn
Horse Press offers many other publications by and about
Avatar Adi Da Samraj, as well as videotapes and audiotapes
of Avatar Adi Da's Wisdom-Teaching. Dawn Horse Press publications are distributed by the Adidam Emporium, a devotee-
operated business offering a wide array of items for meditation,
sacred worship, health and well-being, and much more.

For more information or a free catalog:

CALL THE ADIDAM EMPORIUM
TOLL-FREE 1-877-770-0772
(Outside North America call 1-707-928-6653)

Visit online at
www.adidam.com

Or e-mail:
emporium@adidam.com

Or write:
ADIDAM EMPORIUM
10336 Loch Lomond Road
PMB #306
Middletown, CA 95461
USA

INDEX

NOTE TO THE READER: Page numbers in **boldface** type refer to the Scriptural Text of *Real God Is The Indivisible Oneness Of Unbroken Light*. All other page numbers refer to the introductions, endnotes, and the back matter.

conventional God-religion
associated with space-time
bound point of view, **132-33**
the babble of, **219**
compared with scientific materialism and Way of Adidam,
129-44
credibility threatened by science,
129
fundamentals common to scientific
materialism and, **129-30**,
134, **139**
and insane affirmations, **224**
is about Man, not God, **129**
limitations of its views, **138**
not a means for Realizing Real
God, **129**, **138**, **139**, **141-42**
primary difference from scientific
materialism, **130**
scientific materialist criticism of,
217-18
as search founded on an illusion,
182
serves illusions of mankind, **139**
as subordinate world-view, **131**
transcended by Adi Da, **141-42**
two fundamentals of, **129-30**
utopianism as principal illusion
supported by, **138**, **139**
war with scientific materialism,
130-31
cultic tendency in, **64-65**, **66**
defined, **110**, **149**
dialogue with science, **110-11**
esoteric, **218**
exoteric
controls people more effectively
than scientific materialism,
225
as means for socializing people,
225-26
Great Esoteric Principle of, **71**, **72**
is "cult", **149**
is not science, **103**, **109-110**
is not Truth Itself, **149**
as means by which Divine becomes
"Creative", **123-24**
not in itself true, **184**
ordinary religion seeks power and
control, **215**

practitioners do not require much
involvement with science, **111**
reduction to secular purposes
(social morality), **109**
relation to Adept-Realizer as core of
all, **71**
right academic study of, **103-104**
and science, 51
no conflict between, 52
religion too much submitted to
review of science, **111-12**
science as measure of religion,
109
self-validating process, **104**
should not be absolutized or
forbidden, **150**
as subjective process, **149-50**
true religion, **149-50**
Adidam as Way of, **143**
begins with free heart-response,
175
begins with transcendence of
awe and wonder, **175**
devotion to Realization Master as
only true school of religion,
104
as esoteric process of Realizing
Reality, **134**
as esoteric science, **240**, **241**
is not a science, **240**
is Revelation in the midst of
conditional existence, **221**
is whole bodily "Dance", **184**
nature of, **58**
not in conflict with true science,
221
presently Realizes Fundamental
Light, **221**
Realization as domain of, **218**
true religious requirements, **111**
true science must coincide with,
219-20
Remembrance (of Adi Da), 254
renunciate orders, of Adidam,
defined, 310-11
responsibility, Adidam as an invitation
to assume real responsibility,
278
rituals
religious, **149**

science in dialogue with religion,
110-11
science is not a religious method,
110
true science
Adidam as Way of, **143**
basis of, **224**
as esoteric process of Realizing
Reality, **134**
as free enquiry, **219**
is not scientific materialism, **220**
must coincide with true religion,
219-20
nature of, **58**
not committed to materialism,
219-20
not in conflict with true religion,
220, 221
viewpoint on consciousness, **222**
See also scientific materialism
scientific materialism
associated with space-time bound
point of view, **132-33**
compared with conventional God-
religion and Way of Adidam,
129-44
contrasted with true religion, **240**
control motive of, **240**
defined, 49-50, 316
does not generally criticize esoteric
religion, **217**
as dominant world-view, **131**
doublemindedness about religion,
226
ego-based method of science
summarized, **240**
as egoic science, **224**
its aggressive affirmation of power
and dissociation, **215**
and its offshoot, academic
reductionism, **103**
materialism as principal illusion
supported by, **139**
as modern variation of ancient false
philosophy, **129**
negative results of, **138-39**
not a means for Realizing Real God,
139, 141-42
not effective at controlling people,
225

and religion
common basis of scientific
materialism and conventional
God-religion, **129-30**
primary difference between, **130**
scientific materialism compared
with conventional God-
religion and Way of Adidam,
129-44
scientific materialism is anti-
religious, **220**
scientific materialism's simplistic
criticism of exoteric religion,
217-18
two naive presumptions of, 51
war with conventional God-
religion, **130-31**
seeks to dominate mankind, **138**
serves illusions of mankind, **139**
transcended by Adi Da, **141-42**
two fundamentals of, **129-30, 134, 139**
view of Consciousness, **222**
See also materialism; matter; science
Second Calling, 274
Secret, Adi Da's Divine Heart-Secret, **81**
seeing, **190, 207**
defined, **183**, 305-306
described, **85-86**
seeing practice in Adidam, **207-209**
seeking, 31
abandon by "locating" Adi Da, **82-83**
and first six stages of life, **163**
is dissolved in Satsang, **69-70**
and Lesson of life, 303
as one of two principal tendencies
of devotees, **70**
as preoccupation of heartless body-
mind, **175-76**
and Real God, **176**
and Satsang, **61**
self (individual)
arises conditionally but Inheres in
Real God, **186**
nature of, **160**
not Self-Existing, Immortal, Spark of
Divinity, **185-86**
as self-contraction, 16-17
three forms of, **186**
v. Real God, **185-86**
See also ego/ego-"I"/egoity

I do not simply recommend or turn men and women to Truth. I <u>Am</u> Truth. I Draw men and women to Myself. I <u>Am</u> the Present Real God, Desiring, Loving, and Drawing up My devotees. I have Come to Be Present with My devotees, to Reveal to them the True Nature of life in Real God, which is Love, and of mind in Real God, which is Faith. I Stand always Present in the Place and Form of Real God. I accept the qualities of all who turn to Me, dissolving those qualities in Real God, so that <u>Only</u> God becomes the Condition, Destiny, Intelligence, and Work of My devotees. I look for My devotees to acknowledge Me and turn to Me in appropriate ways, surrendering to Me perfectly, depending on Me, full of Me always, with only a face of love.

I am waiting for you. I have been waiting for you eternally.

Where are you?

AVATAR ADI DA SAMRAJ

1971